Letters of Ellen Glasgow

BOOKS BY ELLEN GLASGOW

The Descendant. Harper, 1897.

Phases of an Inferior Planet. Harper, 1898.

The Voice of the People. Doubleday, Page, 1900.

The Freeman and Other Poems. Doubleday, 1902.

The Battle-Ground. Doubleday, Page, 1902.

The Deliverance. Doubleday, Page, 1904.

The Wheel of Life. Doubleday, Page, 1906.

The Ancient Law. Doubleday, Page, 1908.

The Romance of a Plain Man. Macmillan, 1909.

The Miller of Old Church. Doubleday, Page, 1911.

Virginia. Doubleday, Page, 1913.

Life and Gabriella. Doubleday, Page, 1916.

The Builders. Doubleday, Page, 1919.

One Man in His Time. Doubleday, Page, 1922.

The Shadowy Third and Other Stories. Doubleday, Page, 1923.

Barren Ground. Doubleday, Page, 1925.

The Romantic Comedians. Doubleday, Page, 1926.

They Stooped to Folly. Doubleday, Doran, 1929.

The Sheltered Life. Doubleday, Doran, 1932.

Vein of Iron. Harcourt, Brace, 1935.

In This Our Life. Harcourt, Brace, 1941.

A Certain Measure. Harcourt, Brace, 1943.

The Woman Within. Harcourt, Brace, 1954.

LETTERS OF
Ellen Glasgow

COMPILED AND EDITED WITH AN
INTRODUCTION AND COMMENTARY
BY BLAIR ROUSE

HARCOURT, BRACE AND COMPANY
New York

IN MEMORIAM E.B.R.
IPSA ETIAM DECOREM ET VIRTUTEM
AMABAT

PREFACE

A collection of an author's letters may suggest the atmosphere and temper of his times; it may provide a self-portrait and an autobiographical commentary; and it may serve as a vehicle for his critical and philosophical views. This selection of the letters of Ellen Glasgow should be read as a complementary volume to her book of literary criticism, *A Certain Measure,* and to her autobiography, *The Woman Within.* It is necessarily a selection because it has not been either advisable or practicable to bring together all of Miss Glasgow's letters at this time. Her correspondence is widely scattered among the original recipients, collectors, and libraries; a few libraries have fairly large collections. In particular, the Alderman Library at the University of Virginia, since the Glasgow Papers were deposited there in the spring of 1955, has been building an extensive collection of the correspondence. Also this is a selection because not all of Ellen Glasgow's correspondence is of a nature that would warrant publication. Primarily, the selection has been made with regard for biographical, literary, and philosophical relevance. These letters should be interesting to the reader chiefly for what they show of the author herself, of the relationship of the author to her correspondents, and of her role in the literary and artistic life of her time.

I have not provided a facsimile edition of Ellen Glasgow's letters. I believe the intelligent general reader, for whom this book is intended, does not wish the pedantic affectation of a text liberally sprinkled with *sic's,* asterisks, and daggers indicating peculiarities of syntax, spelling, punctuation, and

[7]

handwriting or typing. Miss Glasgow did not write these letters for publication; I have prepared them for print. I have transcribed the letters from their handwritten or typewritten originals, from photostat or microfilm copies, and occasionally from typed copies provided by custodians when the letters could be obtained in no other way. Passages either impossible to decipher or requiring guesswork are so indicated. Occasional errors in spelling, punctuation, or syntax and other apparent slips I have silently corrected rather than permit such peculiarities to assume undue importance when perpetuated in print. I have, on the other hand, taken care to preserve variants characteristic of Miss Glasgow's practice. This may be noticed especially in the spelling of some words and in the rhetorical punctuation of many passages.

From some of the letters I have deleted portions which were repetitious or which for other reasons seemed not to justify publication. I have used spaced periods to indicate such editorial omissions, except when inconsequential postscripts have been omitted and such spaced periods would be merely a waste of space. I have sought to provide in the footnotes the information the reader may reasonably desire, without cluttering the text with unnecessary commentary.

I wish to express my sense of especial gratitude to Ellen Glasgow's literary executors, Mrs. Irita Van Doren and Mr. Frank Morley.

I wish to thank the following publications for assisting me in the gathering of letters: *American Literature* (Mr. James Woodress), the London *Times Literary Supplement,* the New York *Herald-Tribune Book Review* (Mrs. Irita Van Doren), the Richmond *News Leader* (Mr. John P. Stratton), and the Richmond *Times-Dispatch* (Mr. Virginius Dabney).

The following publishing companies have generously helped me in this project: Doubleday and Company (Miss Clara Claasen and Miss Louise Thomas), Harcourt, Brace and Company (Mr. Denver Lindley), McCall Corporation (the *Red Book Magazine,* Miss Marion Taylor), and Charles Scribner's Sons (Mr. Wallace Meyer and Mr. John Hall Wheelock).

These libraries have generously shared their resources and provided valuable assistance: the Alderman Library of the University of Virginia (Mr. Francis L. Berkeley, Jr., Mr. Jack Dalton, Mr. N. Harvey Deal, and Mr. Russell Smith), Goucher College Library (Miss Sarah D. Jones), the Houghton Library of Harvard University (Dr. William A. Jackson and Dr. Andrew D. Osborn), the Library of Congress (Mr. David Mearns), the Mount Union College Library (Mr. Yost Osborne and Miss Norma Stewart), the New York Public Library (the Henry W. and Albert A. Berg Collection, Dr. John Gordan; the Reference Department, Mr. Rutherford D. Rogers), Princeton University Library (Mr. Alexander Clark and Mr. Alexander Wainwright), the William Allan Neilson Library of Smith College (Miss Dorothy King), the University of Florida Library (the Marjorie Kinnan Rawlings Collection, Mr. Gene Baro), the University of Kentucky Library (Miss Polly Warren), Western Reserve University Library, and the Yale University Library (Mr. Donald Gallup).

I am deeply grateful to these persons for making it possible for me to use Ellen Glasgow's letters as well as for providing information and other assistance: Mr. J. Donald Adams, Mr. Hamilton Basso, Mrs. Stephen Vincent Benét, the late Miss Anne Virginia Bennett, Mr. Van Wyck Brooks, Mr. Lawton Campbell, Dr. and Mrs. Henry Seidel Canby, Dr. Leon Edel, Mrs. D. S. Freeman, Mrs. Edward W. Gamble, Mr. Lewis Gannett, Miss Mary T. Glasgow, Mrs. Ellen Knowles Harcourt, Mr. and Mrs. Henry Hazlitt, Mr. Leslie Johnson, Miss Elizabeth Johnston, Dr. and Mrs. Howard Mumford Jones, the late Dr. Grant C. Knight, Dr. William H. F. Lamont, Dr. Ernest E. Leisy, Miss Rosalind C.

Lohrfinck, Mr. Daniel Longwell, Mr. Harry M. Meacham, the late Mr. H. L. Mencken, Dr. Edwin Mims, Mr. Stephens Mitchell, Mr. John Munford, the late Mr. Robert B. Munford, Mr. Arthur Page, Mrs. Mildred Davies Payne, Mr. Harry Scherman, Dr. Hudson Strode, Mr. Frank Swinnerton, Dr. Allen Tate, Miss Signe Toksvig (Mrs. Francis Hackett), Miss Gertrude Traubel, Mr. Carl Van Vechten, Dr. James Southall Wilson, Dr. James Woodress, and Mr. Stark Young.

I am grateful to Mrs. Anna Belle Close and Mrs. Nancy Ellis Koehler for their assistance in typing and checking material, and to Mrs. Marcella Blount for her assistance in the preparation of the manuscript.

I can, of course, offer no adequate expression of my sense of indebtedness to my wife, Fanchon Rouse, for the many ways in which she has assisted and encouraged me during the preparation of this book.

BLAIR ROUSE

University of Arkansas
Fayetteville, Arkansas
September 5, 1957

INTRODUCTION

Near the beginning of her career Ellen Glasgow wrote a letter to Walter Hines Page, later her publisher, in which she expressed her dedication to her art and her determination to become a distinguished exponent of fiction. She wrote on November 22, 1897, in the year in which her first book was published: "I shall write no more short stories and I shall not divide my power or risk my future reputation. I will become a great novelist or none at all." Later, on January 14, 1902, she wrote to Mr. Page: "The share of the sympathetic publisher in the author's success—the true success so different from the ephemeral—is apt to be overlooked in these blatant days, so it is just as well that some of us should keep it in mind. One cannot lay a foundation by scattering stones, nor is a reputation for good work to be got by strewing volumes about the world; and so when I look ahead in my sanguine hours my vision with regard to my work is much the same as yours—a series of good books each adding to the building of the name I hope for and each testifying to the share my chosen publishers have had in the growing work." Although she would write a few more short stories, and although she would eventually change her publishers, these sentences suggest her purposefulness and her attitude toward her career virtually at its beginning.

Ellen Glasgow, next to the youngest in a family of ten children, was born April 22, 1873, in Richmond, Virginia. Her father was an able representative of the sternest, staunchest, Scotch-Irish, Presbyterian Calvinism. As a young man he became associated with the Tredegar Iron

Works, the ancient Richmond foundry, and eventually directed its operations. Miss Glasgow's mother, on the other hand, was a representative of liberal, gracious, Virginia, cavalier, Episcopal, Tidewater society. From both parents Ellen Glasgow received a full measure of inherited characteristics. Her sympathies were with her mother, whose tastes and attitudes were far more attractive to her; yet her father's character and that of his people, in so far as it meant fortitude and stern determination, attracted her more than she realized and found its way into her work, though their narrow, even cruel, religion she rejected almost instinctively.

Miss Glasgow suffered from uncertain health and actual illness throughout her life. The delicate little girl could not— or would not—go to school. Consequently, she came close to educating herself. Perhaps the result would not be considered a good education in some ways, but it appears to have been excellent for the author's purposes. She learned many things in her severe course of reading which were not included in the curriculums then provided young ladies in Virginia. Not only did she read widely in fiction and poetry, but she became interested in science, history, and philosophy and read far into these areas of study. She was keenly affected by the evolutionary scientific writings and the empirical philosophy of the latter nineteenth century as well as by her reading in metaphysics and oriental lore. These interests remained with her throughout life.

One should not suppose, however, that Ellen Glasgow became a youthful recluse. Despite the early onset of a deafness which became increasingly painful and annoying, she found pleasure in human society and enjoyed friendships with many men and women in whom she noted kindred tastes and spirits. As a young girl she made her debut at a St. Cecilia's Ball in Charleston, South Carolina. As a mature woman and distinguished novelist, she delighted in entertaining in her home at One West Main Street in Richmond, and the excellence of the cuisine there became legend in Richmond and New York. That she enjoyed her associations with a few of her Richmond compeers is clear; it is equally clear that her circle of friends in the city by the James River was always rather small.

She lived most of her life in Richmond because only there did she feel entirely at home; only there did she find the surroundings which she came to believe were necessary for her to carry on her work satisfactorily. However, at least twice in her career she did write away from her upstairs study at One West Main Street: once when she was living in New York for several years (1911-1916); and later, toward the end of her life, when her health made escape from the heat and humidity of Southern summers imperative, she spent several months each summer and fall in Castine, Maine, and there worked upon her last books. Yet it seems evident, as one reads her autobiography, *The Woman Within,* and these letters, that in a sense Ellen Glasgow must always have felt herself an exile even in her own home city. Of course, her deafness shut her away from easy communication with others, and it is evident, with justification or not, that she came to feel her own community had little sympathy for the things she most cherished; that the South generally and Richmond particularly were concerned with matters of art and letters to an infinitesimal degree.

Although Ellen Glasgow resided in Richmond in the old gray Georgian house, she was never closely bound by its walls, physically, intellectually, or spiritually. Until her health made further travel impossible toward the end of her life, she traveled widely in Europe and fairly extensively in America. England she appears to have loved with something of the fervor of the Anglophile. New England and New York State as well as New York City she knew well and delighted in. With other parts of her country she was less well acquainted. She had spent a summer in San Francisco and had fallen in love with that fascinating city. The Midwest apparently she had never known intimately—nor many Midwesterners; hence one may detect more than a note of prejudice growing out of her fancied notions of this region and its people. The South she knew with her mind and heart, but chiefly the latter. It does not appear that she ever understood the Deep South as she did the Upper South, especially her own Virginia. Even Virginia she knew most clearly as a country of the mind and heart; her art of fiction was regional in a useful sense of that term; it was never a "local color" art. She used the people and scenes of Virginia, the inner meanings of lives, and from them extracted universal meanings in the form of novels. In a reply to a woman inquiring about her art, Ellen Glasgow wrote (December 3, 1935): "Knowledge, like experience, is valid in fiction only after it has dissolved and filtered down through the imagination into reality." These realities—these universal meanings —are set forth in the regional terms of character, scene, and action in her novels.

In her nineteen novels Ellen Glasgow created complex patterns which enable the thoughtful reader to understand more clearly the meaning of life in Virginia, the South, and the world during the past hundred years. She wrote of antebellum and Civil War times (*The Battle-Ground,* 1850-1865); of the post-bellum years (*The Voice of the People,* 1870-1898, *The Deliverance,* 1878-1900, *The Romance of a Plain Man,* 1875-1910); of the latter nineteenth and early twentieth centuries (*Virginia,* 1884-1912, *The Miller of Old Church,* 1898-1902, *Life and Gabriella,* 1894-1912); and of earlier as well as of more recent times (*Barren Ground,* 1894-1925, *The Romantic Comedians,* 1923, *They Stooped to Folly,* 1924, *The Sheltered Life,* 1910-1917, *Vein of Iron,* 1901-1933, and *In This Our Life,* 1938-1939).

Miss Glasgow's interpretation of Virginia social history concerned all the people of the commonwealth. Her books

are among the earliest to treat in fiction the lives of the
Southern middle and lower classes—the small farmers, village craftsmen, and the storekeepers—the "plain" people or
"good" people (as distinct from "good families") who make
up so large a proportion of the South's population. These
people had received little attention in literature before Ellen
Glasgow began to write about them shortly before the turn
of the century. Usually they are not the "poor whites" so
excessively celebrated in much twentieth-century Southern
fiction, although occasionally such families find their places
in Miss Glasgow's books.

The aristocrats in Ellen Glasgow's novels represent those
who held social, political, and professional leadership by
heritage and ability. They are not glorified or glamorized,
neither are they despised. Instead, the upper classes are
shown much more clearly in the light of actuality than in
most stories of the South. Notable in Miss Glasgow's presentation of aristocrats is the pervasive meaning of custom
and tradition, the persistent adherence to a code of manners
which is veritably a code of life, shaping lives for evil and
good.

Miss Glasgow's Negro characters are almost invariably
individuals who play important roles in the human dramas in
which they are involved. Rarely are they simply background
or chorus figures. She was aware of the distinctions among
Negroes with respect to class and personal attainment, and
she showed clearly what it meant to be an ex-slave, a "free"
Negro, and a "new" Negro, with all the hopes, fears, and
frustrations these lives contained.

Although Ellen Glasgow sought to show the importance
of a sense of inherited values and the significance of adherence to beliefs and loyalties having deep spiritual meanings
for the individual, she was often more evidently concerned
with the evils of a blind worship of tradition. She condemned,
therefore, any orthodoxy which had stiffened into a set of

relatively meaningless shibboleths. Class distinctions founded
in leadership and ability she did not despise, nor would she
deny that men of lower social status could—and did—rise to
political, commercial, or professional distinction and eventually to social acceptance. She saw the irony in these changes
in social stratification, but this irony is rarely at the expense
of the "plain" man. One may smile at the episode in *The
Sheltered Life* in which a young carpenter's marriage to a
girl of "good family" leads to his "translation" to the Episcopal Church and to the transformation of his family from
"plain" to "quiet," but one's smile is not at the expense of
the carpenter.

Ellen Glasgow used the term "evasive idealism" for the
blind adherence to tradition which she believed led to much
suffering and needless waste in Southern lives. Compounded
of intellectual delusions, emotional bewilderment, and false
sentiment, this state of mind was dramatically embodied in
Mrs. Blake of *The Deliverance,* whose physical blindness
was the symbol of the even more devastating spiritual and
intellectual barrier which prevented many gentlefolk from
admitting the existence of evil in their lives. In *The Sheltered
Life,* so ironically titled, the characters scarcely recognized
the miasma of "evasive idealism." They resented the effluvia
of industrial "progress" which had invaded their once-
fashionable neighborhood, but they did not recognize the
more blighting presence of false sentiment in the midst of
which they gasped and struggled.

Interest in tradition and its meaning in human lives meant,
inevitably for a sensitive novelist, interest in the meanings of
time for men and women. Although concerned with historical
time, involving a climate of beliefs, customs, and changes,
Ellen Glasgow was even more interested in time as an active
force in life, in time enriching and fulfilling lives, or in time
as an eroding and corroding force, wearing away the spirit
and destroying the soul. So in *Barren Ground* the passage

of the years brings fulfillment to Dorinda Oakley while it carries destruction for Jason Greylock, her betrayer; in *The Sheltered Life* the years rob Eva Birdsong of her beauty and leave her life without meaning. *In This Our Life,* however, shows Asa Timberlake experiencing the erosion of time, having it wear away his means to happiness, yet never being wholly destroyed by his misfortunes. For Asa possesses an inner strength by which to resist time and circumstance and so survive spiritually, although apparently defeated in the judgment of his world.

Concerned for the ingredients of civilization or the lack of them in America, Ellen Glasgow could find little of the comic spirit in the writings of her contemporaries. Into her novels, even the darker and prevailingly tragic stories, she brought the balance and relief of high comedy. This spirit pervades that masterpiece among novels of manners, *The Romantic Comedians,* as it does also her comedy of betrayed ladies, *They Stooped to Folly.* In these books, with wit, wisdom, and an irony not always gentle, she brought the spirit of thoughtful laughter, to use George Meredith's phrase, to the illumination of human problems too often drenched in the tears of sentimentality and the violence of melodrama.

Ellen Glasgow could also turn a darker, less amusing irony upon the possibilities for a civilized life in what was perhaps an uncivilized world. Old General Archbald of *The Sheltered Life* may be the most appealing of Miss Glasgow's civilized people, as he recalls what his life *has* been and considers what it *might have* been. As a boy, unable to endure the pain and cruelty of the hunting field, he had shrunk from causing needless suffering. He had aspired to poetry but had followed the law in a world which supported litigation but not literature. He had known the joys and pains of love but had been trapped into a loveless marriage through the code of proper behavior. In his old age he finds that he has been

made to pay the penalties forever exacted from those who
strive against the forces of an uncivilized world. If Ellen
Glasgow rejected a facile optimism, she did not slip into the
blind pessimism with its negation of all values and hopes so
often symptomatic of much twentieth-century fiction. She
possessed an idealism which refused to hide behind preten-
sions or to deny harsh truths, yet which found value in those
lives strengthened and supported by a steadfast courage.
Hers may have been a large measure of disillusionment, but
hers was not the trap of deluded cynicism.

As a young artist Miss Glasgow was aware of the repre-
hensible views of literature and art held by those who considered themselves exponents of Southern culture; she was
sensitive to the mockery of empty claims to cultural pre-
eminence. She decried the absence of any substantial criticism in the South in the early 1900's as well as the frequent
inability of too many Southerners to exercise a clear-minded
discrimination between the valueless and the valuable in
literature produced below Mason and Dixon's line. She was
equally antipathetic to the sentimentally fallacious products
of gentility and post-bellum nostalgia as well as to the violence and horror of more recent fiction, whether exploited
for their own sake or masquerading as psychology or sociol-
ogy. In her own novels she showed the integrity and courage
requisite to presenting the "whole truth" of "the interior
world as well as external appearances." Such phrases she
used in emphasizing the imperative need in the South for
"blood and irony." "Blood it needed," she wrote, "because
Southern culture had strained too far away from its roots in
the earth; it had grown thin and pale; it was satisfied to exist
on borrowed ideas, to copy instead of create. And irony is
an indispensable ingredient of the critical vision; it is the
safest antidote to sentimental decay." [1]

[1] *A Certain Measure,* Harcourt, Brace, 1943, 28.

Introduction

In *A Certain Measure* Ellen Glasgow brought together the critical essays, originally written as prefaces to the twelve novels selected for the Virginia Edition of her works; these were all rewritten, and she added another essay concerning her last published novel, *In This Our Life*. In *The Woman Within,* written several years before her death in 1945 but not published until almost a decade thereafter, Miss Glasgow set forth her spiritual autobiography. In both of these books Ellen Glasgow wrote courageously, often with surprising frankness, about matters of great importance to her and, in many instances, of a painful nature. In *The Woman Within,* especially, she appears to have sought conscientiously to present the whole truth about herself and her life as clearly as she could see it. This autobiography is an interesting and valuable document for the light it directs into the workings of a creative life; certainly it provides useful illumination for the clearer reading and more comprehensive understanding of Ellen Glasgow's novels.

The first letter in this selection was written before the young writer had published a novel, but already she showed the attitude of a professional artist toward her work. The last letters were written a few weeks before Ellen Glasgow died, yet there still remained her courage and her interest in her art. Throughout these letters one may find the novelist's concern with her craft, her devotion to that art of fiction which was for her so high a creative vocation, and those philosophical perceptions and explorations into the meanings of literature as the revelation of life. These letters, written without the conscious formality of work originally intended for print, present a vivid panorama of the life of the author and a lively revelation of Ellen Glasgow as a human being. Comprising her direct communications of feelings and thoughts to her friends, relations, and literary peers, this correspondence reveals the several facets of her personality directly and with a clarity found only in the best of her novels

[*19*]

and then indirectly in the transformations of art. In these letters is the human being who was Ellen Glasgow: the warmly affectionate friend, the sensitive and appreciative fellow worker in the realm of art, the lover of nature and of nature's beauties, the careful craftsman and dedicated professional novelist, the seeker after the civilized soul in a world often seemingly uncivilized and in which she frequently felt herself an exile, the woman who could hate meanness, cruelty, and waste with a good hate. Yet here is also the woman who was cursed—or blest—with a full measure of human frailty, who never supposed herself a paragon of all womanly virtues, who exhibited on occasion a healthy vein of malice as well as irony, who loved dogs perhaps even to the point of sentimentality, whose arithmetic was erratic, whose life may have made her more self-centered than she actually realized yet who never quite lost—even in the midst of the greatest evils—her sense of the comedy as well as the tragedy of existence and a certain gaiety in the face of apparent disaster. Here in these letters is the creator of Virginia Pendleton, of Dorinda Oakley, of Judge Honeywell, of General Archbald, and of Asa Timberlake; here is the hard-working "totally-immersed" novelist of the upstairs study at One West Main Street in Richmond; here is the long-time president of the Richmond chapter of the Society for the Prevention of Cruelty to Animals; here is the Virginia lady who was at the same time a spiritual exile from her land; here is the gaily ironic critic of her time and place. Here and in her books is Ellen Glasgow.

SECTION I

August 29, 189?—June 26, 1908

TO MRS. FRANCIS SMITH[1]

One West Main Street
Richmond, Virginia
August 29th [no year]

Dear Mrs. Smith,

Hearing from my sister Cary[2] the interest that you have kindly felt in young writers, I venture to ask your advice about the following matter.

I have seen your name, unless I am mistaken, in *The Writer* magazine of Boston and the fact led me to suppose that you might chance to have some knowledge of a corporation in connection with it called "The Writer's Literary Bureau," which offers to undertake the sale of manuscripts upon commission.

I wish very much to know if this Bureau is reliable and if a manuscript placed in its hands would have as fair a chance of acceptance by a publisher as if the author undertook the task of finding a suitable publisher herself.

If you could give me any information upon the subject I should be extremely grateful for your kindness.

Cary asks me to send you her love.

Very sincerely,
ELLEN ANDERSON GLASGOW

[1] The wife of a professor at the University of Virginia. The year is not indicated in the dateline, but this presumably is the earliest letter by Miss Glasgow to turn up. It is the only one to which she signed the name "Anderson," and it appears to have been written before she had published any of her work, though apparently she had ready for publication, or was soon to complete, a novel for which she sought a publisher. Whether this was the never published *Sharp Realities* (written and destroyed around 1892 or 1893) or her first published novel, *The Descendant*, it is impossible to ascertain. The latter seems to have existed as early as 1895 and was issued anonymously in 1897 under the Harper imprint.

[2] Mrs. George Walter McCormack, Miss Glasgow's older sister.

TO WALTER HINES PAGE[1]

400 West 57th Street [New York]
[October 28th, 1897]

Dear Mr. Page:

Immediately after receiving your letter, I was taken with a severe cold which confined me to my room for several days and from which I am only beginning to make a sorry recovery. However I shall be quite able to see you, I think, at any time that you should decide to come to New York. I return "The Freeman." [2] Whether I have improved it or not by the changes I have made I am not quite sure. I only know that I find it an easier matter to write a dozen verses than to alter a line.

Yes: I am studying the ground work of *Phases*,[3] and I am also getting most impatient for its completion. There is still a great deal of work to be done, but if I live it shall be finished by the spring.

Sincerely yours,

ELLEN GLASGOW

[1] At this time literary adviser to and associate editor of the *Atlantic Monthly*.

[2] A poem by Miss Glasgow which was apparently being considered for publication in the *Atlantic Monthly*.

[3] *Phases of an Inferior Planet*, Miss Glasgow's second published novel, Harper, 1898.

TO WALTER HINES PAGE

[New York, November 22, 1897]

My dear Mr. Page:

I have already expressed to Mrs. Page my regret that I cannot accept the very kind invitation which she and you extended to me; but the regret is so sincere that I find consolation in repeating it. But this letter is to prove that my mind is upon business bent and to ask you if you will come to my help by forecasting a possible future and giving me a little information in regard to things which may or may not come to pass.

Or very briefly—will you not give me some vague idea as to the terms which Messrs. Houghton and Mifflin would be likely to offer me for my novel provided it proves available for use in the *Atlantic*. This question chances to be an important one with me as you may imagine. I had warned the Harpers[1] that I expected a satisfactory royalty on the book rights and they had not objected, but they had my first book to justify them and whether another firm would grant me the same demands I do not know. They are certainly not exorbitant ones and I hardly think there will be any difficulty. Unfortunately I cannot leave these questions until the book is finished. I must make my decision before that time and I have no desire to use the firms against one another. I only want to do justly and fairly *by my work*—and by my publisher.

I am working upon my book and I have absolute confidence in its dramatic development. It is going to be worth my while and worth your while and if I send it to you and you do not want it for the *Atlantic* you will be very blind and I shall be very wrathful.

So far—and I have forgotten to tell you how helpful I found my conversations with you and what a pleasure I found it to talk with and know you. As regards my work I shall follow your advice in full. I shall write no more short stories and I shall not divide my power or risk my future reputation. I will become a great novelist or none at all. For which determination you are in part responsible.

By the way, if you have no need of your copy of *Phases* will you send it to my Richmond address. I am going home

[1] Harper had recently published *The Descendant*.

the last of the week and as the copy you have is my only revised version I shall have occasion to resort to it in the rewriting. If you have not finished with it, why, no matter.

I hope I have made you understand how sincerely I appreciate your interest in my work and how proud I shall feel to prove myself worthy of your belief in my future. If I have not done so, I must have expressed myself very poorly.

Most sincerely yours,

ELLEN GLASGOW

TO WALTER HINES PAGE [1]

Richmond, March 26, 1898

My dear Mr. Page:

I have intended for several weeks sending you news of *Phases,* and as an excuse for not doing so I have to offer a reason so stale that the writing of it bores me—and that is a physical collapse from which I have been suffering.

I have now corrected about one half the proof for *Phases.* The Messrs. Harper (with whom I have made very satisfactory arrangements) hope to have the book out in the early summer, but it is possible that it may be delayed until the autumn on account of the English edition, which will be published by Mr. William Heinemann. I shall be very glad to get *Phases* off my mind and am anxious to begin on a bigger and more ambitious work[2] which I have been planning for the past six months and which will probably require a couple of years hard work even after I finish collecting my data. Into this book I intend putting my whole strength. If the gods will it to be my last I don't want people to say "she might have done big things," because I am writing this book not to amuse, or to sell, but to *live,* and if it does so I shall be content not to—after it is finished. There is a point, by the

[1] By 1898 Mr. Page had succeeded to the editorship of the *Atlantic Monthly.*

[2] Undoubtedly *The Voice of the People.*

way, upon which I wish you would set my mind at rest when you have time. Given equally good work, do you believe that an American writer has as fair a chance of fame as an English one? An English literary man has written me that I should go abroad to develope my work, that the life I have chosen to portray is more interesting when taken from a French or English standpoint. I confess my own doubts strengthen the position that it is well for a writer to manage to be born in England if he can, but I am distrustful of adopted talent. Then the awful query rises would Hawthorne, himself, be "living" today had fate ordained him a native heath outside of the bounds of *New* England and had he not belonged to what Poe called the "cabal of American literature," and I remember the relative values of Poe and Longfellow and grow more sceptical still. Well, well. "Man is one and the fates are three."

All the same I suppose if I have the stuff in me I will "develope" as well in America as elsewhere; if I haven't it is of no consequence whether it developes or not.

The scene of my new book, by the way, will be laid in Virginia.

Very sincerely yours,
ELLEN GLASGOW

TO HORACE TRAUBEL[1]

Paris,[2] May 25, 1899

To Mr. Horace Traubel

It was a generous impulse which prompted you to tell me that you liked *The Descendant* and I am very grateful—the more so, perhaps, that my work has seemed far off of late and I have sometimes wondered if such things were quite worth while. You may understand from this that your letter has been of help to me when I was in need.

[27]

I was shocked to learn a day or two ago that my admiring, if evidently demented family, had allowed one of my private letters to appear in print in my native town, and that a copy of the paper had been forwarded to you. I can only trust that you did not read it. If you did I can only ask you to believe that it was written to amuse a relative and to forget it.[3]

Gratefully yours,

ELLEN GLASGOW

[1] Mr. Traubel had been friend and "Boswell" to the aged Walt Whitman, and in 1890 had founded the magazine *Conservator* in Philadelphia. He was one of those who recognized talent in *The Descendant*.

[2] This was the year Miss Glasgow spent abroad with her sisters Cary and Rebe, the youngest. The trip was financed by their brother, Arthur Graham Glasgow, the oldest of the family, who had made a brilliant reputation as an engineer and was living in London. The three sailed early in January, 1899, and for nearly a year wandered from country to country.

[3] Miss Gertrude Traubel, daughter of Horace Traubel, notes: "The above letter pasted in copy of *The Descendant*. Also pasted therein the newspaper clipping she refers to marked: '4/23/99 Despatch'—which bears the heading 'Richmonders in Constantinople.'"

TO WALTER HINES PAGE

Richmond, December 2, 1899

My dear Mr. Page:

Thanks for your kind letter.

If you are coming South, I shall be very glad to see you, and hope you will let me know when I may ask you to supper with my family.

As for the book, I can say nothing about it until it is finished, and frankly, my feeling at present strongly inclines me to the Messrs. Harper, if they should care for it in the spring—but, of course, I do not know their plans, and in case I should be forced to leave them, I should wish to give the best possible impulse to the new book. The book represents, to a certain extent, a change of literary base with me, and if it should chance to find a wide reading public, I should probably work upon a series of Virginia novels as true as I believe this one to be.

I should be very glad to have you read the book when it is finished, but it is only fair for me to add that unless a change would unquestionably benefit my book (which seems improbable) I should wish the Messrs. Harper to continue to be my publishers.

I appreciate very much your kind expressions of a wish to serve my book, and I am,

As always,
Sincerely yours,
ELLEN GLASGOW

TO WALTER HINES PAGE

[Richmond], December 8, 1899

My dear Mr. Page:

I am still breathless from your frequent surprises—and in the last one I am wishing you all success.[1]

It is indeed sad the news you give me of the house of Harper and Brothers—it is the one house which I believed to be absolutely secure, and I can but feel that it will rise again.[2]

As for the new book, which I have called (for the present at least) *The Voice of the People,* I am far from sure that you will care for it (it is so unlike the fashionable romantic school) and, perhaps, in that case, it will be as well that a great deal is not said beforehand. At any rate the fact remains that Captain Thorne Harper was the first friend of *The Descendant*—and remembering this I as good as promised him that he should see *The Voice.* Of course I have not

[1] Mr. Page had become a partner in the new publishing firm of Doubleday, Page and Company.
[2] Harper and Brothers was experiencing a period of financial difficulty.

committed myself in any way. I am anxious to keep my books together, and I am especially anxious to give the present novel as wide an audience as its character will permit of.

I shall certainly not take any decisive step until I have consulted you,[3] and, recalling your kind offers of assistance, I shall not hesitate to ask your advice in regard to the other books should occasion arise.

Very sincerely yours,

ELLEN GLASGOW

[3] Miss Glasgow decided to have *The Voice of the People* published by Doubleday, Page and Company (1900).

TO WALTER HINES PAGE

Richmond, April 18th, 1900

My dear Mr. Page:

Your letter did me good. I shall do as you say—write the story just as it comes to me, and I trust that your faith will be justified. I shall spend the summer near the scenes I have chosen,[1] and the work will not be begun till the autumn. At present it is merely taking shape in my mind, but this is a great deal to go on. I may say just here that the usual war novel of our country is detestable to me—I want to do something different—to make, as it were, a picture of varied characters who lived and loved and suffered during those years, and to show the effects of the times upon the development of their natures. The war will be merely an effective setting for a story of life.

Your appreciation of *The Voice of the People* gives me the greatest pleasure. There is nothing that would have disheartened me more than to be in the hands of unsympathetic publishers.

[1] The lower or northern areas of the Shenandoah Valley, which were to provide the setting for portions of *The Battle-Ground*, Doubleday, 1902.

People are saying very pleasant things about it. From Williamsburg I have received invitations to visit and letters headed "Kingsborough" [2]—they—or some of them—are delighted that I showed them to be not progressive. The political part appeals to the Richmond people I have seen or heard from—among them one of our governors wrote me a private note—I imagine, however, that the politicians generally won't care for it. So far no one has denied that the book is "Virginia as it is."

Mr. Marcosson[3] of the *Louisville Courier Journal* sent me a cordial note about the book in response to the photograph, and I have to-day one from the literary editor of the *Brooklyn Eagle*. A friend has written me, by the way, that Mr. Charles Dudley Warner[4] was writing a review for the *Hartford Courant*. I don't know how this will be, though I hear from the same source that he was delighted with the book—especially with the General and the Judge. If anything comes to me that I think you can use I shall send it. So far I have had four or five reviews all pleasant enough, but not very interesting. The man in the *Baltimore News* has been quite vindictive here-to-fore; for this reason I enclose it. The only thing I have learned as yet is that they seem to feel that the romantic novel is not the only kind.

Faithfully yours,

ELLEN GLASGOW

[2] The fictional name of post-bellum, pre-Rockefeller Williamsburg in *The Voice of the People*.

[3] Isaac Frederick Marcosson, a member of the staff and later city editor of the Louisville *Times,* who presumably wrote reviews for its sister paper, the *Courier Journal*.

[4] Essayist, novelist, and editor of the Hartford *Courant*.

TO WALTER HINES PAGE

Richmond, May 12th, 1900

My dear Mr. Page:

Thank you for your letter and the enclosed advertisements.

I suppose I ought to be satisfied that the book has met with so much sincere sympathy. I know, at least, that I would not write down to a sensation loving public for any amount of financial recompense, but I do want my work to be widely recognized. But for all that my methods don't belong to this generation—though I mean to stick to them.

Yes, the new book grows daily. The first chapters have formed themselves so clearly that I shall soon write them out despite myself.

I am glad, by the way, that you warned me against any over haste about serial publication. A representative of the Harpers was down here about a week ago to talk about the book, and would have arranged for a serial publication, but I would not commit myself to him about it. It seems they think *The Voice* my best book—and they think also that it should have gone to them. Of course, I don't think so and I frankly said so. Your belief in this book has meant a great deal to me, and it is the kind of thing that does me good.

Very sincerely yours,

ELLEN GLASGOW

TO WALTER HINES PAGE

Richmond, May 24th, 1900

My dear Mr. Page:

I can't find any decent photographs of Williamsburg. These are the only good pictures of it I have seen, so I send them. I don't know where they were originally used, but I refer you to the enclosed letter. At the same time I am sending you a catalogue of the college—the churchyard is very fine.

By chance we have just found an old photograph of the patriarch of Battle Hall, and an intimate friend of my childhood. He was Uncle Ish[1] and Caesar in one, and, withal, a perfect gentleman by nature. Like Uncle Ish he "moved off" for fear he'd return to slavery (his home was really on Hickory Hill). He united a most devoted attachment to his old mistress with the maxim that "freedom hit are a mighty good thing."

The other little picture is of Duke of Gloucester Street, with the old sexton of the church. I don't know whether they will be of any use or not. If not please send me back "Uncle Will." [2]

Sincerely,

E. GLASGOW

[1] A Negro character in *The Voice of the People.*
[2] The model for Uncle Ish.

TO WALTER HINES PAGE

Richmond, December 16th, 1900

Dear Mr. Page:

It is very kind of you to remember that I live quite away from the world of bookmaking, and to let me hear how things go on. It seems kinder still when I remember that you are one of the busiest men in the world. But it does help me and I thank you very heartily. And the thing I wish most for my books is that they shall have long life—so your plan of keeping *The Voice* upon the market is the one that suits me above all others.

With congratulations upon the success of *The World's Work,*[1] I am,

Sincerely yours,

ELLEN GLASGOW

[1] A magazine of current affairs founded by Mr. Page in 1900.

TO ELIZABETH PATTERSON[1]

Richmond, January 2nd, 1902

Dear Girl:

Many thanks for the dear little copy of the same very lovely sonnets.

We so seldom see each [other] now that I begin to fancy we are drifting in opposite ways until there comes, now and then, some realization that the past is quite as strong as the present and much more sacred. You are bound up, my dear, with some of the happiest memories of my life, and the older I grow the more earnestly I feel that the few intense joys of childhood are the best that life has to give. We may become very successful and very wise, perhaps, but the farther we travel from those first years the faster the freshness passes from us and the dimmer grow our memories of the faces we loved best. May the happiest things the fates have in their hands come to you this year, dear girl.

As always,

ELLEN

[1] One of Miss Glasgow's closest Richmond friends.

TO ELIZABETH PATTERSON

Friday [no date or place]

My dearest Lizbeth:

I was delighted to get your letter and to have news of the return to health of dear Miss Betty. Do let me know when you get back for I am really going to come out and see your mother. You I expect to come to me.

It must be a heavenly place you are at, and you don't know how glad I am that you should have had this pleasure. I can see you now paddling up those blue creeks, and I wish I could catch a breath of the air, and watch the birds. Your description reminds me so much of my beloved Prince Edward Island. This isn't a real letter—I haven't time for one —it is just a note to let you know how I enjoyed hearing from you. Did you know I wonder that my thoughts have turned so often of late to those dear lost springs in the big woods? Do you remember, too, those queer bell-like white flowers we used to find with the blossom growing from the leaf? I have never seen them since.

Best love to Miss Betty—and as ever

Yours,

ELLEN

TO WALTER HINES PAGE

Richmond, January 14th, 1902

My dear Mr. Page:

Your delightful Christmas letter reproaches me with my seeming ungraciousness, and I hasten to make the amends of an apology for not answering it before. The trouble is that I hoped very much to have you cross Richmond on your way north, and it is only within the last week that I have ceased to expect you to drop in upon us some fine day. However, I suppose you had better things to do, and that now, after a most successful trip, you are submerged in the *World's Work* again. That this letter may penetrate to you through your multiplied occupation, I confess I have some little doubt. When I hear—as I do now and then—of the many forms your amazing energies require, I begin, indeed, to regard you as a kind of animated Colossus, or a second Theodore Roosevelt. And this brings me to the point that I'll forgive you anything—even the ineffectual arrows you may sling at Poe—so long as you don't neglect *The Battle-Ground*—or become President.

But what I set out to say at the beginning, and without this tedious preamble, was that I find myself echoing most

[*35*]

heartily the wishes you express that "for many a spring we shall work to-gether." Great joy and solace as my art has become to me, half the pleasure of publishing my books— and this I say advisedly—would be gone were they to bear the impress of another house. The share of the sympathetic publisher in the author's success—the true success so different from the ephemeral—is apt to be overlooked in these blatant days, so it is just as well that some of us should keep it in mind. One cannot lay a foundation by scattering stones, nor is a reputation for good work to be got by strewing volumes about the world; and so when I look ahead in my sanguine hours my vision with regard to my work is much the same as yours—a series of good books each adding to the building of the name I hope for and each testifying to the share my chosen publishers have had in the growing work.

And so,

Always sincerely yours,

ELLEN GLASGOW

TO WALTER HINES PAGE

Richmond, January 29th, 1902

Dear Mr. Page:

About *The Battle-Ground,* No!—No!—No! I didn't forego serial publication in a magazine to have it come out in a newspaper. A hundred times No!!!

About the poems—yes, yes, yes. I have a number of them —enough to make a small volume and I should like tremendously to have them come out. Only they are rather unconventional, you know; but if you don't mind this, I don't; and they are certainly strong besides being good verse. Let me hear more of this plan—I like it.[1]

By the way, it's very hard to get a well taken photograph

[1] Miss Glasgow's poems were published under the title *The Freeman and Other Poems,* Doubleday, August, 1902.

in Richmond, but I'll try if you need another for the exploitation of the book. It's all so silly, isn't it—this craze to look at people!

Suppose I send the poems to you & you go over them and suggest any to be left out.

Very sincerely yours,
ELLEN GLASGOW

TO WALTER HINES PAGE

Richmond, April 18th, 1902

My dear Mr. Page:

The prospect of your hospitality at Englewood is too delightful to come true, I fear, much as we should love it. Indeed, you don't know, I am sure, the burden you are soliciting, for when we start off this summer there'll probably be an Irish terrier added to our party, and four members of one family (even if one happens to be four-footed) are quite too many for a visit even to you. At the same time I am very much afraid that we'll be rather in the condition of "wrecks" by mid-summer, but we can't get off earlier, and so we must leave a large margin for Fate to work in. Of course, you know that we should enjoy above all things coming to Englewood if only for a day or so, and who knows but what we may achieve it yet. At all events let us hope for it. With all good wishes to Mrs. Page. . . .

I am,
Always sincerely yours,
ELLEN GLASGOW

As I care neither for fishing nor sailing Englewood has all attractions for me.

TO WALTER HINES PAGE

Richmond, June 20th, 1902

My dear Mr. Page:

I presume I have your thoughtfulness to thank for *The Rebuilding of Old Commonwealths,*[1] which I have just read with the greatest interest. It is a very suggestive little book, and when I see how forcefully you use your pen I find myself wondering that you haven't given more of your time to the making of literature. The South needs a historian, and why in the name of all that's likely! shouldn't you be the man?

Before the book came my sisters and I were talking of Mrs. Page and yourself, and Cary had said that we must have appeared very ungrateful the evening you were in Richmond. The truth was that we had been keeping the coming of the dog a secret from father (who detests them) and when you invited the little fellow to your kennels we were a little uncertain as to how "the news" would be received. Then, too, I had been quite ill all day, and I have felt ever since that my suffering spoiled a pleasure which I had looked forward to so long.

At present we have another cause for regret in the fact that we must postpone our coming to you—if you will be so good as to let us still look forward to it.

We have all three succumbed to the heat and the doctor is very anxious to get us to the Adirondacks as soon as possible. As it is we can't get off until the 11th of July, spending but one day (the 12th) in New York. If it is not inconvenient for you we hope to catch a glimpse of you then, and when we come back in September you—and Mrs. Page—

[1] By Walter Hines Page. Doubleday, 1902.

will perhaps be so kind as to let us run out for a day or so with you.

With all good wishes,
believe me,
Sincerely yours,
ELLEN GLASGOW

TO WALTER HINES PAGE

Richmond, September 25th, 1902

My dear Mr. Page:

In the midst of the general upheaval of our homecoming, we have spoken so often of Englewood and of the delightful way in which we were taken into your family circle. I enjoyed my two days in New York immensely and most of all I enjoyed our little journey down into the country. Cary is writing to Mrs. Page by the same mail to tell her all this and of another little plan which we have very much at heart.

On reaching here we find that Richmond is fairly bubbling with interest in the horse-show, which comes off the middle of October, and which will really be very much worth seeing —since all Virginia expects to turn out in its best for the occasion, and to bring its horses, too. At first I found it impossible to secure seats, but the President (the capital unintentional) of the Association has offered me his box for a night—the 15th, 16th or 17th of October. Now won't Mrs. Page and yourself come down to see us at this time. We have simply set our hearts on it—Father too—and you will have an opportunity of seeing Richmond at her very best. Not only that—there will be almost all Virginia here—and you can get to know the people better than at another time. Do write me at once that you will come to stay as long as you can, and I will select an evening for the horseshow, and give myself the pleasure of making a few other plans.

Always sincerely yours,
ELLEN GLASGOW

TO WALTER HINES PAGE

Richmond, December 26th, 1902

My dear Mr. Page:

The telegram yesterday brought back to us so vividly the pleasantest Xmas we have ever spent—the one at Englewood last year. Then, a moment ago, your shadow arrived, which, in default of yourself, was one of the nicest things that could happen.—Thank you very heartily.

Now that a New Year is almost here there can surely be no better time for me to send you a letter which will say some few of the many things I am always thinking. It is very nearly eight years since you first wrote to me after reading *The Descendant*,[1] and not far from five since I transferred my interests to the firm of Doubleday, Page and Company. You were, of course, responsible for this, and it may please you to know how sincerely thankful I have been for my choice of publishers. Not only my associations with the firm and the publication of my books, but your personal friendship has been and is today one of the greatest pleasures of my life. I don't know if you realize how truly helpful you have been to me. So now at the season when one may speak sincerely from the heart, I wish to thank you for it. You have made it all seem worth while, somehow—the work and the struggle, and the going on to an aim, which in itself can be but a little thing. But in the highest sense you have given me encouragement, even when you did not dream that I needed it, when you did not know how bitterly I wanted to throw it all away—and life with it. The years have brought a good many things to me, but they have taken them all away again except my work. Whether my own life goes into my books

[1] This would suggest that Mr. Page had seen the manuscript as early as 1895, some two years before Harper and Brothers published *The Descendant*.

I do not know, but such as are in me I must write, and it will always be the quiet, happy souls who will turn out the popular romances, and we others, who have never been able to forget our Gethsemane and our cross, will continue to inflict upon our publishers the books that go down into the heart of things and appeal to those few that have been there before us. And so I have begun upon another big, deep, human document[2] which no one will understand because it is wrung from life itself—and not from sugared romance. I doubt much if even you will care for it, but I could no more help writing it than I could live and not breathe the air about me. It was this or death for me—for I had come to the final choice that some are forced to make—and when I left New York it did not seem to me within the remotest range of probabilities that I should see the New Year in upon this planet. Yet here I am, for the idea saved me, and I can now sit down quietly since the storm is over, and write you this doleful letter of good wishes.

I have said too much, I know, for it is cowardly to put a share of my burden upon so good a friend—but I shall make up for it by praying that only such borrowed troubles may be yours in this coming year—that you may have that fortunate year that you deserve.

Sincerely yours,

ELLEN GLASGOW

[2] *The Deliverance*, Doubleday, 1904.

TO MRS. WALTER HINES PAGE

Richmond, July 2nd, 1903

Dear Mrs. Page:

We expect to sail on the 18th, and if you will let us we want to come to you from the 15th to the 17th. I have no idea what time the Old Dominion gets in, but not late in the day, I suppose—and if all goes well we should reach Englewood on the afternoon of Wednesday, the 15th. It will be such a pleasure to see you again.

With love from us all to you all,
ELLEN GLASGOW

The book grows night and day—a fine spell of work despite the heat—and tell Mr. Page I've changed my mind about renouncing literature just yet.

TO WALTER HINES PAGE

Riegenhotel-Jungfraublick
Interlaken
July 31st, 1903

My dear Mr. Page:

Cary has just announced her intention of sending a letter to Mrs. Page. So she is probably writing all the news in the next room,—but as I never in any circumstances tell anything that happens, I can do no harm by mailing a belated note to you at the same time. You don't know what a difference it made having Arthur and you to see us off and just here I must tell you that we feasted upon the fruit for days and enjoyed it thoroughly down to the last remaining cherry. Our voyage was singularly uninteresting—we left in the midst of a storm (or rather got the wake of one by next day) and for three hours Rebe and I were rather ill. After that all went well, though we didn't particularly care for the line and shan't select it when we come again. We left the steamer with wretched colds, which accounts for our delay in writing, and after madly chasing a lost trunk over Antwerp and spending a few precious moments before the Rubens in the Cathedral, came straight on to Switzerland. At first we were dismally disappointed, and I conceived a hatred for Lucerne (partly owing, I dare say, to the fact that we chanced upon the largest hotel in Switzerland and I'm sure one of the most costly in all Europe). Here, however, it is heavenly; we are sitting at the feet of the Jungfrau and it is the first real mountain, I feel, that I have ever seen. In a week we shall probably go on a little trip and then to Mürren, where we hope to stay. Our visit to Englewood still remains with us as a lovely memory; it is the one place away from One West Main Street where I feel at home.

Rebe and Cary join me in love to you "all and singular," —and each of us sends a good kiss to Mrs. Page. Remember that my address is in care of Brown, Shipley, 123 Pall Mall, S.W., and do get the manuscript from Mr. Schoonover.[1] I am anxious to hear your impressions of it and I am, as always,

Heartily yours,

ELLEN GLASGOW

[1] Frank E. Schoonover was doing the illustrations for *The Deliverance*.

TO MARY JOHNSTON [1]

[No place indicated]
March 22nd, 1904

[No salutation]

It is a far cry, my dear fellow-craftsman, from the gray skies and the naked poplars outside to the eternal summer of which your letter was overflowing, and I hope that the change has rested you all through—has "rested every hair of your head," as my colored mammy used to say. I have just read *Sir Mortimer*[2] and after the resistless sweep and energy in the latter half I would think you needed to stop and draw a long, slow breath. It is full of colour and poetry and quick action and it keeps wonderfully that peculiar golden light, as if of a warmer sunshine, which seems to linger on those days when we turn and look back at them. And Damaris is to me

[1] A fellow Virginian and historical novelist best remembered for such books as *To Have and To Hold* and *Cease Firing*.

[2] By Mary Johnston. Harper, 1904.

[*43*]

the most attractive of your heroines—I like her in that love scene in the garden.

Is your imagination working again, I wonder, and can you really let it lie idle—or are you mentally exhausted and aweary of pen and paper as I have been for months? Those systematic hardy workers who go on day after day with never a pause are the ones I envy—they must escape the fret and fever of sudden spurts and inevitable reactions. Intuition tells me just here that Corolie[3] is downstairs, so I'll leave you for her in a minute. It was very nice to hear from you—I feel that I shall be as glad as possible to know you better— to stand within the gate. Yes, I dare say we are different in many ways—it will be interesting, don't you think, to learn how different. And the main thing, perhaps we both have.

Faithfully yours,

E.G.

[3] Corolie Johnston, Mary Johnston's cousin, who lived in Richmond.

TO MARY JOHNSTON

[No place indicated]

Thursday, [apparently summer 1904]

My dear, dear Mary:

Though I haven't bothered you with letters there hasn't been a day when I haven't thought of you with tenderness and affection. We have seen so little of each other and yet I seem to know you so well and the place you have in my heart is a very deep and real one. Since I have heard that you are beginning to grow stronger and better it has lifted a positive weight of anxiety from my mind. Do keep it up, my friend, there is so much in the power of will—I mean in really wishing to grow well—and then you are so much of interest and pleasure to us all. I can't tell you how often my thoughts will be with you this summer—and I shall think of you particularly whenever I see anything beautiful that you might enjoy with me.

Rebe and I are sailing on the S.S. Bremen on July 6th, so this is only a very little note of farewell for a season. When we are both back again in the autumn, I hope—I do hope that we may be very much more together. Meantime if you are able to write letters remember that my address is in care of Brown, Shipley, 123 Pall Mall. From the other side I'll send you a letter of more interest I trust—but just now my brain has gone to cotton wool. The heat has been so intense that I have spent my time in darkened rooms with volumes of philosophy. Spinoza has seemed best to suit the case. Cary writes that you have been "goodness itself" to her, and her trip has been the very greatest pleasure. Give my love to Eloise,[1] and keep it for yourself, you dear, strong, brave girl.

Affectionately yours,
E.G.

[1] Mary Johnston's sister.

TO MARY JOHNSTON

Richmond, February 3rd, 1905

You have been so much in my thoughts, dear Mary, since you went away, and there seems a very big slice taken out of our surroundings. We haven't even tried to fill in the blank, but in the midst of our snow storms, we have dwelt fondly upon Eloise's postcards, of which Rebe is exceedingly proud. I do hope and pray from the bottom of my heart that those blue skies and palms and the warm air have brought you up again.

I shall never forget the last talk I had with you the afternoon before you went. You looked so much like a little child, and there are moments when one seems almost to see the soul of one's friend shining through the delicate flesh. The people I love best, I love for their spiritual quality, for it shows me God, somehow, and I hunger for him even when I am least positive of his being underneath us all. When I first knew you, do you know, I thought that I could never come quite close to you—that your reserve would be so great, and I am very thankful that I have at last found that there was a way through it. You are different from me in many ways, and particularly in as much as you keep your impulses so firmly in hand while mine so often carry me breathlessly away. And then you have such courage, and suffering, which makes me impatient and ready to rend the universe, has given you a peaceful and strong composure. Well, well, do you remember the Buddhist proverb—"There are many paths down into the valley, but when we come out upon the mountains we all see the self-same sun." The broad roads that are not quite together, but a little of the same spirit is lighting each of us on our way, and it is this that draws us, I hope, together, and will keep us friends until the end. May you lend me a little of your courage, too, dear, when my strength gives out again.

Eleanor Robson[1] has been and gone and I loved her for the sake of something young and tender and pathetic about her. We had a rather nice party, and several times during the afternoon, she turned and said to me, "Oh, I wish Mary Johnston were here!" Cary and Rebe and I wished just as heartily that you had been—you and Eloise. We did persuade your brother to come, and he has faithfully promised to drop in on our Tuesday afternoons. He reminds me very much of you.

Do send me a card, if nothing more privately mine, to tell me how the place suits you now. It is bitterly cold here, but

[1] The actress who played in the dramatic version of Mary Johnston's book *Audrey,* and who later became Mrs. August Belmont.

I am working hard and don't mind it much. Next week I'll probably have a few days in New York.

With sincere affection,
Yours ever,
E.G.

TO ARTHUR GRAHAM GLASGOW

Richmond, March 27, 1905

My dearest Arthur:

Father has just showed us your letter, and you are certainly a most thoughtful and generous brother. I shall never forget how beautiful you were in New York last spring— and ever since then I have felt that I understood you and appreciated you as I had never done before. I suppose Father has told you about Cary's illness and the very serious operation which Dr. Johnston thought was necessary to prolong her life. She has stood it all wonderfully well, and looks already at least fifteen years younger than she did before she went to bed—and so much more cheerful and less nervous. I hope that this will make her better than she has been for five years, but, of course, she must be very careful for a long time. She is now in the hospital and remarkably well when all things are considered. Rebe and I have just returned from two weeks at Chase City;[1] on the 13th of April we hope to go up to the University of Virginia to Dr. Alderman's[2] installation as President, and afterwards I shall probably stop for awhile at Castle Hill with Amelie.[3] The 6th of July (and now I come to the definite intention of all this) Rebe and I

[1] A town in southern Virginia.

[2] Dr. Edwin Anderson Alderman.

[3] Amelie Rives, Virginian writer of popular romances in the early 1900's, was married to Prince Pierre Troubetskoy, Russian portrait painter, and lived at "Castle Hill," between Charlottesville and Orange, Virginia.

[47]

hope to sail on the Bremen for Germany, with the purpose
of my consulting Dr. Isadore Müller, who is said to be the
first living aurist. It may be that he can do nothing for me,
but my ears interfere so with my enjoyment of life that I
should like to feel that I have done all in my power to make
them hearable. Dr. Müller is at Carlsbad for three months
every summer, and we intend to go directly there—Rebe is
engaged in learning German this very minute with her
Hasleff. Apart from the expenses of my trip, I have allowed
one thousand dollars for the charges of Dr. Müller. I do not
think there is the faintest chance of his bill exceeding this
amount, but if it should happen that he should wish to keep
me longer or to perform a serious operation, I might find
that my letter of credit would not suffice, and in this case do
you think that you could advance me, by cable, any additional
amount that I might need? When I say "advance," I mean,
of course, until my new book is published as I hope next
winter or spring.[4] This, you will understand, is dealing with
a remote contingency. I do not think it probable in the least
that my money will give out—I am allowing what I feel to
be a wide margin—but all things are possible and I should
like to feel that I may place my case unreservedly in his
hands and do as he advises. One hears stories of high charges
from doctors, but in my personal experience they have never
exceeded what I considered their due. Of course, I could
always sell the Tredegar[5] stock I hold, but not so long as I
can keep so good an investment; and if I need the additional
money I shall need it by cable. Rebe and I both wish that it
could be so arranged that we could spend a day or two in
England and see the baby, but the passage is made much
more reasonable by going to Bremen, and then I wish to see
Dr. Müller as soon as I reach the other side. I hope you will

[4] *The Wheel of Life,* Doubleday, 1906.
[5] The Tredegar Iron Works, with which Miss Glasgow's father, Mr.
Frank Glasgow, was connected.

not let my request inconvenience you—of course, as it now looks, I make it only that I may have my mind perfectly at ease. What we would do without you to turn to in difficulties I do not know.

With love to Margaret and the baby,

Your devoted sister,

ELLEN

Julia Sully⁶ has been in Spain since February. Father seems well.

⁶ Close friend of Miss Glasgow.

TO WALTER HINES PAGE

The Glen Springs
Watkins, N. Y.
Christmas, 1905

My dear Mr. Page:

It was lovely to have both your letter and the William Watson poems. Into the latter I have already dipped with a great deal of pleasure—some of his earlier poems I am extremely fond of, though, strange to say, I did not possess him in any shape of dress.

I know your Christmas was very lovely at Englewood, and I wish with all my heart that I could have been there. A walk through the lovely Glen in its drapery of ice was the best thing I did today. The air here is really perfect, never sharp but deliciously piney, and the place is very comfortable, though I'm ready to pack my bag and be off at a moment's warning. Cary, I think, has improved somewhat, but she has a long weary road to pull up, I fear.

In my leisure hours, which aren't many, I have been diverting myself with Schopenhauer who is decidedly more interesting than fiction besides being a better training for the muscles of the intellect. Alas, my dear friend, you are speaking with your political intelligence when you counsel

me not to "take metaphysics seriously." If there is one subject upon earth which a human being can take seriously with
dignity it is the soul of man—and what is metaphysics except
the science of the soul? I am a born sceptic, you know, but in
my first period, at the time I first knew you—in my materialistic and pessimistic days, I could not so much as tolerate any
philosophizing that was not hitched fast to the concrete fact.
I suppose I am doomed to pass through as many intellectual
phases as are possible to this planet, but the truth remains
that in the roughest place in my life, I was brought back to
some kind of acceptance and reconciliation wholly through
an interest in the most abstruse and transcendental metaphysics in existence which is that of the sacred books of the
East— But there! I didn't mean to deliver you a lecture.

Give our dearest love to our Mrs. Page and our heartiest
New Year's greeting to each member of the household. We
think and speak of all of you so often—and I am simply
longing to get back to New York. I'm so glad you're going
to advertise *The Wheel* yourself, with your own particular
pen. On my next book I mean to put three year's work.

Always sincerely yours,

ELLEN GLASGOW

TO ARTHUR GRAHAM GLASGOW

Richmond, April 15th, 1906

Dearest Arthur:

I hope you are very much better, and I hate so to trouble
you about business while you are feeling so badly. In New
York you told me that you could always get me a good six
percent investment, and Father thinks it very uncertain
about finding one over here by himself. Some of my invest-
ments have been paid up, so I'll have about nine thousand
dollars I'd like so much to have you put out for me. As I
have so small an income I don't like to let the money lie idle,

for I'd certainly spend it. Somebody told me to invest in the Danville Cotton Mills, but I'd rather trust to your judgment. I hope this won't bother you. Love to both the Margarets.[1]

Affectionately yours,

ELLEN GLASGOW

I've taken a cottage in the Adirondacks for the summer.

[1] Wife and daughter of Mr. Glasgow. The daughter was more often called Marjorie.

TO MARY JOHNSTON

Hurricane Lodge
Hurricane, Essex Co., N. Y.
[Probably summer of 1906]

Dearest Mary:

Ever since Eloise's letter to Rebe, we have rejoiced at the thought of you. It seems as if a load were taken from us, for we have felt your illness more, I think, than we have ever been able to let you know. At such times human affection and sympathy seem always such very little things in the larger presence of pain.

Here we are very sweetly fixed for the summer in a nice fresh little cottage which I wish you and Eloise were here to share with us. It's a lovely country, though not so lovely as my recollections of Maryland. But the chain of mountains is beautiful in outline. The air is sweet with haymaking, and such meadows I have never seen except in the Tyrol or in Scotland. They are fairly pied with flowers, reminding me of nothing so much as of the background in some Pre-Raphaelite painting where each wildflower is painted in with such exquisite delicacy of color. Someday, if all goes well, I may have a very simple cottage in the midst of the fields of timothy and harebells and black-eyed daisies, and then you must certainly come up and spend a long quiet summer with me. This tranquil monotony, somehow, appears to be the only

[*51*]

state for which I am physically fitted, and I suspect it is the same with you. The spring was not a good time with me—I paid an exorbitant price for my last winter's gaiety and it has taken almost two months of this life to bring me back again to the rather unstable equilibrium of sensation which I call health. However, I hope that we will both feel vigorously social again in the autumn, and then, if the gods agree, we'll start the kettle boiling on Tuesday and Friday afternoon. The custom languished last winter, chiefly, I think, because with you and Eloise absent, Berta[1] and Corolie were the only visitors we cared to see.

The rain has stopped at last so I must put on a short skirt and rubbers and climb a rain-soaked hill. Goodbye, dear. If Rebe were here, she would send love to you both, I know.

Affectionately always,

ELLEN

[1] Roberta Welford of Richmond.

TO MARY JOHNSTON

Hurricane Lodge, August 15, 1906

My dear Mary:

Your letter was one of the most delightful and surprising happenings of the summer! What a marvel of recuperation you are—and I can assure you that I have ceased entirely to picture you as an invalid—imagining instead a very lively and elastic little lady who has a good deal of work and play and sweetness and trouble before her yet. Dear, you must set your face forward in earnest and keep always with me in this "small old path" of the *Upanishads,* "difficult to tread as the keen edge of a razor." As for me I can only tell you of the joy—the real joy that your letter has brought me. Tears were in my eyes when I read it—tears of tenderness, of happiness for you. I took up my pen to answer it at once and then—ah, then—well, that is about myself and less interesting to me and far less smooth in a way than your road has been these last few weeks. It's strange, Mary, isn't it that I who have comparative health and strength to work and play and wander about the earth and make friends and enemies if I choose (who can hold also to a hardly bought philosophy even in tragic moments)—that I who have all these things should possess so little of the natural happy instinct for life that today at thirty-two, I could lie down quietly and give it up and pass on to one of the thousand lives I see beyond.

But forgive me, dear, forgive me—I didn't mean to say such things to you and I am ashamed. They sound as if I were unhappy and I am not—oh, far, far from it. For the last year I have been happy for the first time in my life—happy not in the outward shadow part of me, but in my soul which is clear and radiant out of a long darkness.

Ah, I am with you in your feeling about work, and with you, too, in having spent a summer staring (with newly sharpened pencils beside me) at a spotless sheet of paper. *Dolce far niente* is not to my mind but very much indeed to my manner during these last weeks. Day steps after day into the abyss of wasted time. People come and go and instead of an impressionable mind, I seem to present merely the waxen smile of polite features. I've even detached myself in vain from metaphysics—Kant and Bradley stand half read on my desk, and my best beloved Fichte I haven't dared open for a month—yet in spite of everything the eccentric whirl of a summer hotel sweeps me from my moorings, and, for sheer lack of concentration I cannot write. Our cottage is nice, but the hotel is abominable, and driven to desperation at last, we are going to pack up shortly and depart for Montreal and Quebec. The Adirondacks hold no more illusions for me. My four years dream of a camp here has been washed away in rain. I've been here almost three months and we have had barely ten perfect days and nights. Last night the stars were magnificent—Pegasus and Andromeda faced me brilliantly

[*53*]

when I lifted my shade, so I went down and had a friendly reunion with the constellations—but the chances are that they will hide themselves very soon again. Have you watched Venus, I wonder, this summer as closely as I have. She sets now just over our finest mountain and immediately in her footsteps the Great Bear swings into view. I get a wonderful peace and the most exquisite pleasure from my friendships with the stars.

What you say of Italy stirs my pulse, but for me it is not possible because of my bank account and the manner by which I must set about increasing it. Yet for you I hope the plan will work itself into a fact. Richmond will be really Richmond in October—will it not? Then we must arrange to see each other when we can, and you must lose quite the "submerged sensation" you sometimes feel. I've had it often myself and I know just the curious soul-loneliness it brings. I want to draw you, dear brave heart, not only back to work and play but back to me. There's so much of the child in me yet, and life to me means love just as it does to a child—love of many kinds and degrees, but each and all helping us on our way and bringing the journey's end a little nearer the knowledge of God. So love me, Mary, much or little as you can, and I shall love you back in my own measure.

Love from Rebe to you both.

Kiss Eloise for me.

Ever yours,

ELLEN GLASGOW

TO MARY JOHNSTON

Chateau Frontenac
Quebec, Canada
September 15th, 1906

My dear Mary:

Your letter was forwarded to me here, and if I had had the necessary time, I'd have been charmed to meet the people you spoke of—but Rebe[1] and I have both been "invalided" since coming to Quebec, and, to tell the truth, we've done little but eat and sleep and sit about in neighboring hospitable squares. In this way the only acquaintances we've made have been certain sociable dogs that attach themselves in our train and invariably accompany us back into the chateau. Now our visit here is about over—on Monday we leave for New York, and then—if dressmakers and the Gods agree!—we hope to see Richmond about the second week in October. Do you know I shall be really glad to return to those dusty streets and that dismantled house. I want to work—work—work for at least six quiet months.

Your letter, dear, was like a song of joy, so overflowing with renewed vitality and a high heart for life. I know, I *know* it all, for a year ago I passed through exactly the same awakening of myself, though from different causes. Mine was not physical, but spiritual—mental—what you will! For a year I was so dead that I couldn't feel even when I was hurt because of some curious emotional anaesthesia, and, like you, I had to fight—fight, a sleepless battle night and day, not for my reason but for my very soul. Then at the end of a year—at Mürren last summer I came out triumphant, and for three whole months it was as if I walked on light, not air. I was like one who had come out of a dark prison into the presence of God and saw and knew him, and cared for noth-

[1] Rebe married Cabell Carrington Tutwiler in December, 1906.

ing in the way of pain that had gone before the vision. Of course, dear heart, the exhilaration, the first rapture of the mere rebound to physical or spiritual health cannot be permanent, but, I think, the strength of the victory and the memory of it, are built into the eternal forces of one's spirit. We suffered in different ways, but we both suffered to the death—each of us saw at the end of her road the mouth of hell—and each of us turned and struggled back to life—you along your steep path and I along mine. It is something to be thankful for that now at last our roads may run a little while into one. The old sorrows, the old temptations, the old fights are like so many steps by which we go on and upward and always, I hope, to something bigger and higher than we knew before. Ah, Mary, Mary, as I walked alone, just now in this glorious weather, it seemed to me that I could look back not only without bitterness, but with thankfulness upon the way I had come. The exaltation may soften and pass into quiet, but the peace of the soul does not and cannot surrender to the old anguish again.

I can't say more, dear, but this much I must tell you that if my letter gave you an impression of dejection or restlessness it reflected me very falsely. I was born with a terrible burden of melancholy—of too much introspection—but for a whole year, for the first time in my life, I have not known a single instant of the old depression. I am perfectly willing to die, but I can say now, as I never could before, that I am equally willing to live until I come to where my road turns again. The sense of eternity—of immortality that is not a personal immortality has brought me not only reconciliation, but the kind of joy that is like the rush down from the battle of the senses. I have come at last into what Whitman calls "the me myself," that is behind and above it all.

I wonder if you will understand what I've written—but I don't wonder about your sympathy, for I know that I have that always just as you have mine. Our temperaments, our inheritances, our attitudes even may be different—but it is love, after all, that smooths away the edges of personality and makes one *know* another by intuition rather than by knowledge. Goodbye for a time—when we meet you will be settled in your home—and I shall be so much interested in everything about it. We must take up our afternoons very early in the autumn.

Yours always with love,
ELLEN

TO ARTHUR GRAHAM GLASGOW

Greenbrier
White Sulphur Springs, W. Va.
August 14, 1907

My dear Arthur:

Will you do a favor for me if it will not put you to trouble. If it does, just don't think about it again. I have been riding every morning since I've been here, and it has done me so much physical good and given me so much pleasure that I am very anxious to keep it up and to own a Champion and Wilton saddle that really fits me. It has occurred to me that you might order this saddle for me and let it come along with your luggage, free of duty. But, of course, if you can't do it, it will be all right and I will pay the tariff, which is very exorbitant on leather. If you will send the enclosed memorandum to Messrs. Champion and Wilton, 457 and 458 Oxford Street, London, and ask them to make me a saddle to fit me, I shall be so very much obliged. Amelie Troubetskoy gave me their address and says their saddles, made to order, are the best in the world, costing, free of duty, about $90. I should like the bridle and leather saddle blanket also, and if you will order them all for me and have them packed to come with your things, I will be deeply grateful. Let me know if you can do this, and ask the makers to send their bill direct to me, or else I will send the money to you as soon as I know. I am sending a memorandum of all the measurements they are said to require. Nothing I've ever done has given me such pleasure as my rides this summer. Julia Sully is with me now, and she and I go out alone at half past seven every morning.

Our summer has been charming; the cottage as comfortable as possible; and the people very pleasant. We are so much obliged to you for giving it to us, and all of us are feeling exceedingly well. We have tea on our porch in the afternoon, and it is very popular. I've seen a good deal of Effie[1] and am very fond of her. We are planning to take a trip together—perhaps to come over to London someday to see you and Margaret.

Good news comes from Frank,[2] but he has had a terrible summer, and it was pathetic that Father had to go back when he had looked forward to being up here for two months. . . .

Cary writes cheerfully. On her way to the Dolomites, stopping a day or two in Venice. I hope the trip will do her good, but I think her condition a most serious one.

Best love to Margaret and Margy.

> Affectionately yours,
> ELLEN GLASGOW

[1] Effie Branch, sister of Mrs. Arthur Glasgow.
[2] Miss Glasgow's brother.

TO WALTER HINES PAGE

> Richmond, June 26th, 1908

My dear Editor of *The World's Work,*

Don't you think that even for the sake of so utterly impracticable a thing as a mere matter of principle, it is well to inquire into a subject before we indulge in animadversion with regard to its consequences, moral or otherwise? Now personally I have not the slightest objection to being branded as either "sentimental" or "emotional," since it puts me in a

very respectable class from Christ to the first sentimentalist
who suggested that truth might still prevail though the pursuit of it through the rack and the thumbscrew should be
abolished. But the real purpose underlying my gentle protest
is to inquire when and where a bill prohibiting the vivisection
of animals for medical research was introduced into the New
York legislature—or into the Massachusetts one, for that
matter? If instead of listening to the evidently beguiling,
though somewhat Jesuitical Dr. Flexner, you had merely
taken the trouble to read the Cobb-Johnson bill, you would
have discovered that its one aim and object was to prohibit
what you call "the wanton use" of the practice "by persons
who have no serious purpose." The features in the bill which
aroused the hostility of the vivisectors appear to have been
the clause demanding that the animal be under an anaesthetic
and killed afterwards unless the success of the operation
depends on its being kept alive (I am quoting from memory,
so please look up the clause) and that all laboratories should
be open for proper inspection. Now if there is no cruelty, as
Dr. Flexner claims, may I inquire why he should object so
strenuously to the simple passage of a measure which aims
to prevent it? As for the cruelties, may I ask you to read Dr.
Crile's *Experiments in Surgical Shock* or failing that Dr.
Leffingwell's *The Vivisection Question*—or even the late Dr.
Henry J. Bigelow's address on the subject, of an earlier date
than the others. "Sentimental" and "emotional" very good,
my dear Mr. Page, but hardly "ill-informed" when I waded
through miles of medical reports and traced these horrors to
the hands that performed them. And brand us as you please,
you may see from the enclosed clipping that we are becoming
a rather formidable body.[1] That civilization means merely the
building up of "The finer qualities of heart and mind," not
the preservation of life *at any cost,* is what I contend. "Life

[1] Undoubtedly the Society for the Prevention of Cruelty to Animals, in
which Miss Glasgow was active.

at any cost" has become very serviceable as a national motto, and we realize its full significance in the burning of the bazar de la charite, or the wreck of the Bourgogne. I have written this very hastily. Please don't think that I mean to be harsh. I realize that you have heard only Dr. Flexner's side. Ask for Mark Twain's—or for Robert Browning's—or Tennyson's, or a thousand others of equal heart and brain.

Always sincerely yours,

ELLEN GLASGOW

SECTION II

November 1, 1914—December 14, 1929

There is a gap of more than six years between Sections I and II. These were productive years for Ellen Glasgow; Double-day published The Ancient Law *in 1908,* The Romance of a Plain Man *in 1909,* The Miller of Old Church *in 1911, and* Virginia *in 1913.*

They were also years that held heartbreak for Miss Glasgow. While she was abroad in 1910, her brother Frank died; in July of the same year her beloved sister Cary was stricken with her final illness. Cary, whose husband had died in 1894, was living at One West Main Street; she was closer to Ellen Glasgow than anyone else. Following Cary's death in August, 1911, Miss Glasgow, in her grief, left Richmond, forever, as she thought, and took an apartment in New York.

Months later when Virginia *began to take form in her mind, she found that she could not write there, and she went for a visit to Petersburg, Virginia, the Dinwiddie of her novel. However, she lived in New York most of the time during the next five years, returning to Richmond occasionally. Many of her summers were spent abroad. She was in England part of the spring and the summer of 1914 and met those English authors whose work she admired. A few weeks after her return, World War I broke out in Europe.*

TO MARY JOHNSTON

Richmond, November 1st, 1914

Dear Molly,

I've just finished *The Witch*,[1] and it is very fine, I think. You have a wonderful power of re-creating a period, and I feel the Elizabethan Age as vividly as if I were dreaming about it. It is a book of great beauty and nobility of thought.

It seems years since I saw you. Are you well? Are you happy? Are you working again so soon? I know the country is lovely in this weather.

About the 26th of this month I expect to go back to New York. I am somewhat over half through a book,[2] but the flesh and particularly the hands grow weary.

With love to the three of you.

As ever yours,

ELLEN GLASGOW

I like Joan thoroughly. She is the finest of your women characters, I think, and I see her always against the background of the forest.

[1] Mary Johnston's new novel. Houghton Mifflin, 1914.
[2] *Life and Gabriella*, Doubleday, 1916.

TO ARTHUR GRAHAM GLASGOW

Richmond, Thursday [Summer, 1916]

Dearest Arthur:

I was so sorry not to see you when you were in Richmond the other day. If I had had any idea that you were in New York at the beginning of my visit, I should certainly have

[*63*]

tried to find you. Where do you stay when you are there?
After this I think I shall always go to the Vanderbilt. Telephone there if you are in New York about the end of July,
for I expect to be back there for a little while then.

The men have not begun work yet on the house.[1] Will you
let me know, by the way, if any rooms are to be repapered? I
do not want to make any additional expense, but the paper
is so old in some places that I think it would be better to
make less expensive improvements elsewhere, and put on
fresh paper and paint. After this, bathrooms [and] electric-
ity are the essential things—for the gas here is perfectly
dreadful. It is lovely of you to do all this for me—and I hope
it won't cost a great deal.

I have no place yet for the summer, though I may run up
to Bar Harbor for a fortnight later on. Are you coming to
Richmond again during the summer? As soon as we get the
guest room fixed, I hope you will always stay here when you
come.

Lovingly yours,

ELLEN

[1] The war had brought Miss Glasgow to the realization that her wan-
derings were over. She gave up her New York apartment in 1915 and
returned to live in Richmond. After her father's death in January, 1916,
she lived on in the old house, which Arthur Glasgow was having restored
and redecorated.

TO ARTHUR GRAHAM GLASGOW

Richmond, March 26th, 1918

Dear Arthur,

I am sending you the copy of my Income Tax that I find
with the receipts. Miss Bennett[1] left, with a few hours notice,
for San Antonio, Texas. (Camp Travis.) Of course they

[1] Anne Virginia Bennett, a trained nurse, took care of Cary in her final
illness and then became Miss Glasgow's secretary and companion. She
had volunteered for Red Cross service.

had to send all the nurses as far away as possible and thereby add to congestion. She kept all my accounts, I couldn't do a sum in figures to save my life. In looking over my State Tax blank, I find she has put "annuities" from invested funds . . . or trust $5182.71, and I know she was very careful to have it exact. I am sorry, but I am a perfect dunce about business matters. It worries me that my figures should be different. What must I do?

As ever lovingly yours,

ELLEN

In looking over the account book she left, I find $5182.71 —trust fund income!

TO ARTHUR GRAHAM GLASGOW

Richmond, October 11, 1919

My dearest Arthur,

I am in Richmond again, feeling a good deal refreshed by my excursion into the primitive. When I realize how invigorating contact with the earth may sometimes be, I find myself wondering how humanity ever consented to come so far away from the jungle.

It was very nice to have that visit from you, and I seem to grow nearer to you every time that we are together. Whatever comes in the future I want you always to remember that no one could have been better or kinder to me than you have been in the last few years since Father's death. One gets in the habit, I think, of taking such things for granted, but this is as good a time as another to tell you how much your affection and your goodness and just your being over here in America have meant to me. It hurts me sometimes to feel how little I have ever been able to do in return—but I hope it will all be added to your immortal account, and I know that it deserves to be.

One thing more lies on my conscience too, my dear. Never

for a moment regret our last conversation, for I understood that you talked to me as you did because you really had my interest at heart. If things are right what you said will not make any difference, and if things are wrong, you will have said far less than the truth.[1]

A happy and prosperous trip to you—and a return that is not too far off next year.

With devoted love now and always,

ELLEN

[1] This paragraph may refer to Miss Glasgow's relationship with Gerald B——, about whom she wrote in *The Woman Within.*

TO HUGH WALPOLE[1]

Richmond, November 9th, 1920

My dear Hugh,

The book is very, very big, a fragment torn out of life itself. I waited and waited to answer your letter because I hoped every day that *The Captives*[2]—that is a really splendid title!—would come. A week ago it arrived, and I've just finished a careful and most attentive reading. The character of Maggie is a wonderful piece of work. I know her as well as if she were actually a person I had lived with. You have used the religious instinct as a vivid and striking background for the human emotions—but I think on the whole you have made the human part more convincing. Perhaps that is because I am not at home in either church or chapel—but even without experience of that kind, I can feel that you have made a profound and not unsympathetic portrayal. Only Maggie, who is the least religious, or rather pious, of them all, is so much the most interesting. When you realize the vio-

[1] Miss Glasgow's letters to Hugh Walpole are printed through the courtesy of the Henry W. and Albert A. Berg Collection of the New York Public Library.
[2] Doran, 1920.

lence of mental reactions, I suppose it was natural for her to go to Martin. That was quite convincing, and I loved that description of her first evening with him—but somehow I always felt that, loving Martin in that way, she simply couldn't have married Paul.

But the book is intensely human. It has the inevitable note of great fiction, the feeling that every detail must have happened exactly that way—that nothing could have been different. Thank you a hundred times for writing it and for sending it. I feel that it has opened the doors for me into a whole new world of English life—and this will remain with me always—this and the figure of Maggie. The sense of life and of something beyond life is there just as it is in *The Green Mirror*,[3] and all your best books.

For three weeks I was in New York, but now I am at home again and beginning a book.[4] I wish I hadn't begun as early as I did because I might be able to keep my interest better. Miss Cather—who has written a fine book of short stories[5] recently—is still one of "the younger writers," though she is older than I am. I have a very good idea, but somehow it doesn't seem as important and vital a thing to write a novel as it once seemed. That's a pity.

I have been thinking of your house and I hope some lovely English spring day to see it—and you—to say nothing of the staff of servants. I hope they will be constant.

Richmond is just the same, and I hope that it will be the same—that not a tree, scarcely a season will have changed before you come back again. The house and the welcome and Miss Bennett and I are waiting.

Your affectionate friend,

ELLEN GLASGOW

[3] Doran, 1917.
[4] *One Man in His Time,* Doubleday, 1922. Meanwhile, Doubleday had published *The Builders* in 1919.
[5] *Youth and the Bright Medusa,* Knopf, 1920.

TO BOOTH TARKINGTON

Richmond, May 26th, 1921

My dear Mr. Tarkington,

I feel that I must tell you how thoroughly I enjoyed and how sincerely I admire *Alice Adams*.[1] You have achieved two things that I had believed almost impossible in American fiction—you have written of average people without becoming an average writer and you have treated the American girl without sentimentality. The end of the story is very fine and true—and it makes absolutely no concession to the ubiquitous devourer of the second rate. Joseph Hergesheimer and I were talking of the serial not long ago, and we both wondered if you would have the courage to end the story in the right way. Thank you because you had the courage and the art.

Sincerely yours,

ELLEN GLASGOW

[1] Doubleday, 1921.

TO HUGH WALPOLE

Richmond, August 23rd, 1923

My dear Hugh,

Your letter, which has just come, is a real joy. About a month ago I sent you a line through Doran, but I suppose it never reached you. I haven't written because I did not know where you were. Now that you have given up your London house, I should like, if you please, another *permanent* address. The cottage sounds enchanting, but I know only that it stands somewhere "in the Lakes," which is heavenly but indefinite as our visions of heaven usually are!

I am delighted to hear of the book,[1] and I find the title

[1] This may refer to Hugh Walpole's *Jeremy and Hamlet,* 1923, or to *The Old Ladies,* 1924, both published by Doran.

entirely charming. When will it be published? I am awaiting it with ardour. It's queer the way the imagination, having exhausted one field, turns for rest and reinvigoration to another. Like you my one interest, apart from the quality of the thing as literature, is the creation of character—and of course in the most modern of the modernists, there are no cohesive characters, only a stream of more or less vague impressions or sensation. It seems to me all so facile. After all to make a living whole is the difficult thing, just to record ripplings of consciousness is so much easier, and so much cruder. But I think your English futurists are better than our American ones. Nothing I think can be quite so bad, so *pompous,* so utterly devoid of a sense of the ridiculous as Mr. Sherwood Anderson. By the way I've just read *Babbitt,*[2] and I agree with you that it is better than *Main Street.*[3] There is a character in it. Babbitt, common as he is, because of his commonness perhaps, lives.

I have stayed here all summer, working hard, putting my whole heart into a book[4] in which I *believe.* Ah, I've been through the Slough of Despond about my work. After I wrote *Life and Gabriella* about 8 or 10 years ago, I let go and gave up. I was passing through an experience that seemed to drain everything out of me—vitality, imagination, interest, everything. In that time I lost a great deal, and I slipped somehow, naturally I suppose, away from what I had won. Now, I have boiled up, I hope, out of those depths, and I am trying to win back what I have lost. My book is a realistic picture of the poor class of farmers in Virginia—a study of poverty and endurance—a kind of epic plan with a single figure expressing the life and civilization in which she lives. Ah, I do hope you will think it my best book.

Yes, I wish we could all be there, Jeremy[5] too. He feels

[2] By Sinclair Lewis. Harcourt, Brace, 1922.
[3] By Sinclair Lewis. Harcourt, Brace, 1920.
[4] *Barren Ground,* Doubleday, 1925.
[5] Miss Glasgow's Sealyham.

[*69*]

the heat terribly, poor lamb. James Cabell is away, but I never see him when he is here. I hear that he also has finished a book.

As always, dear Hugh,
Your affectionate friend,
ELLEN

TO JOSEPH HERGESHEIMER

Richmond, January 7th, 1924

Dear Mr. Hergesheimer,

I am sending you the short stories,[1] and I only wish the book could be of the English edition because I was able to correct that proof more thoroughly. Several of these you may like. "Dare's Gift" is, I think, a perfectly true picture of the closing days of the Confederacy. I greatly enjoyed my talk with you, and I'm looking forward to "the grim conversation" already, but please, please banish utterly from your mind the idea you gave Hunter Stagg[2] of my books. If I am anything at all I am not an inhabitant of the "realm of romance," and what I have tried to do, (and suffered for doing) is to tell the truth about life as I know it. My *Virginia* is as realistic as any production of the Middle West— only realism of that period in Virginia was tinctured with romantic illusion. But, I have always looked through a veil of irony even in the days when all fiction wore fancy dress. Those were the days when one fattened and waxed rich on illusions, yet I kept even then to the bare and sober reality.

But it will be a pleasure to talk of this and more practical things—for instance publishers!

Sincerely yours,
ELLEN GLASGOW

[1] *The Shadowy Third and Other Stories,* Doubleday, 1923.

[2] Mr. Stagg was active in book reviewing circles in Richmond in the 1920's.

TO CARL VAN VECHTEN

Richmond, [No date]

My dear Mr. Van Vechten,

Emily[1] has given me your messages and she tells me that you expect to be in Richmond only two or three days. As it is difficult, even in the provinces, to meet unless one plans a little ahead, I hope you will keep a part of Tuesday or Wednesday for me. Will you dine with me informally, Tuesday evening at a quarter to eight o'clock? If Mr. Hergesheimer is with you (some one told me he was expected) of course I hope that he will come too. I have heard so much of you from our good friend (and the friend of all the world) Hugh Walpole, that I am sure we are not strangers.

Will you telephone if tomorrow (Tuesday) evening is quite right for you. Otherwise, if your prefer, you might come to tea in the afternoon or to lunch Wednesday. My telephone number is 4199 Madison.

Sincerely yours,

ELLEN GLASGOW

[1] Emily Clark, later Mrs. Edwin Swift Balch, author and onetime editor of the *Reviewer*.

TO CARL VAN VECHTEN

Richmond, April 11th, 1924

My dear Mr. Van Vechten,

Jeremy, who can do everything but write and hopes to do that if he lives long enough, asks me to thank you for the charming photograph. He thinks Scheherazade the loveliest Persian he ever saw, and regrets that she is a cat! He wishes she could tell him all the stories she knows, especially the one about The Talking Bird.

It is a pleasure to hear that you were not disappointed in

[*71*]

your visit to Richmond. Do come again before you have forgotten us, and then we may have a chance to talk to each other. Yes, I shall be glad to let you know when I am in New York. We had a lovely day at Westover, and we missed you.

Sincerely yours,

ELLEN GLASGOW

TO CARL VAN VECHTEN

Richmond, August 1st, 1924

Dear Mr. Van Vechten,

I have had a beautiful time with Ella. It was very kind of you to remember me and to send me the book,[1] which I enjoyed immensely. Even now, with the book securely put away between *The Cathedral*[2] and *The High Place,*[3] I don't seem to be able to shake the democratic dust of Maple Valley from my clothes. You have made it wonderfully vivid, and how I should have hated it if I had been your temperamental heroine! (Poor creature! For I see quite clearly that it came to the Seine at last, and that the freedom minded youth she eloped with ascended to places higher and more unnatural than Mr. Cabell's.) But I delighted in the oblique rays of your satire, and I am not sad after all, that you did not choose the better part for his destiny. When all is said the great denial of a temperament is the denial of a sense of humour, and you made this quite evident in the earlier career of your Countess. What a delightful title you found for the book!

Sincerely yours, and with every good wish for a great success,

ELLEN GLASGOW

[1] Van Vechten's *The Tattooed Countess.* Knopf, 1924.
[2] By Hugh Walpole. Doran, 1922.
[3] By James Branch Cabell. McBride, 1923.

TO DOUGLAS SOUTHALL FREEMAN[1]

Richmond, September 30, 1924

Dear Dr. Freeman,

How can I ever thank you enough? The editorial about the shelter[2] was perfect. If you had looked into my mind, it could not have been more exactly what I wished you to write.

And it was beautifully imagined [and] well written. There was not a word wrong from beginning to end.

In a few days could you, I wonder, add to your kindness by letting a reporter come to see the shelter and write about its aims and methods, or rather the aims and methods of the executive committee? When you can do it, if you will ask some one to call me up by telephone and make an appointment, I should be glad to tell him about the work. To you I can only say again that I thank you from my heart.

Sincerely your friend,

ELLEN GLASGOW

[1] Then editor of the Richmond *News Leader*.
[2] Of the Society for the Prevention of Cruelty to Animals.

TO CARL VAN VECHTEN

Richmond, January 3rd, 1925

My dear Carl Van Vechten,

I was charmed to receive "Red" [1] at the appropriate season, and I have enjoyed the essays immensely. Since I am less musical than literary, my favorite, I think, is the chapter on a theme by Havelock Ellis.

Intellectual audacity always appeals to me, and the manner of your audacity is particularly delightful.

At last my book is finished, and I am on my way to New York! This is why I did not write to you sooner. I wished to

[1] Van Vechten's *Red: Papers on Musical Subjects.* Knopf, 1925.

[73]

be able to tell you definitely where I should be. If the coat of ice in which we are encased thaws by the end of the week, I have planned to go to New York on the 12th and to be at the Hotel Chatham, 48th Street and Vanderbilt Avenue, for ten days or two weeks. I am looking forward with much pleasure to seeing you again and to meeting your wife and the Persian Princess. A delightful Richmond woman, Mrs. Frank Duke,[2] will be with me. I think you met her last spring, but I am not sure.

Ah, it is good to be free—but I have already written the first sentence of a new book, a short ironic thing.[3]

With every good wish for the New Year and every year.

Your friend,

ELLEN GLASGOW

[2] The former Carrie Coleman, lifelong friend of Ellen Glasgow and often her traveling companion.

[3] *The Romantic Comedians,* Doubleday, 1926.

TO DOUGLAS SOUTHALL FREEMAN

Richmond, January 26th, 1925

My dear Dr. Freeman,

You asked me to send you news of my book before it was published elsewhere, so I am letting you into the secret that it is to be published April 15 by Doubleday, Page and Company. The title is *Barren Ground,* and I treat of lives amid the broomsedge [and] sassafras in the abandoned fields of Virginia. An author's opinion, I suppose, isn't worth much when the subject is one of his own books, but everyone who has read the manuscript agrees with me that it is the best book I have written. It is a long novel for these days of hurried writing and reading. The publishers tell me that it contains 161,000 words.

With best wishes,

Sincerely yours,

ELLEN GLASGOW

TO IRITA VAN DOREN[1]

Richmond, March 8th, 1925

Dear Mrs. Van Doren,

Yes, I am delighted with the book on Cabell,[2] and I am now at work on my review.

The 28th will be quite as convenient for me, and I will have the car at the station in time to meet the early train, which arrives before seven o'clock. If Dr. Van Doren will just ask the porter to take you where the cars are waiting, I am sure you will have no trouble, but if there should be any mistake, just come straight to the house. It's a little too early for me to be at the station, as I am not very well and have to consider my strength, but we shall be expecting you about seven and I will order breakfast for eight o'clock.

Do try to stay over Monday. Miss Sully has arranged for the Sabbath Glee Club to sing for you Sunday afternoon (the 29th) and the Cabells will give you a party Saturday evening. It will be lovely to have you here.

Sincerely yours,

ELLEN GLASGOW

[1] Then associate editor of the New York *Herald Tribune Books*. She was the wife of Carl Van Doren, at that time literary editor of the *Century Magazine*. Mrs. Van Doren was a valued friend and adviser to Miss Glasgow, who named her as one of her two literary executors.
[2] Carl Van Doren's *James Branch Cabell*. McBride, 1925.

TO CARL VAN VECHTEN

[Richmond], April 21st, 1925

Dear Carl,

Your letter made me very happy—(I realize that this begins like a love letter, but I beg you to continue fearlessly.) Everything you wrote of *Barren Ground* delighted me,

[75]

and I wish that you could say over again and in print the part about my treatment of the Negroes. That pleased me tremendously.

I am keenly interested in your new book. Someday, somewhere I must write of your work. I wonder if you saw my review of Carl Van Doren's book on Cabell, and if you saw, too, Dr. Sherman's splendid article (or, so it frankly seemed to me) in yesterday's *Tribune*![1] I am barbaric enough to love my friends and hate my enemies!

But, after all, what I like most in your letter is your tenderness for Scheherazade. Of course I am very much disappointed that you can't come in May, and Jeremy is inconsolable because he thinks that, after Uncle Hugh, you are his very nicest uncle. However, what you write of not leaving Scheherazade makes me know that from the beginning God has intended us to be friends. As I expect to be in New York on the 11th of May, we must have that long talk, and Virginia is almost as nice in the autumn.

Greetings to Fania.[2]

As always sincerely,

ELLEN GLASGOW

[1] Stuart Pratt Sherman's review of *Barren Ground* in the *Herald Tribune Books*.
[2] Mrs. Van Vechten.

TO ARTHUR GRAHAM GLASGOW

[Richmond], May 23rd, 1925

Dearest Arthur:

I was overwhelmed by your wonderful invitation which I found here a few days ago when I returned after a brief visit to New York.

Nothing could be more generous; but you are always generous beyond words to me. For twenty-four hours I waited hoping that I might be able to accept your invitation. If I were not tied up here in a dozen ways I should go in a minute; and even then if Rebe could have arranged it I should have dropped everything and gone, whether or no. But Rebe tells me that it is impossible for her to leave the two Cabells.[1] Perhaps if you will postpone your invitation until next June, I shall be able to plan for it, and find some one to go with me who could take at least part of the responsibility. But for my deafness I shouldn't hesitate an instant to go by myself (indeed I should prefer it in many ways; but not hearing is such a terrible handicap, and worst of all it makes you dependent on other people). But of all things in the world I would rather go over for a little visit to you in London and then travel over England or somewhere on the continent for the rest of the summer. So I am hoping that you will ask me next year.

For a while this spring I was quite ill; but I am feeling much better. At my worst I sent for Dr. Brown and he told me I ought not to spend a third summer here. I knew this was true so I have rented (I had done this some weeks before your letter came) a little house at Barnstable, Cape Cod, for eight weeks. Somebody in New York had a friend who was going away for two months and she agreed to let me have her house at the most moderate price—two hundred dollars for eight weeks. She had not intended renting it, but let me have it when she heard I was looking for a place. Most cottages are frightfully expensive.

Anne Virginia is going up with me because she can take Jeremy. She would not leave him; and she has not been at all well, one of my reasons for taking the house was that she could leave Richmond for the first time since she came back from the war. You know she came home as an invalid and had to be sent to a government hospital because they said her lungs were in a bad condition. Now she is getting thin again and seems to feel very badly. I hope the change will

[1] Mrs. Tutwiler's husband and son.

[77]

bring her up to where she was a year ago. I don't know what I should do without her.

When are you coming over? I hope your cure will be all you expect. Whenever I think that I might be over there I begin to feel dreadfully disappointed.

The new book has had a very remarkable reception, everyone says. I spent two years and a half on it, and it is a long substantial book, not by any means "light reading"; but it has had a great success with the more sober minded reviewers and readers. I wish to follow it up with a short ironic thing which I have already begun.

With the deepest gratitude and devotion,

As always

ELLEN

TO CARL VAN VECHTEN

Bow Lane, Barnstable, Mass.
July 18th, 1925

Dear Carl,

Firecrackers[1] reached Richmond after I had left, and making a short stay there in my absence, caught up with me brilliantly a few days ago. I took the Federal Express at Washington and came straight up that same night without stopping in New York. This is why you did not hear from me.

Yesterday afternoon and last night I spent with your [. . .][2] and terrible book. After I once began it, I was oblivious of anything around me until it was finished. The first chapter is amazingly clear. I felt the fascination of [. . .][2] from the moment he entered until the end of the book. The whole thing is diabolically clever, and so profoundly depressing as any "realistic" novel ever written. I

[1] By Mr. Van Vechten. Knopf, 1925.
[2] Indecipherable.

[*78*]

have, too, after reading it with much interest and pleasure the curious feeling that this is a trackless wilderness under you, a desert-hell, not garden but jungle—that I do not know and have never even had a glimpse of. Someday I must talk with you about this, and try to discover how many Carls there are in reality, and if my Carl has any actual relation to the innumerable other Carls. But you have an extraordinary power of [. . .]² terror. Not since Balzac has there been a more terrible scene than the ending of the Countess.

I hope you are having a pleasant working summer. Up here in this retreat I am idling away July and August. I can't work, but I play . . . every morning and . . . afternoon. . . .

In September I hope to be in New York for a few days, & if you are there, I shall look forward to seeing you and talking more about your book.

Sincerely yours,
ELLEN GLASGOW

² Indecipherable.

TO EDWIN MIMS [1]

Richmond, May 12th, 1926

Dear Doctor Mims:

I wish that every Southerner between the cradle of the Confederacy and the grave of Fundamentalism could be induced to read *The Advancing South*.² Nothing could be more civilizing, and I, for one, would gladly see it placed in the schools as an impressive contribution to the awakening of thought in the South.

Yet, even as I read, I wonder if the whole country, not the South alone, is becoming intoxicated upon the same ancient

[1] Then head of the English Department at Vanderbilt University.
² By Dr. Mims. Doubleday, 1926.

[*79*]

deadly brew of fanaticism, intolerance and hypocrisy? Is this witches' cauldron beginning to boil over again in the Land of the Free? And are we preparing for ourselves a mental intoxication compared to which the simple pagan drunkenness from wine was a harmless frolic?

Well, I am grateful for the balance and sanity and most of all for the intellectual honesty of your book. I hope it will have the great appreciation that it deserves.

Sincerely yours,

ELLEN GLASGOW

TO CARL VAN VECHTEN

Richmond, July 28th, 1926

Dear Carl,

Yesterday after your book[1] came, I shut my study door and read it straight through from the first page to the last without putting it down.

It is an amazing thing, vivid, barbaric, and so alive that it bleeds. At times it is comic, at times tragic, at times revolting in its horror and pain, and I may add that it seems to me the best argument in favor of African slavery that I have ever read.

I hope that I shall be well enough to write a review of it. Already I am planning one; but I was quite ill in New York, and the doctor has made me stop all work for the summer. Ever since I came home I have been unable to write a line. Still there are many things I should like to say of this book, and I hope that I may be able to write at least a brief review. What interested me tremendously is the way the Negro reacts to the freedom of Harlem.

Only in the father of Mary (a very appealing character) do I find the slightest trace of the Negro that I know. The

[1] *Nigger Heaven*, Knopf, 1926.

serene fatalism, the dignity of manner, the spiritual power, all these qualities decayed, it appeared, with the peculiar institution.

I should like so much to talk to you about this book. Though I am too close to it to form a final opinion, I believe it is the biggest, the most vital thing that you have written. There is a fire at its heart.

> With best wishes your sincere friend,
> ELLEN GLASGOW

TO CARL VAN VECHTEN

Richmond, July 31st, 1926

Dear Carl,

I shall be ever so glad to have you use the quotation from my letter. I wrote several paragraphs of a review, but I came down with one of my headaches and had to surrender to the heat. But I hope to write something later on, while it may still do good, for the autumn rush. Meanwhile my comment may be just as useful.

No, I don't mean that you are trying to prove anything. You are too much of an artist for that. But the book has the accent of realism, and I cannot help comparing the world of Harlem as you present it with the life of the Negro as I have known it in the South. This, I think, is tremendously interesting.

I am (God permitting) leaving next week (the end) for Yama Farms, Napanoch, Ulster County, New York.

I shall be one day in New York, and if I am well, I shall telephone you. Otherwise, I hope to see you in September, if you are in town the last week.

Yes, my book[1] is to come out in September. I almost died over the proof sheets, and this is what made me ill. You know

[1] *The Romantic Comedians.*

how it is when you finish one. I believe you will like it, and I shall send you an early copy.

Sincerely always,

ELLEN GLASGOW

TO ANNE VIRGINIA BENNETT

Hotel Majestic
Harrogate [England]
July 26, 1927

Dearest A.V.

I wrote Rebe about Durham and Fountains Abbey, and the high points in our trip so far (and I think always will be) are York, Fountains and Durham. I'll try to tell you about Whitby, but before I begin, I must arrange a small business trifle. Will you write to Mrs. McCormack, 1401 Stockley Gardens, Norfolk, and ask her what my niblick cost, and send her the money. Alas, the gay clubs and bag I bought at Selfridges have never been unwrapped. The little time I've had free from cure, I've wanted to see something beautiful! We rent the cheapest little two seater car we can get, and with a very good driver who knows the country well, but the car is the only reasonable thing here. I never realized that things would be so expensive over here, and there are so many extras—belonging to the cure. The doctor also is very expensive, not very good. . . .

Sunday we had a glorious day. The doctor told me not to take any treatments. So we motored 150 miles to Whitby Abbey. Whitby is one of or, I believe, is really the oldest seaport in England, and it is said to be the place on the North Sea where the Saxons landed. There is a great Saxon Abbey there, which was ruined by the Danes in 800 or so, and then refounded by some Norman Baron under William the Conqueror. It is a wonderful ruin, and still dominates the land as well as the sea. For my part nothing is comparable to the

[*82*]

ruined abbeys of Yorkshire, and no churches ever built by man approach the English cathedrals in sublimity and beauty. The drive home was one of the loveliest we have ever taken. Over glorious moors and by a place called the Hole of Halcum. . . .

The way this velvet turf spreads under the thickest trees, and down to the very edge of the rivers is perfectly marvellous. And as for the roses that we imagine cannot live without the sun, they surpass any I have ever imagined for richness, color and beauty. We have collected seeds of rare flowers, but I suppose they will never put up. Here everything that is scattered to the winds appears to blossom. I wrote Rebe about the poppies in the wheat, and the wild foxglove and snapdragons by the woodside. . . .

TO ANNE VIRGINIA BENNETT

Langham Hotel
Portland Place, London
[August 7, 1927]

Dearest A.V.:

Here we are in London again, with the difference (Oh, what a difference!) of having a car of our own. I was so glad to find your letter here, and so glad too that you are having the hall done before my return. I think now, since we have the car (though of course I'll have the expense of running it and Hasley's[1] board on the trip of two weeks), that I can manage all right, and shan't need any more money. But everything costs so much that I have no temptation to try it but once. There are so many ways I could spend all that money more permanently. If you have time while the house is being cleaned, will you try to straighten my drawers in my study as well as my bedroom. When I get home I must settle down to work as soon as I can.

[1] Miss Glasgow's chauffeur in England. The name may be Hastings.

I felt splendid the last week or so at Harrogate, but since reaching London I have ached all over from exhaustion and lost my appetite. We both feel breathless and weak and get tired so quickly. I suppose I've overdone it, but I hope to get back my strength on the boat, if not before. I know now why people take "an after cure."

It is damp and very chilly here today, so I suppose what they call "the heat wave" is broken. Ever since we came the papers have been writing about "the heat wave" "London gasping with no relief in sight" because the thermometer "has not fallen below 58 degrees for several days"! All the time, while London panted, Carrie and I have shivered if a window were open at our back, and never gone out without a coat and a woolen robe over our knees.

We came to this hotel because we heard it was good. . . . The rooms are nice, and more reasonable than most (fifteen dollars a day) but the food (extra of course) is very poor and that may be the reason I don't eat much. We try to go out, but I have never enjoyed restaurants as Rebe does—and I get so tired I'd rather have my meals at the hotel, especially dinner. Tuesday, if it is fair, we expect to motor (a day's trip) to Rochester and Canterbury—and then on Thursday to Waltham Abbey, Epping Forest and Chigwell, to see Dickens' Maypole Inn. The 17th we intend to start on our motor trip, and I have lengthened it to include Tintern Abbey, Gloucester, and Oxford. I don't care particularly about going to Oxford, but Carrie has never seen it, and I thought she ought not to miss it. I am eager to be off, but I cannot believe that any other part of England will seem so beautiful to me as Yorkshire.

Our first disappointment came with the interior of Lincoln and Ely. I had heard so much of Lincoln's being the most beautiful cathedral after York that it was a blow to find the nave low and small and out of proportion with [the] Norman exterior, which is fine and wonderfully impressive. Ely, too, is beautiful on the outside, but absolutely spoiled by modern (1850) mural decorations within. The marvellous octagon roof, which must have been very impressive in its original state, has been painted to look like the interior of an Italian church. Anything less in harmony with the structure of the building or the English Gothic architecture it would be impossible to imagine. As for the two towns, we did not care for Lincoln and were glad to leave. This may have been because we went to the wrong hotel, The Saracen's Head, when we ought to have stayed at the White Hart close by the cathedral. We hated the Saracen's Head. It is modern and pretentious and entirely bad. On the other hand Ely is a charming, sleepy, perfectly typical English cathedral town, and the Lamb is an old inn that you love from the moment you enter it. We enjoyed it very much, the food was all good and typically English.

The first train Thursday brought us to London and Hasley met us at Liverpool St. Station. He is splendid and so much interested in anything that we see and wherever we go. He told us we must certainly see "the churchyard where the elegy was written." He said he had learned a good deal about "little old shops" from the daughter of Mr. Pierpont Morgan, who was "always looking for them." Our first two days we spent looking for a coat for you. We went everywhere, and I changed my mind twenty times.

At first I thought I'd get a gray or brown tweed, but the gray did not look smart, and the tweed they make now is very loosely woven and bulky and made coarse and we both look so large that I decided not to get [it] for you. Finally, after going back three times and spending hours there, I ordered a black coat of the best black material, rough, that I could find, and Jay is now making it. We are going Friday to see it tried on a very nice woman who says she is five feet seven, which as well as I remember is your height. I selected the only coat that seemed to me to have any room about the hips.

They are all made so straight and tight and narrow. Then I put all the trimming into a very good big collar of Persian lamb, the best black fur they had. I certainly hope it will fit you and that you will like it. I gave a great deal of time and strength to trying to get the best one, and I am sure black will be so much more becoming to you than the light tweed, which does not give in to the figure at all. The darker shades of tweed are not worn and all were ugly. But this black rather wooly material was the only pretty black I could find —I also bought, or rather ordered, for they have to be made, Jeremy and Billy[2] paraphernalia. They don't have fancy things here, but I hope they are well made. There wasn't any pretty blue, it was too gray. So I got Billy a very pretty green instead. He will have to get his blue in America. I got Dimple[3] a little plaid collar, though they said the plaid were for Scotties especially.

My back aches so I'll have to stop. Sunday is as dreary in London as in New York, but we'll go to the London Museum after lunch. I hope I'll feel better after a while.

Tell Rebe again her miniature is, I think, the prettiest that I have seen. I like it best of all. It is really beautiful. Love to Lamb.[3]

As ever,

E.

[2] Billy, a white poodle, had been acquired as a companion for Jeremy.
[3] "Dimple" and "Lamb" were terms of endearment Miss Glasgow used for Jeremy.

TO FRANK SWINNERTON

Langham Hotel, London
August 10th [1927]

Dear Mr. Swinnerton,

That is delightful! It will be a very real pleasure to meet you and Mrs. Swinnerton, but I should hate to put you to the trouble of coming up to London.

Fortunately, a good fairy has placed a car at my disposal while I am in England, and on August the 17th or 18th I am starting with a friend (also from Virginia) on a long motor trip. Our first day brings us to Dorking, and I wonder if it would not be easier for you to let us, if you can have my friend too, stop and see you there. I am not sure about distances, but you will know whether it can be arranged and still enable us to reach Winchester in time to see the Cathedral. Of course if you and Mrs. Swinnerton are coming up to London in any case, this might not save you the journey, but I suggest the different plans for your choice.

You see I am so very keen about meeting you both.

Sincerely yours,
ELLEN GLASGOW

TO ANNE VIRGINIA BENNETT

Imperial Hotel, Torquay
August 25th [1927]

Dearest A.V.:

We spent last night here at this very good hotel. Torquay (pronounced *Torkie*) is a beautiful place on the Devon Coast, with the most glorious air. We have had a good deal of rain, but today, and the day we spent in Dorchester could not have been better. Saturday morning we left London in a pouring rain, and it poured hard and fast for the past two days of our trip.

We had a delightful lunch with the Frank Swinnertons, in their charming antique cottage (500 years old) at Cranleigh. There is a lovely garden in front of it, but the rain poured so we could barely see it. When we got there they had a big wood fire in the immense old stone fireplace, and Mrs. Swinnerton, (who is very sweet and much younger than he is) took off our wet clothes! Just coming from the gate, where he met us bareheaded, had got us dripping, and [she] gave us a delicious glass of sherry. I don't think I have enjoyed a lunch more. After restaurant fare it seemed so good and homelike. They waited on the table themselves. Everything was ready and the table all waiting when we arrived, except the hot dishes, which he took in from kitchen door and carved and served. It was all so sweet and informal, and he is very delightful to talk to, so much more interesting than his books.

Later, I was writing before breakfast, and Carrie was not dressed. She came down and we went into the dining-room and had breakfast (the finest Devonshire cream) at a table looking out on a beautiful view of the sea and rocks. It is heavenly outside, and I am going out to sit in the sun until eleven o'clock, when we go on to Two Bridges, where (God permitting) we shall spend the afternoon and night. I want to take a walk on Dartmoor and to spend a night there. If they can't take us, we'll try Tavistock—and go on tomorrow to Tintagel.

Tea with Mrs. Conrad [1] was rather dismal. She has become enormously stout, and so very complacent, poor soul, clinging to the shadow of fame which he shed over her. On the contrary the Hardys were lovely and simple, and seemed so glad to see me. She is very shy, but a thoroughly nice sensible woman. I missed Wessex, the wire-haired terrier, and they

[1] Widow of Joseph Conrad.

said their hearts ached whenever they thought of him. He died of old age a few weeks ago, and he was a puppy of six months when I saw him in 1914. I never saw so attractive a man of his age as Thomas Hardy, which proves that it is intellect, after all, that counts as one goes over the hill of life. He is far more modern and advanced than most men of twenty-five, and age has not deadened his sensibility in the least. I was so glad I went after hesitating to do so. It must be the last time, and I shall like to remember how he was when I saw him so near the end of life. He is profoundly civilized and sympathetic about animals just as he is in his books—and especially in *Jude*.

I wrote Rebe about Sherbourne, a lovely little town, which she saw, I think, and about Mr. Phillips, the prior of the old men in the almshouse. It was very touching, and I am going to send him some Virginia tobacco, if I can pay the duty, as soon as I get home.

Two weeks from yesterday we sail. . . .

E.

TO HELEN MacAFEE[1]

Richmond, January 31st, 1928

Dear Miss MacAfee,

I was very glad to have your letter two days ago. And I hear that you will see England in June. I had an enchanting summer there last year, and after motoring from North to South and East to West, I look back with the greatest longing to beautiful Yorkshire and the ruined abbeys of the North. I hope you can go there. Fountains Abbey, Durham, and a visit to Thomas Hardy, the youngest old man that ever lived, were the high points of my summer.

Yes, I think it is time for me to begin work on that article. As soon as I have rounded a difficult part of my novel, I shall

[1] An editor of the *Yale Review*.

honestly try to turn in the direction of criticism. The trouble is that I have too many ideas and too little industry.

Sincerely yours,

ELLEN GLASGOW

TO WILLIAM H. F. LAMONT[1]

Richmond, February 9th, 1928

Dear Mr. Lamont;

Many thanks for your interesting letter. Within the next five years I hope to do another book like *Barren Ground*— but not yet. A novel like that grows slowly. For ten years I carried that idea in my mind, and I gave three years to the actual writing.

The Romantic Comedians bubbled out in one year, though it wasn't nearly so easy to write as it appears. Every word in that book (and in *Barren Ground* too) was carefully chosen; for in literature as in life I prefer words to deeds.

As for the idea—well, I was worn out with having men write what they know or don't know about dangerous ages in women. But the way it was done, the style of the writing, was what I gave most thought to from the first page to the last.

Sincerely,

ELLEN GLASGOW

[1] Member of the English Department at Rutgers University.

TO HENRY SEIDEL CANBY[1]

Poland Spring House
South Poland, Maine
August 18th, 1928

Dear Doctor Canby:

It would be very interesting to review the books you mention. I have the greatest admiration for Mrs. Peterkin's[2] work, and certainly Mr. Heyward's *Porgy*[3] deserves to become a classic. Unfortunately, however, I am deeply envolved in the problem of how to write a novel without declining to do anything and everything else. I have been for the last eighteen months at work on a book,[4] and until this is finished, I must put the idea of an article, however interesting, completely out of my mind.

It would be very pleasant to see you again. From the 9th to the 15th of September, I expect to be at the Hotel Chatham in New York, and I hope that you and Miss Loveman[5] will come to lunch or to tea with me one of those days.

Sincerely yours,

ELLEN GLASGOW

[1] Scholar, critic, essayist, and at this time editor of the *Saturday Review of Literature*.

[2] Julia Peterkin won the Pulitzer Prize for her novel *Scarlet Sister Mary*, Bobbs-Merrill, 1928.

[3] By DuBose Heyward. Doran, 1925.

[4] *They Stooped to Folly*, Doubleday, 1929.

[5] Amy Loveman, an associate editor of the *Saturday Review of Literature*.

TO DANIEL LONGWELL[1]

Richmond, May 26, 1929

. . . No, no, no. This drawing cannot go on *The Battle-Ground.*[2] It is not only a dreadful thing in itself; but worse than that, it is, or appears to be, a caricature of a very remarkable painting. Not only would everyone in Richmond be made furious by it, but I think there is too little genuine art in the world for us to wish to desecrate it like this. I am sorry, but I am also perfectly positive.

If you wish to know my idea of the right kind of wrapper for *The Battle-Ground,* look at the dust-jackets of *Drums*[3] (a wonderfully artistic thing) and *Marching On.*[4] If I cannot have something artistic, and not cheap, I'd rather have simply a plain cover.

As always

E.G.

[1] An editor at Doubleday, Doran and Company.
[2] This apparently concerns preparation of the volume for the Old Dominion Edition of Miss Glasgow's novels which Doubleday, Doran and Company was bringing out.
[3] By James Boyd. Scribner, 1926.
[4] By James Boyd. Scribner, 1927.

TO GRANT C. KNIGHT[1]

Richmond, June 29th, 1929

Dear Mr. Knight:

Your letter is a difficult one for me to answer—so difficult, indeed, that I fear I shall be obliged to evade it. After all, what can one say of a friend? I knew James Lane Allen[2] very well (though he had other friends who were much closer than I) and I find myself hesitating before the cold fact of

[1] Professor of English at the University of Kentucky.
[2] Kentucky novelist.

a biography. Yet I have never belonged to the sentimental school either of biography or fiction, and it seems to me that the only excuse for writing the life of a person is that truth shall be served.

Did I find "Emblems of Fidelity" amusing? If I ever said so, I hope that I was speaking the truth. Did I find Mr. Allen capable of generous friendship? Well, fortunately, I was never called upon to test his friendship. I do not like testing human relations, and he was, I think, the last man in the world to respond to any kind of test or demand. He had, I feel sure, much that was fine and generous in his nature. Others, probably, saw more of this finer side that I did; but I was attached to him if one can be attached to a person one offends every few days without being aware of it. After seeing me very frequently and writing very charming letters every week, he would suddenly refuse to speak to me for months because I had in some way, without meaning to be rude, done something that displeased him or that he considered an affront to his dignity. This morbid sensitiveness finally came between us, and in the last years of his life we drifted entirely away from each other. Being his friend was too arduous for a woman who likes to take human beings naturally—or not at all. I have kept a few of his many letters, and these are all beautiful—and, well, literary. Even when I knew him best (and I repeat that I was never, I think, one of his closest friends) it never occurred to me to expect anything from him in the way of sympathy or understanding; yet there were occasions when he moved me deeply by revealing a stronger friendship than I had believed him capable of feeling.

Yes, I think he was misanthropic—but why shouldn't he have been? It is a very interesting thing to be. I recognize of course, your "famous journalist." We have often discussed this "obsession"—and others.

I hope I have been sufficiently frank, generous and discreet. The real trouble between us was that, try as hard as I could, it was impossible for me to admire his style of writing as ardently as all the sentimental young men of the nineties had admired it. Since we were both bred in the Southern tradition, I tried, in the classic feminine manner, to do what was required of me in the way of adulation—but I invariably failed! It was natural, I suppose, (surrounded as he was by adulation without effort) that he should resent my failure to live up to his expectations. Yet he was very noble at heart.

Sincerely yours,
ELLEN GLASGOW

TO GRANT C. KNIGHT

Richmond, June 30th, 1929

Dear Mr. Knight:

Since writing you, I have found many letters from James Lane Allen. It is a rule of mine never to keep letters after their first freshness has faded; but for various reasons, I seem to have put by not a few of Mr. Allen's. In reading them over, I find that they express the man, as I knew him, completely.

When I met him he was, of course, no longer young; his great dreams were over; and the grand manner, so much admired in his youth, had become slightly pompous. He seemed to me to have hardened in a fixed pattern of the great tradition; and in New York, where I knew him, the great tradition was a little lonely. Yet his letters show none of this. They breathe a warm and generous capacity for friendship; and I reproach myself when I read them because I may have seemed unsympathetic in the description I gave you. Let me repeat that he was fine and noble and very faithful at heart. Only that perverse streak of sensitiveness, or egoism, or—what shall I say?—made so many of his human associations end in disaster. For example, he could write, "I allow myself to believe that I know you better, know *more* of you, than any other human being in this stupid, harsh, blindfolded, and largely contemptible world"; and yet within the next few months, I might receive, and indeed did receive this note:

"I am wondering whether a letter written some weeks ago found you in Richmond or has found you at all. If it has not reached you, this is a letter. If it has reached you, this is not a letter.

Sincerely yours,

James Lane Allen"

And since I had received his letter, but had been unable to answer it, there would ensue a long and very haughty silence on his part.

But we must remember that he was an ill man when I knew him. There were times (though he would not have liked to hear this, and very naturally) when his craving for wider recognition or his appreciation of very trivial honours, was almost heartbreaking in its pathetic eagerness. And not only was he ill and disappointed, but (I was distressed to hear this after his death) he was also very nearly impoverished, I am told, at the end of his life. Yet he bore all this with superb gallantry. Taken all in all, he was, I think the most gallant figure I have ever known. Upon these qualities, I hope you will lay particular stress in your biography—upon his courage, his tenderness of heart, his patience, his fidelity, his fortitude in affliction and disillusionment.

Sincerely yours,

ELLEN GLASGOW

TO DANIEL LONGWELL

Richmond, July 10, 1929

. . . Virginia was as far removed from "a Victorian wife for whom love was *not* enough" as she could well be. On the contrary she embodied the Victorian ideal for whom love *was* enough. Her story[1] may be called a tragicomedy of manners, but not a comedy.

I wish you would announce these books as the earliest volumes in what I intended to make not only a continued comedy of manners, but a complete social history of Virginia since the Civil War. . . .[2]

As Always

E.G.

[1] *Virginia.*
[2] Another reference to the Old Dominion Edition of her novels.

TO GRANT C. KNIGHT

Richmond, July 15th, 1929

My dear Mr. Knight;—

The first quotation was from a letter that Mr. Allen dated simply "Monday," but it was postmarked February 4th, 1918.

The second letter, being more formal and indignant, was dated May 29th, 1918. I do not know what letters came between or what caused the sudden resentment.

Among the letters I have kept there are a number that might interest you, and if you should come to Richmond while I am there, I should be glad to have you look them over. They are filled with plans for his books, and reveal a very touching eagerness for understanding and appreciation. For example, in one dated "Sunday," but postmarked March 28th, 1914, he writes at length of a novel he is beginning.

What book he meant I do not even recall, if I ever knew, but he wrote in a rich vein of enthusiasm;—"Since you went away I have taken my future in my own hands—at whatever cost —and in peace and quietness have settled down to do one *great thing*—as the rest of my life's work. Just to finish all the years of struggle and effort with the greatest thing of all —greatest for me! So there I am, and here I am! At work on a real novel, a long, very long novel, of the first magnitude in every way—as magnitude goes in our American literature. This is a recital that will be known to but few even as a plan. When you return, I shall wish to tell you about it in some all-comprehending way. It is to be dedicated to you if you will be able to say that you so desire."

Can you place this book? As I read over this letter, it seems to me deeply moving, almost pathetic; yet if he ever began the novel, the war must have broken it off. After this letter, I must in some way have offended him, for we seem to have drifted away from each other. A year later, however, we were good friends again, and I saw him often in New York. But he was never the same man after the war began. Even before America went into the struggle, he had given himself heart and soul to the cause.

I remember very well our first meeting, though I have forgotten the year. It must have been about 1910—or perhaps 1909. Of this I am not certain, for I cannot find his earliest letters. We were both at a dinner given by Ruth McEnery Stuart[1] in New York, and that was the beginning of one of those sudden friendships which seem to have no relationship to time. Indeed, I think he was as unreserved with me as it was possible for him to be with any one—and yet I never felt that I knew what to expect from one day to the next. With the best will in the world he simply could not be natural. The grand manner encased him like chain-armour. . . .

[1] Southern writer of short stories.

[*97*]

Will you tell me please, in return for the trouble I've taken, if Evelyn Scott is a Southerner, and where she was born. I am preparing an essay for publication in book form (you may have seen it last Christmas in *Harper's,* "The Novel in the South") and if Miss Scott is a Southerner I should like to include her in a list of authors.[2]

Sincerely yours,

ELLEN GLASGOW

[2] Evelyn Scott is the Tennessee-born author of the Civil War novel *The Wave,* Smith, 1929, and other fiction. The essay referred to was later included in the preface to the Virginia Edition of *The Miller of Old Church,* Scribner, 1938, and in *A Certain Measure,* Harcourt, Brace, 1943.

TO CARL VAN VECHTEN

Richmond, September 19th, 1929

Nothing that has been written about my book,[1] dear Carl, has pleased me more than your letter. Do you know that you are the only reader or critic who has even suspected that Victoria is really the figure of the pattern. Yes, she was, indeed, so subtle and difficult that you alone perceived what I meant by her.

I am ill now and cannot write, but I shall hope to see you in New York this autumn.

Your affectionate friend,

ELLEN

[1] *They Stooped to Folly.*

TO JAMES SOUTHALL WILSON[1]

Richmond, December 14th, 1929

Dear Doctor Wilson:

Alas, I have embarked again upon the sea of trouble! After being ill more or less all the autumn and the greater part of the summer, I am trying to begin work on a novel.[2] Even your delightful letter to James Cabell (and there never was, I am sure, a more delightful letter) cannot turn my mind from fiction to criticism.[3] Perhaps in the future the spirit may possess me; but that must be after I have finished at least the first part of my book. Won't there come in time, or in the nature of things, a tenth, and even a twentieth, anniversary? If I write one article, it seems I must write two—for there is an older promise to Doctor Canby, and he has been blessed by Fate with a memory as accurate as yours. However that may be, I have an obscure feeling that I can write only novels.

With every good wish for you and for the anniversary number, and the hope that I may see you and Mrs. Wilson the next time you are in Richmond,

I am,

Always sincerely yours,

ELLEN GLASGOW

[1] Professor of English at the University of Virginia and editor of the *Virginia Quarterly Review.*

[2] *The Sheltered Life,* Doubleday, 1932.

[3] Dr. Wilson had asked for a contribution for the fifth anniversary issue of the *Virginia Quarterly Review.*

August 24, 1930—August 17, 1934

TO CARL VAN VECHTEN

Old England Lake Hotel,
Windermere
August 24th, 1930

Dear Carl,

Miss Bennett writes me that your book[1] has come to Richmond ahead of me. Ever so many thanks. I am looking eagerly forward to the pleasure I know it will give me.

Since that delightful glimpse of you and Fania I have had a severe illness, and a part of my summer has been spent in a hospital, or, as they call such places over here, a nursing home.[2] The day we lunched together I was really in great pain, and a day or two later I came down with acute neuritis. Unlike you, however, I had no Chinese robe to cover me and no admiring English "Lady Authors" (isn't that what they call them?) to cluster about me. Devoid of adulation, with only an uninteresting doctor and a calm-featured nurse, I confronted adversity.

Tomorrow, driven by wind and rain, we are returning to London. I am still not able to do very much, though it was worth the trip to Edinburgh just to see the Scottish War Memorial. I, who dislike both war and memorials of war, was deeply stirred by the abundance of imagination and insight. But, then, the Scottish mind seems always to have had imagination and a keen understanding that austerity and beauty

---

[1] *Feathers,* Random House, 1930.

[2] Mrs. Duke had persuaded Miss Glasgow to go back to Harrogate, where the treatment three years before had been good for her. They spent a week in London, which was very tiring for Miss Glasgow, and on arrival at Harrogate, the doctor ordered her to a nursing home.

are not incompatibles. And, after all, how much better bronze warfare, or even symbolical warfare in stained glass, is than a bullfight, with burning sulphur poured into the bleeding wounds of an animal!

Well, it would be good news indeed to hear that [you and] Fania are in London again before sailing. If you are, by any chance, in town, won't you call us up at the Berkeley Hotel.

Yesterday we motored all day over this enchanting Lake country. On our way, we passed Brackenburn,[3] and saw the fine view and the borders of gaily blooming flowers. No, we did not stop, and thereby hangs a story! There was a time, as you know, when Hugh and I were very good friends. I was really attracted to him, and he seemed to like coming to visit me. Once, even he arrived at Christmas with no warning except the maid's hurried announcement that "Mr. Walpole was downstairs in the drawing-room." Then, and gladly, I put my nephew out of his room, and Hugh was quite delightful and appeared to be depressed by some occurrence in California, which he forgot almost immediately. To go on, last year was the first time I did not see him, though I had many affectionate letters urging me to visit him at Brackenburn. No, this isn't the point. The point is that I accepted. When I found we were really coming to England I told him we should be charmed to stay two days with him either before or after our cure at Harrogate. But to this letter, though he had written me constantly till then, there was no answer! So do you wonder that we did not stop but were content to admire the gaily blooming flowers as we sped by?

And it is useless to deny that, unless you have Chinese robes to spread over you, Englishmen can sometimes be as funny as Punch! But you, dear Carl, have learned discretion in a school that was not easy, and perfect discretion admits nothing as long as Chinese robes may be bought.

[3] Hugh Walpole's home overlooking Derwentwater in the English lake district.

Well, I have let myself quite run away.

With affectionate greetings to you both, and every good wish in the world for the book.

As always
Sincerely yours,
ELLEN GLASGOW

TO SARA HAARDT MENCKEN[1]

Paris, September 14th, 1930

Dear Sara:

I send you my love and every blessing it is in the power of affection to bestow. You have always seemed to me to be one of the few real persons born into this shallow-hearted literary generation. Never have you asked of life more than you are willing to bring to it.

Mr. Mencken is wise and fortunate, I think, in his love— or, it may be, those who love wisely are always fortunate. May the future bring to you both all the fine and lasting gifts of the gods that watch over us.

After a long illness and a summer that has been more trying than pleasant, I am sailing for home in a few days. Perhaps the autumn may find you in Richmond.

With kind regards to Mr. Mencken and the heartiest good wishes,

I am to you as always,
Affectionately,
ELLEN GLASGOW

[1] The young Southern short-story writer and critic who married H. L. Mencken, August 27, 1930.

TO ARTHUR GRAHAM GLASGOW

Richmond, December 30th, 1930

Dearest Arthur,

I am so sorry I did not see you again, and only after you had gone did it occur to us that you left just at lunch time. But, surely, you would not have waited to be asked to stay! I always think of the house and everything in it as more than half yours, since without you we shouldn't be here at all.

Before the year is out (and well out, thank Heaven!) I do wish to thank you again for your great generosity, and to tell you that I appreciate it as much as I am able to appreciate anything in this world. In your place, I doubt if I should be nearly so generous; and in my own mind I have never been able to see what return it ever brings you. The reward of virtue has always seemed to me to be greatly exaggerated.

However, you have chosen of your own free will, to be good to me, and I thank you for this splendid Christmas gift, as well as for everything else, from the bottom of my heart. Anne Virginia is going down this morning to pay off part of the note. If we pay it before the first of the year, I shall avoid that much tax on my income—or at least on the amount I have in bank January the first.

I hope your cold is much better. Christmas is always a nightmare to my nervous system, and this year, because of the throbbing pain in my back, it has been even more trying than usual. I am writing this on the typewriter in order to avoid the strain of a pen.

I wrote to Margaret yesterday, and this is just a line to you before the new year begins.

With every good wish that is possible from a grateful heart,

Your loving sister,
ELLEN

[*106*]

TO BESSIE ZABAN JONES[1]

Richmond, March 29th, 1931

Dear Bessie,

I was so glad to have your delightful letter, but, alas, a few days afterwards I came down with influenza, (for the second time) and I am only beginning to feel well again. This is just a line to send my thought of you, and to say that I hope you and Howard will really come to Virginia this spring. If you do, and when you do, of course you will make me a visit. I should love to see the house in Ann Arbor "on the edge of town," and to stay in it. It is charming, I know, and I am proud to imagine an "Ellen Glasgow room" or even shelf. Howard's article was very able and I like immensely, too, the essay he had in *Scribner's* "On Leaving the South." The other article furnished me with a splendid quotation. I suppose he received the paper I sent him—(*The Herald-Tribune*). So few persons have understood the South so thoroughly.

I meant to send only a word or two, and see how I have rambled on. If I had known I should write so much, I should have taken a typewriter.

No, my very next book[2] is somewhat, but not entirely, in the vein of *They Stooped to Folly.* After this, I hope to write a companion piece[3] to *Barren Ground.* That is the one of my books I like best.

Affectionately yours,

ELLEN GLASGOW

[1] Wife of Howard Mumford Jones, then professor of English at the University of Michigan.
[2] *The Sheltered Life.*
[3] *Vein of Iron,* Harcourt, Brace, 1935.

TO BESSIE ZABAN JONES

Richmond, May 16th, 1931

Dear Bessie,

It is always delightful to have one of your charming letters. You and Howard are such real persons that I feel as if I had known you forever.

It was a great disappointment that you could not come to Virginia this year. Never was there a more lovely spring, belated but filled with fragrance and bloom. However, I think you were right to buy that house, I know it is charming and homelike, and I hope to see it some other spring. Only I am sure rural Michigan would break my heart. I was born to worship trees, and I cannot bear to see one destroyed. The roads in Virginia are a tragic sight to one who, like myself, must have been a dryad, not a mermaid, in the age of fable.

I was very grateful to Howard for making that translation, and I am looking eagerly forward to his article in the *Virginia Quarterly*.[1] I hope it will be in the next number.

What you tell me of your classes is most amusing. Please, for my sake, love *Tom Jones*. I have always considered it the greatest of all English novels. Nowhere else can one find such vividness, such vitality. And *Amelia*! Do you suppose I am the only person left who has read *Amelia* straight through from beginning to end, not once but twice, and adored every word of it? But, even then, I like *Tom Jones* best of all English and American novels. The Russians, of course, are in a different world, and supreme. Yet I find the latest Russian novels hard reading.

[1] "Discussions of New Books: Mr. Lewis's America," *Virginia Quarterly Review,* July, 1931.

Do write to me again when you are not too busy.
With affectionate greetings to you both,

As always,

ELLEN GLASGOW

TO ARTHUR GRAHAM GLASGOW

Richmond, June 19th, 1931

Dearest Arthur:

I was so glad to have your letter which must have crossed mine. Every one says the cure at Bad Gerstein is excellent, and I feel sure it will do you a world of good. Do let me hear as soon as you feel some decided benefit. I shall be anxious to know that you are better. . . .

Everybody is depressed in Richmond, and things appear to grow worse all the time. This morning, to my consternation, I was informed that the Dan River Mills would not pay the July dividend on preferred stock. I wish now that I had sold mine last summer, but I was strongly advised not to do so.

After all, I gave up Glen Springs because I found it was too expensive. I tried to stay on here; but the first heat made me ill again, and Dr. Tompkins told me I simply must not attempt to remain here through the summer. So Carrie and I are going to Nantucket for July and August. I have never been there, but it seemed the most reasonable thing to do. Of course not being able to go alone makes everything cost more; but I hope the change will enable me to finish my book next winter.

But for you I could not have done this, for your helping me to pay back some of the money I borrowed last winter has made it possible for me to arrange to go away. I shall have to borrow a little more; but if I can ever get strong enough to finish my book, I hope to be on my feet again.

With dearest love and gratitude,

Devotedly,

ELLEN

TO HOWARD MUMFORD JONES

Richmond, July 17th, 1931

Dear Howard Mumford Jones:

As usual, you went to the point. Your article in the *Virginia Quarterly* is the best thing I've seen on the cherished American belief that the surface is greater than the whole.

I make my bow. One sentence, "Her concern is with the life of the soul amidst the eternal problems of existence" sums up my work in a phrase. Many thanks.

As always sincerely yours,

ELLEN GLASGOW

TO LEWIS GANNETT[1]

Richmond, September 25th, 1931

My dear Mr. Gannett:

Thank you very much for your letter and (shall I say?) for your fairness.

Of course, as usual, the whole truth is something that cannot be said in print; but, since you are in a better position to spread gossip than I am, the least you can do, I feel, is to create a special and choice blend of your own. Here and now, I appoint you my official dispenser of gossip; and I hope that you will avail yourself of every opportunity to administer justice and to contribute broken doses of truth to the discussion of prizes. So long as you don't say it in print, I

[1] Book critic for the New York *Herald Tribune*.

think you can safely report that I was the last of the three judges to yield to the decision and that I went so far as to withdraw my name from the contest because I did not think that any book submitted deserved an award.[2]

Well, after all, in a world like this—a world in which people are starving or burned up in prisons, nothing, not even the scheme of things in general or the dignity of literature, seems of the slightest importance. But you are really very nice and I wish you all the good in the world.

Sincerely yours,

ELLEN GLASGOW

[2] Presumably a reference to Miss Glasgow's participation as a judge for the Harper Prize Novel contest.

TO STARK YOUNG[1]

Richmond, Saturday [No other date]

Dear Cousin:

I have just read with pure delight your letter to Shaw. The penetration is yours alone, and yours alone is the perfection of manner. Everything that you write has that quality of unerring insight—your interpretation of plays, your understanding of the South as a part of the world, and your deeper understanding of the humanity that makes the world as a whole.

Bless you,

ELLEN

I read your dramatic criticism every week with unfailing joy.

[1] Then a member of the editorial staff of the *New Republic*. Mr. Young has supplied the following comment about Miss Glasgow's addressing him as "Cousin": "I called Miss Glasgow Cousin because she would not have liked to be called Miss Ellen, old style and what doubtless seemed old maid style. We did, however, have some connections Southern style, but not blood kin."

TO STARK YOUNG

Richmond, January 12th, 1932

Dear Cousin:

Your letter warmed my heart, but I am distressed to hear of your loss,[1] and I send you my deepest and tenderest sympathy. Love like that is so rare in the world today; all ties except the ties of material possessions seem to have grown so brittle. I wish I could have a long talk with you. Perhaps, when the spring comes, you may run down for a visit.

You were a darling to remember me in Italy. I love that shadow work, and I shall treasure the handkerchief.

Yes, I read and enjoyed and admired the articles by Allen Tate. They are fine and true. More power to him. I was tremendously drawn to him at the University.

But I have always wanted to put my best into my books— to make them compensate, in a way, for the kind of life I have had. Strangely enough, I have a feeling that my best work is ahead. In spite of the long tragedy of my life, I do not think I have exhausted the creative part of my mind. Now, when everything else matters so little, I may give my whole self to that. The only thing I have saved out of the wreck is the gift of work, and I shall cling to this as our ancestors clung to the Rock of Ages.

Indeed I know how hard it is to live easily. I, also, am economizing, and that keeps me at home. Then I can't rid myself of a sense of responsibility, which means that I am very old-fashioned, for all my advanced ideas. Christmas, we (Miss Bennett did the work) got together fifty-two small Christmas boxes for people who had none (just candy and nuts and fruit and cake) besides thirteen baskets of provisions, and stockings for the children of all the servants. That

[1] The death of Mr. Young's nephew, Stark Young Robertson.

[*112*]

takes time and patience, but there are so many people out of work here, and the descendants of all my mother's servants (she never used, nor did her grandmother ever use, the word "slaves") are still in touch with me—at least when trouble approaches. But I don't like the world. Never can I remember a time when I liked the world. Everywhere about us there are people who we know are in desperate poverty.

Yes I remember Mr. Bowman[2] with pleasure, though I had only a few words with him that afternoon. I should like to see him again and to know him better. When I'm in New York again, I shall love to come to tea with you both. However, I have taken a solemn vow not to go anywhere until I have finished my book.

Affectionately yours,

ELLEN

[2] William McKnight Bowman, an architect and friend of Mr. Young, who had visited at Miss Glasgow's house with him.

TO ALLEN TATE

Richmond, Wednesday [1932]

Dear Allen Tate,

Bless your heart, I am not only pleased but enchanted. An elaborate and technical discussion delights me even when it is about somebody else. So you can imagine how much I shall enjoy reading that criticism of my own edition![1] . . .

Do come to Richmond in the autumn and stay over to see me on your way to the University. I am impatiently eager to see your book—yours and Stark's are the two I look forward to, and Mrs. Tate's if it compares at all with *Penhally.*[2]

My own book has a splendid theme, I think, if only I can

[1] Presumably the Old Dominion Edition of Miss Glasgow's novels.
[2] By Caroline Gordon (Mrs. Tate). Scribner, 1931.

command my strength and feel the rush of wings through
my mind.

As always,

ELLEN GLASGOW

Yes, I learned long ago that the only satisfaction of author-
ship lies in finding the very few who understand what we
mean. As for outside rewards, there is not one that I have
ever discovered.

TO ALLEN TATE

Richmond, March 6th, 1932

Dear Mr. Tate:

Though I ordered your poems[1] as soon as I saw them announced, they came only this morning. I have just read the
book from cover to cover and back again; some of the poems
I read several times. Strangely enough, I had not read your
"Ode to the Confederate Dead" (though I read a great deal
of poetry, very little of this is modern verse), and this poem
has impressed me deeply. I was prepared to find your mood
sympathetic to mine. After meeting you at the University, I
felt that we were in a way, if I may call in my Scottish strain
of mysticism, predestined to be friends, but even then I did
not realize that our attitude to life was so nearly the same.
After all, the bond of philosophy is a strong one, since every
writer worth his salt must have a philosophy.

I have waited impatiently for your Lee. Is it coming soon;
and are you and Mrs. Tate coming with it to Virginia?

Will you thank Mrs. Tate for her letter. I am much interested in her new novel, for I enjoyed *Penhally* and thought
it a very able piece of work. Tell her I know only too well
how hard it is to write about poor white people—or, indeed,
about any people, rich or poor.

[1] *Poems: 1928-1931*, Scribner, 1932.

Your articles in the *New Republic* have been extraordinarily good, I think, and very well worth doing. I wish Southern writers could understand and interpret one another more frequently. We have left all that to Northern and Western writers, and they have taken every advantage of their opportunities.

Well, perhaps, that will come later.

Sincerely yours,

ELLEN GLASGOW

I meant to tell you how much I like the last sonnet in "Inside and Out." Two lines in that stand out and will stay with me. Then, too, I particularly like "Ignis Fatuus" and "The Wolves" because both speak to something within myself. My philosophy? Perhaps.

TO CARL VAN VECHTEN

Richmond, March 23rd, 1932

Dear Carl,

You have found a perfect title, and the book[1] has a magic quality. The gem of the collection is the first essay. I loved that, and I see your mother and father, especially your mother, as vividly as if I had known them in life.

There is a lovely pensiveness in that scene of your youth, a tender contour and a delicate colour that blend in the distance. But I enjoyed the whole book. Many, many thanks.

I have agonized all winter over my new novel. Ah, the vanished joys of illiteracy! If this book is ever finished, I hope to go to New York, and to see you. . . .

Affectionately yours,

ELLEN

[1] *Sacred and Profane Memories,* Knopf, 1932.

TO DANIEL LONGWELL

Richmond, [Probably spring, 1932]

Dear Dan,

At last—at last I have written the end of *The Sheltered Life*. After three years with one idea, I feel as if the movement of life were suspended and I were sitting in a world that had turned over. Of course I must go over the book carefully, but I hope to send the manuscript to you before the last day of May. One thing I know: this novel is good, more intense than *They Stooped to Folly*, more sympathetic in treatment, and, I think, deeper and richer in substance.

Will anyone suspect, I wonder, that I am writing again, not of Southern nature, but of human nature, that I am writing, not of Southern characteristics (whatever that may mean!), but of the springs of human conduct and the common heritage of mankind? Will anyone even begin to suspect that always, whether I wrote social history or fiction, I was treating the South as a part of the world, that I was concerned neither with a failing system nor with class-consciousness (to which I am profoundly indifferent), but with universal experience? I have included the Southern scene, it is true; I have tried to be accurate in detail, to achieve external verisimilitude; and yet the meaning of my work has never been on the surface. To me, the novel is experience illuminated by imagination; and by the word "experience" I am trying to convey something more than an attitude or a gesture. In *The Sheltered Life,* as in *Barren Ground,* my idea has been to give the scene an added dimension, a universal rhythm, deeper than any material surface. Beneath the lights and the shadows, there is the spirit of place; beneath the region, there is the whole movement of life. Chekhov has used this motive perfectly in *The Three Sisters*. Many plays and most novels of imaginative reality have touched or suggested it. To me, the Southern landscape contains this living quality, this depth of mood, and all that is needed is the true insight of the novelist.

Is it too much to hope that somebody will at last begin to suspect? Well, no matter. Nothing would astonish me, after all these years, except to be understood.

Thank you for your very, very agreeable letter. Yes, it is true that I have put more of myself into this book.

As always,

ELLEN GLASGOW

TO DANIEL LONGWELL

[Richmond], June 22, 1932

. . . I need money more than I ever needed it, I think, and if you know of a fairly decent magazine that would pay me thirty-five thousand dollars, I might accept the offer.

But I simply cannot see myself or my book in *The Cosmopolitan*. All my life at a sacrifice, I have stood against the commercialization of my work—for my work is the only thing in the world that makes life endurable. If I lose that integrity, I am lost indeed. . . .

As always

E.G.

TO ARTHUR GRAHAM GLASGOW

Richmond, July 1st, 1932

My dearest Brother,

You are certainly wonderful to me. I cannot thank you and Marjorie enough for the very welcome addition to my income. It was lovely and generous of Marjorie to let me have her part for my life. Will you tell her, with my love, how much I appreciate her sweetness and thoughtfulness.

[117]

As for you, nothing can express the way I feel about all you have done.

I am rejoiced to hear that Margaret is so much better. She has been so brave and patient, and everything around her depends on her unselfishness and resourcefulness. Give her my love and all the good wishes in the world.

I hope the cure will be a great benefit. Write to me about it.

Your devoted sister,
ELLEN

My book is to be published August 23rd. The publishers are very enthusiastic. They think it is my best work—but I am like a squeezed orange—or lemon!

TO DANIEL LONGWELL

[Richmond], July 12, 1932

. . . The proofs of *Barren Ground* went back yesterday.[1] In reading this book over again, after seven years, I felt, as I had felt when I was writing it, that it is the truest novel ever written. Not true to a locality only—I don't mean that —but to life and to the inevitable change and fall of the years. That book deserves to live. It is a perfectly honest interpretation of experience, without illusion, without evasion. . . .

As always
E.G.

[1] Revised for the Old Dominion Edition.

TO ALLEN TATE

Richmond, July 18th, 1932

Dear Allen Tate,

After all, in spite of a letter from the editor urging me to read the magazine, the copy of *Hound and Horn* never came.

[118]

I shall look for a copy in Richmond, but I doubt if there is one to be found here.

Stark Young told me you were going abroad, and I am glad for you and your wife, though it is a disappointment not to see you in Richmond. I had looked forward to your visit, and I wished to tell Mrs. Tate that I tried to win for her the Prix Femina Americain. Not that it would do anybody much good.

Do let me have your address in England. My book is coming out in August, and I wish to send you a copy.

With every good wish in the world,

ELLEN GLASGOW

The magazine has just come, and I have read your article with much interest. I wish I could discuss [Hart] Crane's poetry and his life with you. I have not read all that he wrote; but nothing of his that I have read seems to me so touched with genius as your great Ode.[1] What you write of his death appeals to me very much.

[1] "Ode to the Confederate Dead."

TO ALLEN TATE

Richmond, August 12th, 1932

Dear Allen Tate,

It is the greatest pleasure to have your letter from Paris. I shall think of you there, and hope that you will both have the happiest eight or ten months. How I shall miss you at the writers' gathering in Charleston next October!

In a few days I shall send you a copy of my new book. I pray that you may like it, for I value your opinion tremendously. A great deal of myself has gone into this book, and I put three years into the actual writing. However, it is not in the popular mode of *rough stuff*—or what I have named the Ravelled Sleeve School of fiction. That was what I liked so much about Caroline Gordon's book, it is distinguished and beautifully done.

By the time you return, I hope to have for you some volumes in my definite [*sic*] edition. When I read my early books over, I weep because I began writing so young, before I had learned how to write. But in this edition I have revised one or two of my books, and I should like you to read the better versions.

Many thanks for your suggestion to *Hound and Horn.* After I wrote to you, I read your essay over again; and I got a great deal more out of it than I had found in that first rather hurried reading. It seemed to me to reach beyond Crane into a very fine understanding of personality in its relation to life. I have tried to touch on this in *The Sheltered Life.*

> With best wishes always,
> ELLEN GLASGOW

TO ANICE COOPER[1]

Richmond, Sunday, August 12, 1932

. . . By the way, did you ever go to see Henry Hazlitt of *The Nation,* as I asked you to do? I am so afraid the book[2] there might get into the hands of some young communist, who judges every book by whether the author is "well bred" or not; and regards every "ill bred" author as "superior." . . . There is so much pure malice in reviewing among this young group of radicals. I was radical myself once and I am still in spots, but the bad manners Communism breeds have about cured me. . . .

> Sincerely yrs
> E.G.

[1] Member of the staff at Doubleday, Doran.
[2] *The Sheltered Life.*

TO DANIEL LONGWELL

[Richmond], August 12, 1932

. . . I am not a popular novelist, and I cannot be turned into one. Isabel Paterson[1] scolded me in New York because she had heard (the editor of *Good Housekeeping* had told her) that I had turned down the offer of thirty thousand dollars for a serial. All I said was, why didn't they make it forty thousand? . . .

As always

E.G.

[1] A novelist who for many years conducted the "Turns with a Bookworm" column for the New York *Herald Tribune Books*.

TO J. DONALD ADAMS[1]

Richmond, August 24th, 1932

Dear Mr. Adams,

Nothing that can be said or written of my book will mean more to me than your letter and the review for next Sunday's *Times*. They came at the right moment, just when I needed such perfect understanding of why and how I write novels. Now, the superficial and flippant reviewer may do his worst. I shall not let any misrepresentation depress me after what you have written.

When I talked with you in New York I realized that we look at life and literature from the same point of view. This makes your appreciation so comforting to me—this and the penetration you show in every line of your criticism—for it is perfectly true that my early books lack something, and that something is myself. So long as I was held fast in the toils of life, suffering within my own ego, it was impossible to project my whole self into my novels. Only yesterday,

[1] Literary critic and editor of the New York *Times Book Review*.

strange to say, I had written this, or very nearly this, in a preface to *Barren Ground*. That book, I was unable to correct in the final proof sheets, and in this definitive edition there are many minor improvements in style.

Yes, I shall certainly let you know when I am in New York again, and I hope then to meet Mrs. Adams. Is there a happy chance of your coming to Virginia?

Sincerely yours,

ELLEN GLASGOW

TO J. DONALD ADAMS

Richmond, August 28th, 1932

Dear Mr. Adams,

How kind you were to send me Mr. Soskin's review! It gave me such pleasure; but I should like to tell you again that I appreciate your criticism more than anything that has been written about *The Sheltered Life*. Your insight was deeper because you know all my work, not just the one book you were reviewing. What you said of "The Deep Past" warmed my heart. That chapter is the whole book in a crystal; yet so many reviewers have passed it by without seeing its significance.

May I thank you, too, for placing the criticism on the front page where it could not be missed. My first copy came from Miss Cooper, but yours reached me later.

Sincerely yours,

ELLEN GLASGOW

TO SARA HAARDT MENCKEN

Richmond, August 29th, 1932

Dear Sara,

It was good of you to review *The Sheltered Life,* and it pleased me very much to know that you like it best of my books. One should grow as long as one lives and writes.

I should love to see you again, for you came close to me on that brief visit. Are you ever coming this way again?

Will you give my cordial regards to Mr. Mencken, and tell him that his *Treatise on the Gods*[1] is still one of my favorite books. Because it is different, I think people failed to realize how profound it is beneath its brilliant surface. I have had many discussions about it. Are you writing anything now? Do not give up.

Affectionately yours,

ELLEN GLASGOW

[1] Knopf, 1930.

TO ALLEN TATE

Richmond, September 22nd, 1932

Dear Allen Tate,

I cannot even begin to tell you how much pleasure your letter has given me. There is no American critic whose opinion means more to me than yours. Every one tells me the book has had a wonderful press, but of course very few reviewers have known what I was writing about. By this time, I suppose you have seen Stark's review in the *NR* [*New Republic*]. He was writing his review, when through a misunderstanding, a Communist got in the only disagreeable review the book has had. Stark's article expressed perfectly what I had had in mind. I had asked him to do it from that angle, and to lay stress on the points the other reviewers would never see. The chief point was one you bring out in your letter—that I am not writing of Southern nature, but of human nature. By the Sheltered Life, I meant the whole civilization man has built to protect himself from reality. As you perceive, I was not concerned with the code of Virginia, but with the conventions of the world we call civilized. In General Archbald, the real protagonist, I was dealing with the fate of the civilized mind in a world where even the civilizations we make are uncivilized. I like tremendously what you write of the Birdsongs, and especially Eva. The flaw in human nature, the way personalities bend and break one another, not from selfishness alone, but from the highest motives also—this was in my mind throughout the whole book. I was thinking, too, as you discern, of the Greek feeling that character is fate.

There is only one thing that you have not quite understood, and I realize that this has been my own fault, that I have been afraid of making myself too explicit, and have, therefore, not made myself perfectly clear. But in the preface to the definitive edition of *Barren Ground* (now in press) I had written:

"As a young girl, thinking over my first book, I had resolved that I would write of the South, not sentimentally, as a conquered province, but dispassionately, as a part of the larger world. I had resolved that I would write, not of Southern characteristics, but of human nature. Now, at this turning-point of my life, these early resolutions awoke again with a fresh impulse. It is true that I have portrayed the Southern landscape, with which I am familiar; I have tried to be accurate in detail, to achieve external verisimilitude; but this outward fidelity, though important, has never seemed to me essential in my interpretation of life. The significance of my work, the quickening spirit, would not have varied, I believe, if I had been born anywhere else. For me, the novel is experience illuminated by imagination, and the word "experience" conveys something more than an attitude or a gesture. In *Barren Ground,* as in *The Sheltered Life,* I have worked, I felt, with an added dimension, with a universal rhythm deeper than any material surface. Beneath the lights and shadows there is the brooding spirit of place, but, deeper still, beneath the spirit of place there is the whole movement of life."

This extract will give you an idea of what has always been in my mind, even though I have not been able to bring the thought out very clearly in my books. But you are right in thinking that the tragic years I passed through (I mention this in my preface) changed my approach, though not my intellectual attitude to my subject. I cannot write of these things now, but some day, when you are in Richmond, we will talk them over. So many of my books were written with only half of myself—at least four or five—written simply in the effort to escape from too much living. The one you mention, *One Man in His Time,* was the worst of these, I think. I was in the midst of a nervous breakdown, and desperately unhappy. But the books I wish you to read again are the eight volumes in my definitive edition. Shall I send all these to France? They are so heavy that it seems better to keep them for you. We plan to bring them out in November. Do you know, by the way, no one else has even alluded to John Welch.

This letter is entirely about myself, and I feel ashamed. You will understand, however, and you will realize that I am deeply interested in your work, and that, whenever I find an opportunity, I try to make other persons share my interest and pleasure. I have just placed your poems second in my choice of books of the year. This was in a list for the *Herald-Tribune,* and I was glad to have another chance to speak of it, and to include *Penhally,* too, among the novels.

Nothing could delight me more than what you write of "the tragic vision" in *The Sheltered Life.* That was what I meant the novel to be—an expression of the tragic vision which is the end of all vision.

I have been too hurried in this letter, and the typing is inexcusable. But I am sending it as it is, with all my errors, because neat typing wouldn't really convey my feeling.

Kindest regards to Mrs. Tate. As always,

ELLEN GLASGOW

Will you give my regard to John Peale Bishop[1] when you see him.

[1] Author and contributor of articles, verse, and fiction to magazines.

TO SARA HAARDT MENCKEN

Richmond, October 17th, 1932

Dear Sara,

That was a charming lunch yesterday, and I enjoyed every moment. You were just as I remembered you, and I felt instantly at home with your Henry and very congenial. He is so natural and genuine that I can scarcely believe I have not been friends with him for years. Your marriage seems to me ideal, as my Amanda[1] would say, only I mean far more than she would imply by the word. Do come to Richmond before the autumn is over.

My love to you and my affectionate regards to "Henry."

As always yours,

ELLEN GLASGOW

[1] Miss Amanda in *The Romantic Comedians*.

TO ALLEN TATE

Richmond, January 30th, 1933

Dear Allen Tate,

I was so glad to have your charming letter and to hear that you are reviewing my book for the April *Hound and Horn*. Nothing written of *The Sheltered Life* gave me more genuine satisfaction than your letter about it. I find myself turning definitely toward your point of view and away from the raucous voice of the modern industrial South.[1] The most disheartening thing in life to me just now is to be obliged to live and work in an age that seems to have lost not only all standards but even all respect for what we used to think of as artistic integrity.

Deep in my mind, however, there is a smothered hope (I scarcely dare speak it aloud) that Southern writers may withstand the violent aspect of "Americanism" now in fashion and create an entirely different attitude in literature. Your articles in the *New Republic* made a fine beginning, I think. Perhaps others will join in the movement of recoil. But first we must live down the literary oligarchy of the Middle West, and that isn't so easy, with all my friends the Van Dorens writing about one another—and about Mr. Sinclair Lewis. Have you read *Ann Vickers,*[2] a whole mob of a book? And, still worse—oh, far worse, have you read Carl Van Doren's *Sinclair Lewis?* "Mr. Lewis," remarks Mr. Van Doren, "is America writing."

Perhaps—Meanwhile, Stark has begun his new novel,[3] and I am glad that he is writing, not of Mr. Lewis as America, but of the War Between the States—and his own South.

The next four volumes in my definitive edition have been postponed until March. Do you really wish me to send you eight large books, or shall I keep them? I wish you to read the later prefaces, but I fear all those books will make trouble in packing. When you come back to the South, I hope you will bring Mrs. Tate to Richmond for a visit.

Will you tell her, by the way, that I liked her Indian tale. A relative of my great-grand-father—or rather "a connec-

---

[1] This might suggest that Miss Glasgow was turning toward the Agrarian view, but she never became a wholehearted Agrarian, or an Industrialist either.

[2] Doubleday, 1933.

[3] *So Red the Rose,* Scribner, 1934.

tion," as we say in Virginia too—was carried off by the Shawnees from Tazewell County, and this story reminded me of her history. I hope the novel about poor people comes on well. My own new book[4] treats of the poor too, but not of the poor white class. I have seen so much destitution among educated people in this depression, and before, that my poor persons belong to the class the breadline seldom reaches. But I think the theme is good and I should love to talk it over with you.

It is good news that you are working. Only the other day I was reading your poems aloud.

Always sincerely yours,
ELLEN GLASGOW

[4] *Vein of Iron.*

TO STARK YOUNG

Richmond, February 14th, 1933

Dearest Cousin,

You are an ever present help in trouble and out of trouble. What a beautiful letter that was about your housekeeper, and how alike we are in the way we feel toward persons and events! I was deeply moved, and I wished I could have known Mrs. Melville. Things like that, persons so helpless and so unselfish and kind, tear the heartstrings. And there is so little that one can do, though knowing you and having your friendship and sympathy and understanding must have made all the difference in the world in her life. I know the lovely things you were always doing, things that other persons forget or neglect.

Well, writing that letter to you did me good, though it was a blow to find I couldn't send the prefaces[1] I wished you to see. When I wrote for them, because of a nervous apprehension when I was ill in bed, I found they had been made

[1] The Old Dominion Edition prefaces.

up in plates and sent to press for the last time. I hope they are right. Not that anybody will read them except the author and her cousin; but they will have at least two intelligent and discerning readers, and that is more than can be said of a number of books.

I hope your book goes well. I am in the mood now when I see no reason for ever writing another novel, and very little reason for ever reading one—unless that one is yours. I have a good theme if I can ever feel that the effort is worth while. What depresses me is the inevitable way the second rate forges ahead and the deserving is left behind. I shouldn't mind it if I saw the admirable sweep on to success, or immortality, but always it seems to be the ordinary, the vulgar, and the average, or the lower average, that triumphs.

This may not be a noble spirit, but it is very human. To comfort me, do tell me something of your book. When it comes out, you must select your paper, and I am going to write that article if it [is] the last thing I ever undertake.

Bless you! How I should love to talk with you.

Affectionately yours,

ELLEN

I am up now and better and less troubled by apprehensions. Isn't it queer how big little things can seem when one is ill with a malady like influenza?

TO ALLEN TATE

Richmond, March 11th, 1933

Dear Allen Tate:

I am simply delighted to hear that you are home again. Not only because I like to know that you are working in this country, but especially because America needs you now more than ever. Like you, I feel that there must soon come a change in American life. Surely the tide of materialism, of cruelty and vulgarity, is beginning to turn; and after it has once begun to recede there is so much that you can say, and, I think, you alone perhaps in the South, to bring about the realization of change. If a new era begins in literature, it must be because some writer, some critic, who has the ideas and the power to convey their meaning repeats over and over that civilization does not end in noise and many inventions.

All winter I have been rather ill, and I have just returned from New York where I was in the hands of doctors for ten days. I saw Stark several times and we both spoke of you with pride and admiration. He has just begun his new book, and the beginning is always difficult.

My books are held back until April because of this financial strain. Four are already published, and I may send these, though the prefaces are much lighter and more impersonal. In the second four prefaces I may have been too egotistical —but there is more thought in them anyway. I shall have the first four books, early novels, sent to you in Kentucky, and the others will follow as soon as they appear. Later, after the spring opens, I hope you will come to Richmond, and I should love to have Mrs. Tate and you come to me for a week end. Life is very much less amusing in Richmond than it used to be, but I know that you do not look for amusement. For my part, I like the way of living better now because it is simpler even for those among us who have tastes that are still luxurious.

I hope Mrs. Tate's book[1] has gone well. This is a bad time to bring out a book, I suppose, yet in my heart I believe that the whole collapse of a materialistic structure will be a benefit to literature rather than a disaster. Certainly the state of letters in America could scarcely have been worse.

With kind regards to you both,

Always sincerely yours,

ELLEN GLASGOW

[1] Caroline Gordon was working on *Aleck Maury, Sportsman*. Scribner, 1934.

TO ALLEN TATE

Richmond, March 13th, 1933

Dear Allen Tate:

I forgot to tell you in my last letter that you must not think I expect you to read all these books. This would be entirely too much. I am sending them because the edition is a good one and I thought you might read one or two at the most of my earlier novels. Only I wished you to have them in the definitive edition. Of the first four, *Virginia* is my favorite, and *The Battle-Ground* was the most popular, especially in the South. This book was written, however, when I was very young and was published so long ago that it seems to me to be the work of a stranger. Perhaps I like *Virginia* because it was the evocation of an ideal and is always associated with my mother and the women of her period. I describe Virginia in the beginning exactly as I was told my mother looked when she was a girl.

In these first prefaces I tried to be light and impersonal. They will mean little to you. The next four will come in April, and in these I have a sensitive feeling that I may have given myself away perhaps a little too frankly. There is cold comfort in the thought that few will read them and those few, with the exception of Stark and you and one or two others, will know as little about me as ever. Is your Lee[1] coming soon?

Sincerely yours,

ELLEN GLASGOW

[1] Allen Tate did not complete his projected book on Lee.

TO ALLEN TATE

Richmond, March 25th, 1933

Dear Allen Tate,

I am delighted as well as astonished, and I shall keep the news in confidence until it is made public.[1] Only yesterday I was asking if the time had not come when the South might begin to do its own thinking. Perhaps at last we may abandon the attitude of defense and apology, and refuse to borrow our standards from the Middle West. What I have always resented, with a kind of smothered indignation, is the way we have continued to regard the South as a lost province, to be governed, in a literary sense at least, by superior powers. But, of course, in order to assert our independent spirit, we shall be obliged to begin to think instead of borrow our opinions. Without knowing anything of this movement, Stringfellow Barr[2] and I decided that our chief hope lies in you. Winkie [Mr. Barr], by the way, is much more sympathetic than you might suppose, and a thoroughly fine fellow.

I am intensely interested. You have my sympathy and support, and, so far as I am able, my cooperation. When I am able to begin work again, I shall be glad to write an essay that will fall in with your subjects.

Sincerely yours,

ELLEN GLASGOW

When you write to John Peale Bishop, will you tell him how heartily I liked his article in *The Virginia Quarterly,* and several of his poems I read in *The New Republic.*

This is carrying on the note you first sounded in Southern

[1] The *American Review* was being planned.
[2] Editor and at this time professor of modern European history at the University of Virginia.

poetry. When I read your book of poems, I said, "Even poetry in the South is having ideas."

TO ALLEN TATE

Richmond, April 3rd, 1933

Dear Allen Tate:

I hasten to tell you how much I like the name *The American Review*. This seems to me to strike exactly the right note. Do not—oh, do not let anyone try to start a Southern magazine for Southern readers, or attempt to revive the old *Literary Messenger*. As far back as I can recall somebody in the South, usually in Virginia, was always trying to do this; but it was a mistake both in policy and in psychology, and could lead nowhere but into the grave.

Now, in another period, your group has an opportunity to create an influence that may give the South a new place in American letters. To do this, it seems to me, you must demand, which means assume, a share in making American standards. Of course the critics of the Middle West, and before that of New England, realized that they could win power only by inventing the label "Americanism" and dominating the whole of America. They were shrewd enough, too, to perceive that, in literature at least, the way to the whole of America lies through literary New York.

I agree with all you say of propagandists in literature. Very heartily do I agree with your assertion, "An artist vindicates his tradition not by arguing for it, but by assuming it, and that assumption permits him to take all the world, even when he sees it in terms of a single country, as his province." This expresses, without altering a syllable, what has been my faith from the beginning. I believe, too, that literature must be free to feed in strange pastures, and must remain alive to the world even when it draws inspiration from

[*133*]

dying and death. Your chief advantage, I think, lies in what I may call affirmation, as opposed to negation, of life. At present what other group has an idea that is rooted and living? Only the Communists have a vital faith and that faith appears to lead to standardization of thought.

Stark has another superb piece of criticism in this week's [*New*] *Republic*. What a critic he is! This other side is the only thing, I feel, that prevents his giving himself entirely to fiction. I have great hope of his new novel. Do you, by the way, see *The Nation*. The spring book number, April 12th, has a short essay on what I believe. I wrote the article for a series, and if you do not see the paper, I will send you a copy.

Yes, *Virginia* comes very near to the idea I had in my mind. The theme of the book is concerned with the fate of perfection in an imperfect world. Virginia is the incarnation of an ideal, and the irony is directed not at her, but at human nature which creates an ideal only to abandon it when that ideal comes to flower. She was not a weak character, but her vision was that of the heart. Her strength was the strength of selfless devotion.

The Battle-Ground, one of my very earliest books, has always held its place in the South, with a still earlier book called *The Voice of the People. The Deliverance* is a true, and I think vivid, picture of the decade that followed Reconstruction. All these early novels were written in my early twenties and seem strange to me now. One or two, like my first book, did not appear in print until two or three years after they were written. The early volumes were all included in a social history of Virginia I planned long ago. For years I worked with this idea, but gave it up just before I wrote *Barren Ground*.[1] Until I wrote *The Sheltered Life* I liked

---

[1] This appears to contradict James Branch Cabell's assumption that he gave Miss Glasgow the idea for thinking of her work as a social history of Virginia, as he asserts in his *As I Remember It*, McBride, 1955.

Barren Ground best of my books, and after that I liked *The Romantic Comedians*. I am sending you these volumes in the new edition, with several rather egotistical prefaces. But I have been so much misunderstood that I took Stark's advice and simply "let myself go"—a little way anyhow.

Sincerely yours always,

ELLEN GLASGOW

TO LEWIS GANNETT

Marlborough-Blenheim [Hotel]
Atlantic City, N.J.
May 25th, 1933

Dear Lewis Gannett:

You have been very good to me, and I send you my grateful appreciation.

Although I am still imperfectly reconciled to a world in which the noisy, the timely, and the second best almost invariably wins in the race, I have learned, after thirty years of watching, that the race itself is far from important. Nothing really matters but to preserve, at whatever cost, one's own sense of artistic integrity.[1]

But you help, and I thank you.

Sincerely yours,

ELLEN GLASGOW

Will you read Stark Young's article[2] in *The New Republic* for May the thirty-first. The doctor in Baltimore banished

[1] The Pulitzer Prize committee had just passed over Ellen Glasgow's *The Sheltered Life* for T. S. Stribling's *The Store* (Doubleday) as the prize novel for 1932. Mr. Gannett had written in his column "Books and Things" in the New York *Herald Tribune:* "*The Store* is a lively, full-packed tale; but beside Miss Glasgow's work it seems roughshod." He had also praised Miss Glasgow for her "finely-drawn portraits of the borderline between the Old South and the New. . . ."

[2] "Prefaces to Distinction," an article on Ellen Glasgow and her work, appeared in the June 7 issue.

me here for a few days. How artificial it all is! Even the ocean is like the ocean on the screen.

TO ALLEN TATE

Hotel Stafford
Baltimore, Md.
June 4th, 1933

Dear Allen Tate,

I am delighted to have your foreword, which followed me here, where the doctor is doing painful things to my head and ears. The impressions I write now are hurried ones, after a first intensely absorbed reading. But I cannot really think when I am out of Richmond. I should like to keep this chapter and think, or rather brood, over it until I am free from pain and at home in my study. Will you need it before the last week in June or the first of July?

I think the idea is extremely interesting and significant, and I like the comprehensive design. One question I may answer immediately. The first chapter makes me eager to read the whole book.[1] I feel that the interpretation will be rich and imaginative, and unlike other books that deal with our past. My own novel, for example, the one I am now writing, treats a part of your subject, yet I feel that the approach will be different because you have varied themes and mine deals only with a union of the Scotch-Irish and Tidewater and the place of love in a world that has surrendered to the worship of things. This, of course, makes your book significant to me, but this is far from the chief reason of that significance. (The pain in my head twisted that sentence, but you will understand.)

I really ought to wait and write later, but I am eager to have you know that my response has been immediate and complete and enthusiastic. When I am well, I will take up

[1] *The Fathers,* Minton Balch, 1938.

the details. For instance, I thought pages "2" and "4" particularly suggestive. I wished you had added a little more to the first paragraph on page "4". All this needs to be brought out clearly and fully—and I thought, too, that the way you wrote this paragraph particularly good and vivid. Also, I felt that your very last sentence (the closing one of the chapter) might be made more impressive if it were divided or changed a little. But it is all intensely interesting, and the book will be, as you say, different.

I wish we could talk over our two books. My father's ancestors fought at Bothwell Bridge and my mother was a perfect flower of the Tidewater. In my novel these strains are mingled in a woman who is almost the opposite of Virginia.[2]

Remember that I am writing you after one reading. This is only the beginning of what I shall have to write when the doctor has finished his work and I am able to go back to mine.

You know, however, that any possible help that I am able to give (even the smallest) is yours freely and gladly.

Sincerely always,

ELLEN GLASGOW

Did you see Stark's very beautiful and distinguished review of my prefaces in *The* [*New*] *Republic* for June 7th? What a wonder he is!

I have so much to say of the new magazine, but that must keep.

I am not able to look over this letter, but I have a feeling that it does not convey the enthusiasm that carried me on from page to page in your chapter. It is all, I think, fine and sound and impressive in outline. More later.

[2] The heroine of Miss Glasgow's novel of that title.

TO ALLEN TATE

Richmond, Tuesday [No other date]

Dear Allen,

That is a lovely thing, made of delicate implications and tinted shadows, in the *Hound and Horn*. With the end of the first sentence you create a scene, an atmosphere, that encloses the story in a subdued light "in October when the warm days were few, and the fallen leaves under the thick shade stuck to the dampness on the walk that the sun could not dry." A hundred times I have seen just that, and the association weaves its own peculiar background, a mingling of autumn and sunshine and futility that is ageless. Altogether a delicate and moving piece of work.

Did I tell you how much I like the title of your book. "Ancestors of Exile" [1] is very fine, I think. It interests me to find that you are working on that theme; for I thought I was almost the only American who had had always that feeling of exile, of being not only in a strange country but on a strange planet. All of which makes me look ahead to the finished book.

Always sincerely,

ELLEN GLASGOW

I am so sorry I missed Mrs. Tate's story in the *Yale Review*, but I stopped taking that magazine some months ago.

You made, too, a masterly use of the old woman and the string, the fumbling of age, and the saving of useless ends for oblivion. I shall always remember the picture of those old hands winding bits of string into a ball.

[1] An earlier title for *The Fathers*.

TO ALLEN TATE

Richmond, July 4th, 1933

Dear Allen Tate,

I have just returned to Richmond, and one of my first acts has been to read and reread the Foreword to your book. I find that it has grown upon me in the interval. It is all admirably written, and to me very suggestive and full of the shadowy outlines of characters and ideas. Only one criticism occurs to me, and I offer it merely as a casual suggestion. All the time I was reading I felt that I wished there were more of it, that the ideas might be more explicit and less implicit in certain passages. In my own case, I find that I always leave too much to the understanding of my readers, and this is especially true of my prefaces. I regret that I did not make them, or some of them, longer and fuller, without fear of repetition or overstatement. So few persons ever seem to understand what I mean, because of a quality of reserve in expression—a quality that belongs to one's personality, I suppose. You, I think, have this instinct for reticence and subtlety. It is, I feel, essentially the outer covering of a sensitive and an artistic nature; but such natures are always, like your "obscure Americans" more or less exiles.

The analysis of your recoil from the situation abroad is so fine that I should like to see it drawn out, and then that fine paragraph on page four could be lengthened, as I wrote you from Baltimore. Every sentence has distinction, and it is a distinction of ideas, not merely of an outward grace. I feel that you have a theme that is sound and fine and true, and I am eager to see the whole book.

I hope you are well again and at work, and I hope, too, that Mrs. Tate's novel is going as it should, even in midsummer.

I never thanked you for what you said of the Pulitzer

Prize Committee, but I appreciated your indignation. So many different persons seemed to feel that indignation over the choice. Dr. Canby, Donald Adams, William Soskin, Lewis Gannett and quite a number of others wrote to me. Such expressions give me pleasure—but I have lived too long in a world that "encouraged mediocrity" and in a country that consistently preferred the amateur to the artist. After more than thirty years of this one becomes accustomed, if not entirely reconciled, to the national apotheosis of the average. But I still resent the kind of books the North considers representative of the South.

I wish we could talk over your work and mine. Shall you go North this summer? After six weeks of hotels and doctors every day, I feel that another vacation must wait upon work or an improved financial condition. However, I am, I think, much better.

As always sincerely yours,

ELLEN GLASGOW

That was a perfect essay of Stark's in the *Virginia Quarterly*.[1] So rich in feeling, so unerring in touch, and so true to the deepest experience.

[1] Apparently Mr. Young's "Theatre 1932 New York," April, 1933.

TO ALLEN TATE

Richmond, July 5th, 1933

Dear Allen Tate,

I wrote to you yesterday, and this morning your letter comes!

Yes, I greatly prefer that you should do the long article for the January number of the *Virginia Quarterly*. I shall write to James Wilson at Bread Loaf.

It is excellent news to hear that your book is going so well. Don't let anything interfere with that, I beg of you. I wish I could have given more suggestions; but the Foreword seemed to me too nearly perfect for carping criticism. I felt the coming book through it and in it. This is what any preface should convey, I think, and I know you meant one to gather exactly this understanding of the book as a whole. Let me know if I can help in any way when the book is published. Though I am not in the least a born reviewer, I am always ready to do anything for Stark and you that will bring a clearer insight. The public is incredibly stupid about Southern writers, and it is very important that the Southerners who have a point of view and a philosophy of life should stand together and interpret one another.

By the way, I enjoyed your article very much in the first issue of the *American Review,* but I must confess that I was disappointed in the announcements for the future. The trouble with the *Bookman* was that it never ceased to be insufferably dull, and in this age one may be wicked but one cannot be dull and live. I still feel that Irving Babbitt and Paul Elmer More would sink any craft. It isn't what they think, but the way they think it—the iron armour they wear over ideas— Oh, well, I may be mistaken, but it seemed to me the clanking was still a little too loud. But your piece and the other Southern articles were new and different.

As always sincerely yours,

ELLEN GLASGOW

I am at home again, thank God, and much better, I think.

After writing this letter, I find myself wondering if it would not be better to have that article from you in the *Hound and Horn.* What do you really think? It is so much easier for me to reach a public through the *Virginia Quarterly,* and you could tell James that you are writing the criticism for another magazine. This feeling grows on me; but I am thankful to have one of your splendid essays anywhere and at any time.

So, after all, I am leaving the matter in your hands and not writing to James until I hear from you. Only I beg of you to wait until you have finished your own book and have time on your hands.

E.G.

TO HENRY HAZLITT

Richmond, September 8th, 1933

Dear Mr. Hazlitt:

The Anatomy of Criticism[1] is brilliant and exciting. I admire the tone of the discussion because it is critical without being contentious in the modern manner. There is, indeed, no book in recent American criticism that seems to me so distinguished. When the present fashion of irresponsibility in letters is over, I hope you will emerge more and more clearly as a "lover of reason in a fevered age."

Naturally, I like some chapters better than others, and find myself usually in agreement with Elder or Middleton. Yet you have given all theories an equal opportunity, and this makes your book deeply significant in an epoch when tolerance is the rarest of virtues in criticism. I particularly liked the discussion of "Objectivity or Subjectivity." Yet I enjoyed quite as much the chapter on "Tradition and Rebellion" (especially Elder's remark, "new forms are eagerly embraced by persons with nothing to say, for those with nothing to say can distinguish themselves only if they find a new way of saying it"), and the illuminating essay on "Realism versus Romance," in which Middleton seems to me to solve the ancient problem in a masterly fashion.

There is so much in the book I should like to talk over with you. Is there a chance that you will come to Richmond with Mrs. Hazlitt this autumn?

With kindest regards to you both,
Sincerely yours,
ELLEN GLASGOW

[1] By Henry Hazlitt, literary critic, essayist, and editor. Simon & Schuster, 1933.

TO IRITA VAN DOREN

Richmond, September 8th, 1933

Dear Irita,

I should like to help you with your Fall Book Number; but where can I possibly find fifteen forthcoming American novels that I should consider worth recommending? Other books I might choose. I am carried away by *Flush*[1] (but Virginia Woolf is a genius and English); I am reading with much interest Henry Hazlitt's *Anatomy of Criticism*; I am looking eagerly forward to *The Fathers* by Allen Tate. Yet these three books would be left out of a list of "forthcoming fiction."

The sad truth is that I find most American novels of to-day hard and bitter reading. I passed my peasant stage early (while other people, who were in the fashion, read Henry James and Oscar Wilde and even Edith Wharton), and the peasant mind, even at its lowest in modern fiction, no longer excites me. I dislike sophistication, especially sophisticated barbarism; but I am sufficiently out of the mode to prefer a civilized style. I suppose the fashion will pass sooner or later. Meanwhile, I am not sure that it is wise for me to choose fifteen or twenty titles when these titles are confined to American fiction that has not yet appeared. It is true that I might like *The Farm*[2] which I have not read; I respected the New England backbone in *As the Earth Turns*;[3] but the Southern peasants in *South Moon Under*,[4] and even the Florida swamps, all seemed to me to be made of wool. Also, I may confess, Faulkner's school of Raw-Head-and-Bloody-Bones sends me back, not to real-

---

[1] By Virginia Woolf. Harcourt, Brace, 1933.
[2] By Louis Bromfield. Harper, 1933.
[3] By Gladys Hasty Carroll. Macmillan, 1933.
[4] By Marjorie Kinnan Rawlings. Scribner, 1933.

ism anywhere on earth, but to the Weird Tales of Hoffmann. Gothic tales have their place; but, after all, why do all
mushrooms have to be toadstools?

Affectionately always,
ELLEN GLASGOW

. . . It is true that I am looking forward to Isa Glenn's
book.[5]

[5] *Mr. Darlington's Dangerous Age,* Doubleday, 1933.

TO IRITA VAN DOREN

Richmond, Friday [September, 1933]

Irita dear,

Partly for love of you and partly for love of Flush, and
the fear that he may fall into the wrong hands, I will try my
pen in a review. But I cannot attempt to do justice. I am at
the hardest turn of my book, and I cannot take much time
away from it. Then I feel that I write better when my pen is
barbed with satire, and I cannot be satirical about Virginia
Woolf. Now, if only it were Mr. Ernest Hemingway and his
school of sophisticated barbarians.

I have written Alfred Harcourt a letter which he intends
to quote. Do you think it would be better for him to wait
until I write the review? If you do think this, will you telephone him.

Always affectionately,
ELLEN

I hope you will let me mention five books in the Christmas
number instead of three.

How I wish you could drop down this autumn!

TO JAMES SOUTHALL WILSON

Richmond, September 15th, 1933

Dear James,

I have just read your review[1] with interest and appreciation. It is pleasant to know that you prefer my later books (so do I) and think that my work has not declined with the years.

I should like much to have a good talk with you. Is there a chance of your coming to Richmond?

Sincerely yours,

ELLEN GLASGOW

[1] "Ellen Glasgow's Novels," a review of the Old Dominion Edition, *Virginia Quarterly Review,* October, 1933.

TO ALLEN TATE

Richmond, September 30th, 1933

Dear Allen Tate,

I am awaiting your book with eagerness. When will it be published? What I read about it in Sunday's paper sounds as if it might be the historical background of my new novel, which is now half written. Only my book is placed in the Upper Valley of Virginia, and yours is in Kentucky, isn't it? But I feel as if I cannot wait to see it.

I have just returned from a wonderful trip to Rockbridge, where my father's people of the Glasgow name settled, on the old plantation of Green Forest (Glasgow means Green Forest in Gaelic) when the country west of the Blue Ridge was still scarcely more than a wilderness. The fine old house (1780) is still standing, with immense pillars. It was burned once [in] 1820 and rebuilt on the original foundation, with the original columns and the old brass locks and some of the old woodwork. What a spirit those pioneers had! Of course

[*145*]

Arthur Glasgow was not among the earliest, but he was one of the earliest in the Upper Valley. The Indians were still fighting there when he came about 1766. My father was born in the old house (there was a plantation of between 4,000 and 5,000 acres) but my mother was from the Tidewater. I saw two "boom" towns, one only pretending to be a town, twelve miles apart, which had both been included in the plantation.

I was so much interested in the snapshots you sent. It is strange how feeling seems to swing back to the past when one goes on, after the first recklessness of youth is spent or wasted. But the War Between the States destroyed the greater part of the records.

I hope you are coming this way before the autumn is over, and that I shall be in Richmond. Another dreary time with a doctor awaits me, but I don't know just when.

My kindest regards to Mrs. Tate. She takes almost as long as I do to write a book.

Did you see Stark? I was immensely interested in what you told me about the essay in the *Virginia Quarterly*. I have not seen that book of Edmund Wilson's.[1] The name was too much for me. But I shall glance over it when I have a chance.

As always sincerely yours,

ELLEN GLASGOW

You must come when I am here because I expect Mrs. Tate and you to stay with me.

[1] Probably *The American Jitters,* Scribner, 1932.

TO DOUGLAS SOUTHALL FREEMAN

Richmond, October 10th, 1933

Dear Doctor Freeman:

I am delighted to hear from Julia Sully that you have finished your *Lee,*[1] and that the four volumes will be pub-

[1] *R. E. Lee,* four volumes, Scribner, 1934-35.

lished this autumn. You cannot imagine how eagerly I am awaiting the work. Do let me know as soon as you have heard the date of publication. I should like to ask several editors to be on the watch for it and to place it in the hands of able historians for review.

Now that your long work is over, for a time at least, I wonder if you would be willing to become a member of the board of the S.P.C.A. Of course you would not be expected to attend meetings; but there is no one we would rather have as a director. I know how many things you have on your mind and heart, and you have already been of the greatest possible help to us.

Sincerely yours,

ELLEN GLASGOW

TO STARK YOUNG

Richmond, October 30th, 1933

Dearest Cousin,

It was delightful to see you on my brief visit to New York. You always give me a sense of exhilaration, and my one regret is that I left so much still to talk over.

I shall be happy to read your book whenever it seems best to you—either in manuscript or in proof and to make any slight suggestions that occur. But your work has that rare finish of thought and style closely woven that makes me regard criticism as an impertinence.

I talked over the review with Irita Van Doren. She will put an article, not dealing with one book alone, on the front page of *Books*—or I could do the review of just this book for Dr. Canby. When the time comes, please write me exactly the points you wish to bring out in a review. I shall probably catch them myself, but I may as well have your suggestions. Will you, too, send me a copy of *The Three*

Fountains.[1] You promised this to me, but the book never came. I should like also to see your poems. I have been writing about you several times to the members of something called the Institute of Arts and Letters. All such groups seem to me ineffectual, but it was an opportunity to speak my mind on the subject of your work—and I am careful never to let such an opportunity slip by. Such things mean nothing to you, of course, and as little to me.

But be sure to let me know about the book.

Always affectionately,

ELLEN

[1] By Stark Young. Scribner, 1924.

TO J. DONALD ADAMS

Richmond, November 2nd, 1933

Dear Donald Adams:

. . . It was a great disappointment not to see Alya[1] and you in New York—but I understand perfectly. I was there only three days, and a good part of every morning was spent in the office of Doctor Faulkner. The town seemed to me to wear a dejected look. How I wish you could bring Alya down to Virginia before the autumn is over!

With affectionate regards to you both,
Sincerely yours,

ELLEN GLASGOW

I have liked so much several recent reviews in the *Times* by Eda Lou Walton, especially her able analysis of *The Romantic Agony* and her understanding review of *Flush.* An ugly misprint in my review of *Flush* in the *Herald-Tribune* gave me a bad moment; but since three editors had let it slip by, we decided that it might as well pass without correction. How annoying such mistakes can become when one has given careful work to an article.

[1] Mrs. Adams.

There is a book I had intended to ask you to look out for in the spring. Stark Young is writing a novel of the Civil War, and because of his long immersion in the subject and the period, I feel that it will penetrate far deeper than any fiction of the Raw-Head-and-Bloody-Bones school. After all, the Gothic tale may have its superficial place, but it is not indigenous to the soil. Nor, for that matter, is the civilization in the South today exclusively a social order of inhibited peasants.

TO J. DONALD ADAMS

Richmond, February 4th, 1934

Dear Donald Adams,

I have read several times your admirable essay on "Literature and Individualism." [1] It is by far the best thing I have read on the subject, and I thank you for saying superlatively well so many things that ought to be said. I like it all (though I regard Mr. [Ludwig] Lewisohn as a wild-eyed Freudian), but I particularly like your penetrating remarks about science and the need for an affirmation of other values. However, it is all sound and convincing and, in some strange way, encouraging.

I hope you have had a good winter, and I wish that your lovely Alya and you could come to Virginia. It would be a pleasure to show you the remarkable historical restoration at Williamsburg. I am happy to hear that you are friends with the Brickells. [2] They are very dear to me, and so are Alya and Donald Adams.

Sincerely yours,

ELLEN GLASGOW

[1] In the *Saturday Review of Literature*, February 3, 1934.
[2] Herschel Brickell, the literary critic, and his wife.

TO BESSIE ZABAN JONES

Richmond, February 7th, 1934

Dear Bessie,

Another good talk with you before the fire in your living-room. This is the way I felt when I read your delightful letter. And how proud I am to know anyone who has read even a single book of the *Old Testament* in Hebrew! Not that I should prefer it in Hebrew. As I like it best, it has "had the advantage," so Lytton Strachey observes, "of being translated by a board of Elizabethan bishops." But it is my favorite book, I believe, taken as literature and discarded as prophecy, especially the *Old Testament*. Yet even the *New Testament* seems to me finer as literature than as religion. I cannot accept a creed that divides man from the rest of creation. Evolution was in my blood and bone long before I had ever read Darwin. But the literature of the *Old Testament* is superb, and even Christianity might not have failed if it had ever been tried.

Yes, I enjoyed *Peter Abelard*.[1] It is a fine re-creation which is quite as difficult, I suppose, as a creation. I agree with you that the Gothic horrors of William Faulkner are legitimate material for grotesque tales, like the Weird Tales of Hoffmann, but not considered as realism or even as naturalism. He says in his introduction to *Sanctuary*,[2] "To me this is a cheap idea because it was deliberately conceived to make money." That covers a good deal of that kind of writing nowadays in the South. If anything is too vile and too degenerate to exist anywhere else it is assigned to the "honest" school of Southern fiction, and swallowed whole, bait and all, by Northern readers, who have never been below Washington, but have a strong appetite.

[1] By Helen J. Waddell. Holt, 1933.
[2] Smith and Haas, 1931.

Do you, by the way, really feel that people, especially "poor white" people talk and think as they do in the books of Elizabeth Madox Roberts? Are they convincing to you? To me they are a strange breed, and I find them singularly repulsive, except in *The Great Meadow*.[3] This book is impressive; but, as Dorothy Van Doren remarked of it, "the characters are lost in a fog of language." Strangely enough, since it moved so many other readers, *The Time of Man*[4] left me cold and even sceptical. Her writing seems to me overstrained and unrelated to the life she portrays.

And now *Marcus Aurelius*! It has been twenty years or more since I looked at him; but he carried me over one of the worst times in my life. I have a little volume, heavily underscored, which I used as a girl, and bore with me over Europe, as Byron bore "the pageant of his bleeding heart." I had marked it in Egypt, in Greece, in Constantinople, in Italy and in the hands of God generally. As "an ever-present help in time of trouble," I have found stoicism a greater comfort than any religion that one cannot believe in. But, in the end, nothing outside myself has ever really helped me very much.

This brings me to your question:—"Have you liked your life?" And I answer, not one day, not one hour, not one moment—or perhaps, *only one* hour and one day. When I read of D. H. Lawrence and all the other strutting, sadeyed martyrs of literature, I tell myself that they do not know the first thing about suffering. So long as one is able to pose one has still much to learn about suffering.—No, I haven't read Horace Walpole for years, and I have almost forgotten about Byron. I read constantly the letters of Keats —my poet among poets. Recently, I read the letters of Mrs. Carlyle over again, and I liked her and loved her. Another favorite of mine is Dorothy Wordsworth. I love the way she

[3] Viking, 1930.
[4] Viking, 1926.

wrote of beggars and of picking up sticks with Wordsworth to make a fire in Dove Cottage. I shall never forget those damp stone floors in Dove Cottage. They needed a fire—but they were happy! There are few things more heartening to read than Dorothy's Journal.

I wish I could write on, but I must stop for lunch. My love to Howard. When—when—*when* shall I see you both again?

Affectionately yours as always,

ELLEN

TO J. DONALD ADAMS

Richmond, February 19th, 1934

Dear Donald Adams,

Many thanks for the fine review of *A Nest of Simple Folk*.[1] I had read it with much admiration, (for I see the *Times* every day), and I was just wishing that you would write a book from this point of view—extending and expanding your essay on "Literature and Individualism." There is a vital and increasing need of such work in American criticism, and, I think, a superb opportunity for any able and honest and important critic who has no Marxian axe to grind and no purely personal ends to serve. I cannot understand why the few responsible critics become so timid in the presence of loud irresponsibility.

So please, please, please, please fight the good fight to a finish.

I appreciate what you say of my work. That is what I have at least tried to do, whether I succeeded or failed.

It delighted me to hear that you may bring Alya to Richmond in the spring. Do let me know whatever time will be

[1] By Sean O'Faolain. Viking, 1934.

most convenient. I shall take the greatest pleasure in making you both feel at home in Virginia.

With affectionate regards to you both,
Sincerely yours,
ELLEN GLASGOW

TO J. DONALD ADAMS

Richmond, May 23rd, 1934

Dear Donald,

Your review of *Escape from the Soviets*[1] interested me intensely; but I have not been able to secure a copy of the book. One has been ordered for weeks. I cannot understand why Dutton has not given this book a chance. . . .

I have just finished the advance proofs of Stark Young's new book—*So Red the Rose*.[2] It is by far the best thing he has ever done, and the very best novel of the Deep South in the Civil War ever written by anybody. He has succeeded where DuBose Heyward failed in *Peter Ashley*.[3] When it is published I hope Alya will read it. I know she will like it because it is fine and sincere in tone and without the popular glandular maladjustment. I hope, too, that it will fall into sympathetic hands in *The Times*.

The Unpossessed[4] is exceedingly clever, though I think Virginia Woolf is a great artist but a fatal influence. I found the people in the book as boring as they would have been in life. The trouble with most Young Intellectuals is that they are neither young nor intellectual. If these persons were intellectual—well, God save Socrates!

With love to the three[5] of you.

As always yours,
ELLEN GLASGOW

[1] By Mme. Tatiana Tchernavin. Dutton, 1934.
[2] Scribner, 1934.
[3] Farrar & Rinehart, 1932.
[4] By Tess Slesinger. Simon & Schuster, 1934.
[5] This includes the Adams's daughter Mary.

TO IRITA VAN DOREN

Richmond, May 23rd, 1934

Dear Irita,

On Sunday I am leaving for Philadelphia, and by the end of next week I hope to be at the Hotel Weylin in New York. . . . I am looking forward eagerly to a nice quiet talk with you, world without end. Will you keep an evening, or lunch if you prefer, and let me know by June the first. I shall be in town only a few days, and it will seem like getting back to sophisticated barbarism after the more civilized provinces. A visit from Emily Clark yesterday gave me the impression that, unless one enjoys burglars, New York and Philadelphia had best be avoided. I hope to see Pat,[1] and I shall write to her soon. Also to Lewis Gannett, if he is in town. Do you, by the way, know where the Hazlitts are now, and what he is doing?

I have just finished advanced proofs of Stark Young's new book. It is by far the best thing he has ever done, and it is, in my opinion, the finest novel of the deep South in the Civil War that has ever been written by anybody. Where DuBose Heyward failed, Stark has succeeded. Of course it gives the point of view of the far Southern planters; but, after all, they had a point of view, and they paid a great price for the privilege. Certainly, they have as much right to a fair presentation as have the sodden futilitarians and the corncob cavaliers of Mr. Faulkner.

I assume that you still wish me to write this review.[2] If you have any one else in mind that you would prefer, please send me a telegram. I am trying to write it before I go away, and so clear the ground for my own book[3] when I return.

---

[1] The name by which Isabel Paterson was known to her friends.
[2] Of *So Red the Rose.*
[3] *Vein of Iron.*

After two years of hard work and complete immersion, I have just finished the first draft. That is why I am taking a short rest. I think this novel will be a triumph. It is different and yet not different from my others, and I am tremendously interested in writing of a fresh background and a different stock. Yet I know both quite as well as I know the Tidewater.

Much love always,
ELLEN

I hope I may have at least a glimpse of Carl.

TO DANIEL LONGWELL

Richmond, May 24, 1934

. . . I have a weakness for historical novels especially when they harbor plenty of Indians. . . . Well, Virginia Woolf is a great artist but a fatal influence. And all the Young Intellectuals of whom the only thing to be said with certainty is that they are neither young nor intellectual! But, of course only morons would ever think or speak of themselves as intellectuals. That's why they all look so sad. It's a tremendous effort to be either a natural moron, apparently, or a false intellectual.

Well, well, some day, after we are all contented dust America may grow up and cease to be taken in by amateur theatricals. But not yet, O Lord! . . .

As always
E.G.

TO IRITA VAN DOREN

Richmond, June 9th, 1934

Dear Irita,

You have heard, of course, that Dan[1] has left Doubleday, Doran. This means that I shall go with this novel (my best or one of my very best) and not wait for the autobiography.

Whenever an opportunity occurs, will you take up the question with Harcourt or Houghton, Mifflin. Everything will depend upon the terms offered and upon what I feel to be a proper enthusiasm for my work. It was dear of you to say that you would represent me in my absence.

I was so sorry that you couldn't come to see me again and bring Mr. Davis[2] to tea.

With much love always,

ELLEN

[1] Daniel Longwell had at this time become associated with *Life.*
[2] John Davis, a personal friend.

TO STARK YOUNG

Richmond, June 12th, [Probably 1934]

Dear Cousin,

In New York, where I spent a crowded week, I thought of you constantly. As soon as your letter came I wrote to Mr. Perkins[1] and had a nice answer. And didn't I take care of my cousin? I know how much it means to awaken expectancy for a book, and I talked to every one I knew of *So Red the Rose.* Donald Adams wrote me he was "greatly impressed" by what I said of the book and was taking it to read on the boat. Emily Clark is deeply aware that she is to review the finest novel of the South in the Civil War ever

[1] Maxwell Perkins, editor at Charles Scribner's Sons.

written. Also I found that the *Saturday Review* had given the book into the good hands of Josephine Pinckney.[2] I had a long talk with Irita and I hope that she will put my review on the front page. She asked me please not to mention all of the merits and not [*sic*] of the flaws—but I didn't want to hunt up things to carp about, and I told her so. Let me know the "points" we spoke of, but I think I have all I need.

How are you and yours?

I hope you found your aunt much better. Give her my love, and to your sister too.

Have you an idea of staying in the South all summer? I wish I could have a long heart-to-heart talk with you. Now, I shall go back to my review and finish it before I motor into the mountains next week.

Affectionately,
ELLEN

[2] Novelist of Charleston, S.C.

TO IRITA VAN DOREN

Richmond, June 18th, 1934

Dear Irita,

What a treasure you are, and (unlike some other treasures I have known) how unerringly wise and intelligent!

I agree with every word you write, and I can prove this in no better way than by taking your advice from beginning to end. Certainly, if I go to Alfred Harcourt,[1] I shall do so because I believe in him and have faith in his word and in his ability as a publisher. The mere idea of consulting any one else after I have chosen A.H. for my publisher, is simply ridiculous and, as you say, would be ruinous. No, I shall not make trouble of that kind for him or any one else. . . .

[1] Cofounder of Harcourt, Brace and Company.

Of course, I shall have to have very good terms. Since so much that I put away has been lost, I am obliged to make up what I can in a diminished income. I shall talk over any contract with you, and there are many small details to be considered. But for the major points in the contract do you think an advance of twenty thousand on a straight twenty per cent royalty, and a guarantee of fifteen thousand to be spent in advertising the next novel would be right? I have just written to Raymond Everitt [2] that I could not have an agent act for me. It pained me to write the letter; but I think A.H. is right, and I must not, at this time, when I need to act with wisdom, let anything stand in the way of my professional interest.

I have just reached home. Everything is in confusion, and I am rushing this off to you without reading it over.

Much love and many, many thanks, dear Irita.

Ever yours,

ELLEN

[2] Then connected with Curtis Brown, Ltd., a literary agency.

TO STARK YOUNG

Richmond, July 28th, 1934

Dear Cousin,

I am so glad my review[1] gave you pleasure. That was why I wrote it, and I wouldn't have taken so much trouble for any one else. However, I must confess that the article does seem rather fine when I read it over in print. If it helps the book, I shall be more than compensated for the effort.

Yes, when I look out over the literary field in America, I become profoundly discouraged. Was there ever such flatness anywhere else on earth? There is a positive vindictiveness

[1] Miss Glasgow's review of *So Red the Rose* appeared under the title "A Memorable Novel of the Old Deep South," in the *Herald Tribune Books,* July 22, 1934.

toward any aspect of distinction. Ortega notices this in his *Revolt of the Masses*,[2] so the distressing symptom cannot be confined to this country. If I had my way, I should give up writing for good and all, and escape into some desert beyond the reach of vulgarity and obscene cruelty. But I am bound to the wheel. I can do nothing else, and if I stopped writing I should probably find a way out of life. After all, I exist on the surface and live deep down in some world of inward creation. After more than thirty years, I feel lost when I try to absorb myself, even for a few weeks, in other interests. I do find a satisfaction that keeps me alive, and I have never expected any returns or rewards that were not restricted to the work in itself. Neglect, abuse, wilful misrepresentation— I have had all these, but they have all been as external as the stings of an insect—

I have so much to talk over with you. Have you any idea what time in August you may come? I want you to myself; but if you do not expect to come the 21st or 22nd, my nephew may stop on his way to camp.

So often I think of your aunt and your sister and you, and wonder how it is in Texas at this season.

Affectionately,

ELLEN

[2] By Ortega y Gasset. English translation, Morrow, 1932.

TO IRITA VAN DOREN

Richmond, August 2nd, 1934

Irita dear,

Your letter came at the right moment and has finally decided me. I cannot tell you how much I appreciate your interest and sympathy and all the trouble you have taken with my problem.

Alfred Harcourt came down on Tuesday, and we had a perfectly satisfactory talk. He told me I might write my own contract, but I did not wish to do that. I asked him to tell me what he would feel justified in offering me, and then to let me take his offer or leave it. In the end, though he said he had never given any one a straight twenty per cent, he would do it for me if I asked for it. Instead, I suggested fifteen per cent up to thirty thousand, and he made it twenty-five. So these are his terms. An advance of twenty thousand on a basis of fifteen per cent to twenty-five thousand, and twenty per cent afterwards, a guarantee of fifteen thousand to be spent on advertising this novel. All the other points I could think of were decided agreeably, and I was impressed by the man's conviction and integrity. He would handle all my marginal rights on a ten per cent basis, as any other agent would do. I liked him very much.

I suppose he will talk to you, and I told him I wished you to see the contract before he sent it to me. But I have not said positively yet I shall go to him. I am waiting until I hear from him because if his enthusiasm has waned since he returned to New York, I could be perfectly satisfied to change to Houghton Mifflin. I like Mr. Greenslet,[1] too, and he seemed quite as appreciative. The terms are almost the same, though A.H.'s may be a little better. The Houghton Mifflin guarantee is for the least that they are to spend and only on newspaper publicity, not on promotion. Then they offer a bonus, which brings the royalty advance to very nearly the same figure.

But I have decided for Harcourt, and on the understanding that I cannot promise to deliver the manuscript at any specified date. If I did that, I should never be able to write the book at all.

I have worked harder than I have done for years, and I am staying here all summer for that reason. Never has any of my novels taken so strong a hold on me as this one. It is a big book, not a slight one, and it has a great many char-

[1] Ferris Greenslet, a director of Houghton Mifflin.

acters. The whole idea and handling will be a new departure for me. I have a sense of mastery which I trust will not mislead me.

Much love, dearest Irita. How I wish I could see you. I know the country did you good. That is just the kind of summer I like best.

ELLEN

TO DOUGLAS SOUTHALL FREEMAN

Richmond, August 3rd, 1934

Dear Dr. Freeman:

I am delighted to have good news of your *Lee,* and I shall be proud and glad to have the inscribed volumes.

This morning I am writing to Dr. Canby to remind him of his promise to ask Littell Hart[1] [*sic*] to review the book, and I shall write, too, to the editor of *The Herald-Tribune* and suggest Stephen Benét. I wish it were possible for me to review *Lee,* but at present I am in a state of total immersion in my new novel, and, besides, I should not feel competent to write of the battles.

Affectionately yours,
ELLEN GLASGOW

[1] Probably Captain B. H. Liddell Hart, British specialist in military history.

TO IRITA VAN DOREN

Richmond, August 12th, 1934

Irita dear,

A book like *Lee* will receive so much technical reviewing that I think it would be well to have it interpreted by a poet who is familiar with the subject. There was so much pure poetry in Lee's nature.

A letter accepting Mr. Harcourt's offer lay for a week

[161]

on my desk while I was having a correspondence with Garden City.[1] At last the letter has gone, but the whole thing has been difficult and rather painful. Nelson [Doubleday], so far, has been really lovely, and shown a side that is human and appealing. But they could not understand in the firm that I had reached a decision. Last evening Dan came down and talked for two hours trying to persuade me not to leave. He brought two contracts, one blank but signed for me to fill in. It had never occurred to me that they would take my going as "a personal blow." I do not like to write of this, but I know I am safe with you. And it is just as well that Harcourt, Brace should realize that, good as their terms are, I am able to command them elsewhere.

Will you go over the contract before Mr. Harcourt sends it down to me. Two matters I should like cleared up. First, what can be done to save my definitive edition from being "remaindered." Secondly can H.B. handle the foreign rights as well as a London agency might handle them? Personally, I should rather have Alfred Harcourt take care of them if [he] has had such experience.

How I wish I could see you, dearest Irita, and I am looking forward to being with you in the country next summer, if only for a day.

Much love always,
ELLEN

I do not expect Harcourt to spend money on my old books. Last night I heard again that they would not be sold. But I am anxious.

[1] Where the offices of Doubleday, Doran were then located.

TO ALFRED HARCOURT

Richmond, August 14th, 1934

Dear Mr. Harcourt:

I appreciate your very nice telegram of yesterday and your even nicer letter this morning. In spite of the sad prophecies I am receiving by every mail, I am feeling unusually cheerful. I believe we shall work well together, especially if you will undertake to do all the work. My prayer is to be left free from business worries but to have perfect confidence that my interests are looked after with enthusiasm and unfailing ability. If I never, never have to nag anybody to do anything, I shall be happy. But, of course, this blessed state can occur only when I *know* that everything possible will be done for my books.

I hope, too, that I shall carry into my new associations all the good will I found in my former connections. A letter from Garden City yesterday says, "Our whole organization has an abiding affection for you and your work. You would miss such enthusiasm." So, please do not let me miss anything.

I am enclosing a few notes. The next time you come down I hope to show you several chapters of *The Will to Live.*[1] If you do not feel about it as I do, you may cancel the contract.

Sincerely yours,

ELLEN GLASGOW

[1] Working title for *Vein of Iron.*

TO IRITA VAN DOREN

Richmond, August 17th, 1934

Irita dear,

I intended to write to you yesterday, but I spent the better part of the day with Nelson, and in the afternoon I had a headache.

[*163*]

It was dear of you to call me (by the way, you must charge that call to me) and I was worried from what Anne Virginia told me because I was afraid you might not have had an entirely pleasant time. I sent the telegram as you suggested, saying positively that I had signed the agreement and it was useless for him to come down. That is settled, I thought, and put the matter out of my mind. But the next morning at nine o'clock James came up to say that "a gentleman was downstairs and he had offered him breakfast." I was dreading a storm and as I went down I reminded myself that an old friend used to tell me my greatest gift was the ability to take the sting out of people. But, believe it or not, and even attribute it if you please to my sting-extracting gift, he was perfectly angelic. It's a nuisance to be forever putting yourself in some one else's place; but I came to understand him so well in those few hours that I felt as if I had been born in his skin in some other life.

Well, he asked first of all if I would authorize him to "go to Alfred and buy that contract." And he would really have done it. He would have spent any amount of money, thrown it away, in order to gain his point. If he had come to upbraid, he stayed to lunch, instead, and at the critical moment Anne Virginia brought in large and fragrant mint juleps in my finest Georgian goblets. It was the first time I had ever seen him alone, and I liked him better than I had ever done in my life. He talked to me of his difficulties and said "I know I do a lot of things that seem to you cheap; but I don't do them from choice, I have to make that plant pay its expenses. My father invested nine million dollars in it in all, and it employs eleven hundred people." I could feel sympathy in all that; but of course it did not change my feeling that he was not the right publisher for my books. I do not want to make my living out of the mass mind.

I was glad, though, that things ended pleasantly. He reassured me entirely about my edition. Nothing would induce him to remainder them, and he would do anything I wished and protect my interests in every way. He even offered me an advance on my old books, and was eager to give me enough money to go over to my niece's wedding in October. It is useless to deny that he has very generous impulses, and is as mild as a May morning if you know how to take him, which is rather as one would take an over-grown child.

I told him that you had nothing whatever to do with my changing publishers, that I had decided to go before I talked with you. You will be amused to hear that you made a deep impression upon him. He said, "She is fine. I wish I knew her better. She is worth a dozen of Carl." Needless to say, he did not draw an argument from me by that statement.

The agreement has gone to Harcourt, and I cannot tell you how grateful I am to you for all your trouble. You have been perfect as always.

Much love, dearest Irita,

ELLEN

My review of *So Red the Rose* has brought me endless bother. Every publisher (to say nothing of the writers) in the country appears to be animated by a desire to have me review a book. And I hate doing it above all things.

SECTION IV

September 27, 1934—July 8, 1937

TO DOUGLAS SOUTHALL FREEMAN

Richmond, September 27th, 1934

Dear Doctor Freeman,

Great was my joy when I reached home last night to find your gift of *Lee,* with the beautiful and generous inscription. This will always be one of my treasures. I am indeed proud and grateful.

I shall read the book slowly and thoughtfully, as such work deserves to be read, and I shall write again when I have finished the two volumes. The "Foreword" is very fine, and I am so glad that you begin the biography with the note of human chance, not with a genealogical record. My eagerness to begin this book has made me push aside a whole morning's work.

With deep appreciation,
Affectionately yours,
ELLEN GLASGOW

TO ALFRED HARCOURT

Richmond, October 26, 1934

Dear Mr. Harcourt:

I really don't know what to say about dates. That is why I did not write to you when you asked me.

I should be glad to have you bring Mr. Lorimer[1] to Richmond and to talk with you about the book and show you as much as I have ready. I might be able to let you read a hundred and fifty pages of manuscript; but there isn't any-

[1] George Horace Lorimer, editor in chief of the *Saturday Evening Post.*

one on earth who could read the writing of that first draft except myself. Even Miss Bennett, my secretary, couldn't read my first writing, because it is in a kind of personal script.

If you do decide to come, week after next would be better. By that time, I may have a little more writing done. But this is the difficulty that always occurs in the matter of a fixed date, and much as I need the money, we may have to give up the prospect of serialization.

There is something else, too. I never have but one copy of a book. This always drives my publisher distracted; but I cannot help that. I try to have two. I begin with a carbon and end invariably by discarding that and putting all my work on the single copy I am correcting. Some pages are copied only once, and some leave Miss Bennett still working over the same paragraph at the end of the day. However, in spite of the struggle, the book does get written sooner or later. I am tremendously enthusiastic about this novel, and I shall not be satisfied until I have made it as nearly perfect as possible. It doesn't really matter to me that people, especially in America, prefer bad writing.

Sincerely yours,

ELLEN GLASGOW

TO DOUGLAS SOUTHALL FREEMAN

Richmond, January 2nd, 1935

Dear Doctor Freeman:

A too generous spirit prompted your lovely letter; for nothing could have held back your *Lee* in any world that had not gone blind to excellence. Far be it from me to imply that merit always wins. I know my human nature too well to accept that fallacy. But your *Lee* was predestined to success by a peculiar combination of the right qualities.

However, the little I could do to help in the beginning was not inspired by a general interest in what you call "obscure writers." I was animated by my friendship for you and by my firm conviction that you had given twenty years of your life and your learning to the making of a great biography. May the coming year bring you and yours every blessing.

Affectionately yours,

ELLEN GLASGOW

TO BESSIE ZABAN JONES

Richmond, January 8th, 1935

Dear Bessie:

I was so glad to have your letter, for I think often of you and Howard, and always with interest and affection and the wish that it were possible to see more of you.

For the past two years I have been completely absorbed in my novel, and the actual world has receded. There is another year's work ahead and yet I dread the time when I shall finish this book and send it out into the world that "knows not Joseph." No novel has ever meant quite so much to me. It is, I feel sure, my best book, completely realized and created before I put pen to paper. After my three comedies of manners, I have returned to my earlier kind of novel. This book is like, and yet utterly unlike, *Barren Ground*—if you know what that means. It is long, thoughtful, tragic, but not melancholy (though I like melancholy novels when they are genuine), and saturated through and through with reality. Modern but not sprawling.

Do tell me more of yourself and your life. Your personality interests me more and more, and whenever I have a letter from you, I seem to catch a fresh slant of light on your mind. I wish I could see you, though I really have no life except in my work. There, and there alone, have I found peace. But it took years and years of anguish and of seeking to find peace even within. The agony of the world has always pressed in upon me, even when I was a child, and the curious

[171]

part is that my power of suffering, both personal and vicarious, has not diminished as I have grown older. I still blaze with rage at the injustice and cruelty of life. Only I realize now that it is all wasted, like Heaven's rage at the sight of a robin redbreast in a cage. Do you love Blake as I do? Especially that poem, "A robin redbreast in a cage, Puts all Heaven in rage." and the "Milton"?

Do write to me again and tell me of yourself. No, my book has not been delayed. I have lingered over it because I shall be sorry to reach an end and find only a blind alley ahead of me. Sometimes it is hard for me to write; but this novel has not been difficult, except of course that the effort to find the exact right word and phrase is always difficult. I wrote the first draft very quickly, for me, though it sounds long because it took me almost two years. That was the vital and living whole. Then I went back, and I have been on the rewriting ever since last spring. Did you, I wonder, see my essay[1] in Dr. Canby's series in the *Saturday Review*? It appeared in the Christmas number, December the 8th? So many teachers of English have told me that it was an article they needed. You might be interested if you would look it up in the library. And I think Howard would be, too.

Love to Howard, and every good wish in the world.

Affectionately yours,

ELLEN

[1] "One Way to Write Novels."

TO CARL VAN VECHTEN

Richmond, January 30th, 1935

Dear Carlo:

What a gift for friendship you have! Years go by, but one always finds you where one left you. I am always pleased and touched when you send me a card from the same place in

London every summer and tell me that the spot brings me to your remembrance.

It will be lovely to see you next Tuesday. If you think I shall like Miss Stein,[1] I am sure to do so. And even if I shouldn't like her, I should still be polite, because I was so unfortunate as to be born that way. I can be rude as anybody if I am prepared; but it takes me at least twenty-four hours to make ready. Usually, I avoid modern Fads and People Who Lecture. However, I have nothing against G.S. except what is popularly known as her "Influence." My private opinion is that the writers she has influenced, (especially Hemingway) couldn't have been much worse if she had let them alone. They remind me of spiteful children who feel, after they have been slapped, that they must run out and pull the cat's tail.

James[2] has had a hard time with influenza; but I hope he will be able to come out to dinner Tuesday. I shall have only a very small dinner, and ask a few people to come in for eggnog. As you know, there are no "literary" people in Richmond. We stand or fall by our human quality.

Love to Fania. I wish she could come too.

Affectionately yours,

ELLEN GLASGOW

For the first time in fifteen years, I went to the movies yesterday. And how I wished I had stayed safely at home with my Dickens! There is entirely too much Walpole in this David Copperfield.[3] Not only was Hugh in the pulpit, but he was spread thick over the rest of it. Dickens was sentimental; yet his final flavour is as robust as beef and ale. Hugh

[1] Gertrude Stein.

[2] James Branch Cabell.

[3] David Selznick's motion-picture production of *David Copperfield*, released by Metro-Goldwyn-Mayer in 1935. The script was written by Howard Estabrook and adapted by Hugh Walpole, who also played a small role.

has his quality, and that is not robustness, though it is quite engaging in its time and place. Or, perhaps— Well, no matter—.

TO ALFRED HARCOURT

Richmond, February 7th, 1935

Dear Mr. Harcourt:

I am glad you wrote me about Miss Stein. She came down with my old friend Carl Van Vechten, and they dined with me a night or two ago. I like Miss Stein and Miss Toklas[1] very much. Though I do not take Miss Stein's prose seriously, her personality won me, and we became very good friends.

My book is going well. I am eager to have you read it as a whole and to begin to make plans. . . .

Sincerely yours,

ELLEN GLASGOW

[1] Alice B. Toklas, Gertrude Stein's long-time secretary and companion. Miss Stein used the title *The Autobiography of Alice B. Toklas* for her own autobiography, published by Harcourt, Brace in 1933.

TO ALFRED HARCOURT

Richmond, March 20th, 1935

Dear Mr Harcourt:

I deeply appreciate your invitation to come to New York as the guest of Harcourt, Brace and Company. I wish it were possible for me to make that speech at the dinner of The Friends of the Princeton Library; but I am deeply absorbed in my book and I feel that I cannot break off until it is finished. There are many things I should like to say, though I shall never say them in the company of the radio and the flashlight. . . .

My novel is coming on beautifully—at least for me. I hope to have it completed by early summer, and then I shall try to arrange for the two copies. That will require a little time. Would it be possible for you to come down after the work is done and before the typist begins to copy. I am impatient to have you read the whole novel. Next time you must come straight to us and not go to a hotel. Perhaps you may arrange to stay over a second day in order to read the book from beginning to end. As August is my publishing month, it looks as if there would have to be another postponement. I have a superstition against the spring for publishing.

Anyway, it is "thumbs down" on the popular magazines. I have looked over several of them (*The Woman's Home Companion, The Ladies Home Journal, The Delineator,* etc.), and I simply cannot see myself surviving in that atmosphere, beneath those moving picture captions. After all, if I am respected now, after thirty years of struggle against commercialization, it is because I have followed my own course, regardless of fashions, and held to my own standards. If these magazines wanted my work, it would be only to use my name, and, besides, I should always feel that there is something wrong with me or they wouldn't have looked at my writing. *The Red Book* may be better; but I haven't seen a copy.

Well, we shall have time to discuss this when I see you.

Sincerely yours,

ELLEN GLASGOW

TO ALFRED HARCOURT

Richmond, March 21st, 1935

Dear Mr. Harcourt:

After writing this letter,[1] several things that I feel ought to be said popped into my mind, and I have decided to accept the invitation to speak at the dinner of the Friends of the

[1] The letter of the previous day to Mr. Harcourt.

Princeton Library. But I make one condition. I may say what I please and not merely pay after-dinner compliments. It isn't worthwhile to leave the South in order to make or hear compliments.

It will be nice, and I shall be grateful, if H.B. & Co. can arrange to have me as the guest of the firm at least coming and going and for a day in New York. For the rest, I shall look after myself and the friends who will be with me. Will you arrange to have her receive an invitation to the dinner. Her name is Mrs. Frank W. Duke.

I hope we shall have an opportunity for a long talk, and I hope, too, to meet the other members of H.B. & Co.

Sincerely yours,

ELLEN GLASGOW

TO ALFRED HARCOURT

Richmond, May 5th, 1935

Dear Mr. Harcourt:

I was so glad to have your letter and to know that my little address[1] appeared well in print. I have not yet seen a copy.

Everyone was so nice to me in New York that I was obliged to enjoy my visit. It was a particular pleasure to see Mrs. Harcourt and you, and I was delighted with the luncheon on Wednesday. We shall all work well together, I am sure, and I liked everyone and everything in the firm.

By the way, while it is still in my mind, will you make a note:—"large, clear type for *Vein of Iron.*" Even if the pages run on, please have good print and paper. My idea of a well-made book is *To the Lighthouse.*[2] It has a special

---

[1] "Heroes and Monsters," Miss Glasgow's address before the Friends of the Princeton Library, was published in the *Saturday Review of Literature*, May 4, 1935; also in *What Is a Book?*, Dale Warren, ed., Houghton Mifflin, 1935.

[2] By Virginia Woolf. Harcourt, Brace, 1927.

feeling that appeals to me, and I like the general appearance and the lightness of weight in the hand. That has distinction and so has *Passage to India*;[3] but, if you will forgive my saying this, I dislike the type, paper, and binding of *Siesta*.[4] I cannot abide a woolly paper and intense black small type.

I am hard at work again, and I hope to finish my book by the first of June. Then I shall ask you to come down before I take a breathing spell and have the manuscript copied. There are many things I wish to discuss. Next autumn, after this rush of work is over, I hope you will bring Mrs. Harcourt to see me. I should like to show you Williamsburg and some other things in Virginia.

Miss Bennett sends you this little sum. She says she hopes it was justified. Of course, I took care of Mrs. Duke and the other days.

Sincerely yours,
ELLEN GLASGOW

[3] By E. M. Forster. Harcourt, Brace, 1924.
[4] By Berry Fleming. Harcourt, Brace, 1935.

TO STARK YOUNG

Richmond, May 11th, 1935

Dear Cousin,

Ten minutes after your letter came, a note to Irita was in the post. She may think me interfering; but I believe the only difficulty will be that your book is a collection of short stories.[1] All papers slight short stories, and seldom give them to outside reviewers. But I did all I could, and we shall see.

I am nearing the end of my book, and I think it is all beautiful and wonderful. How I wish I could talk over some of it with you! There is not a human being in the world to whom I might read a chapter, or discuss any part of the work. I envy your good fortune in knowing people who will listen

[1] *Feliciana*, Scribner, 1935.

intelligently to chapters when you read them aloud. Are you going to be in New York this summer? Is there any chance of you being able to come to Richmond? I am so distressed that you are still suffering with that foot. If only I could think of something to do for you!

I think my book will come too late for this autumn. After September, I think it is too late for a serious work. I dislike spring publication, but next year is an election year, and the autumn would not be a good time. Probably, we shall decide on January. As soon as I hear positively what my publishers think of that time, I shall let you know. Certainly, I can believe anything of the *NR.*, and I am depending on you to see me over those rapids. My idea is not to let the publishers send a copy to the magazine, and to send you an early one. I can stand propaganda in novels, but not in criticism. And the paper has become so dull and sheepish that I have stopped taking it.

When does your new book appear? I feel that it is a little close on the splendid success of *S.R.R.* [*So Red the Rose*] but I know publishers like to "follow up," though I am always doubtful about the practice, and try to avoid it. However, I hope you will have proof very soon that my theory is wrong. They tell me that I wait too many years between books. Yet I still wait, and I still hear what they tell me.

Affectionately always,

ELLEN

Can you think of anything I could do for this new book— yours, not mine?

TO STARK YOUNG

Richmond, May 21st, 1935

Dear Cousin:

I am so glad to have your note this morning. It will be all right, I think, about Mr. Commager.[1]

At last—at last—I have finished my book! After three years. I began it in May, 1932, several months before *The Sheltered Life* was published. It had been simmering in my mind for many years.

I am disposed now to bring it out in the early autumn—August or September. As soon as I see my publisher, I will write to you. I should like so much to have you read the early proofs. Do you suppose this could be managed? But if you hate galleys as I do, it would be too much to ask. The book is different from anything I have done—but I am thrilled by its quiet power and its poetic insight.

Affectionately always,

ELLEN

[1] Henry Steele Commager, then professor of history at New York University. Presumably Mr. Young suggested Mr. Commager as a possible reviewer for *Vein of Iron*.

TO ALFRED HARCOURT

Richmond, May 29th, 1935

Dear Mr. Harcourt:

Instead of sending two sets of galleys down to me, will you please have the *second* galleys (complete) sent to Stark Young, 320 East 57th Street, New York.

The time you allow me is so short that it is important to save every hour. I wish Stark to have the proofs when I have mine, not later, and I have told him to expect them next Wednesday or Thursday.

Many thanks for your letters, and especially for the questions that show careful reading. That remark about Mrs. Waters' age is very useful. I will check that, and John Fincastle's age too. My recollection was that he thought of the past, or that the book was published when he was fifty—but all these points are well taken, and these are just the kind of details my mind is disposed to overlook.

As soon as the galleys come, I will begin to read them; but I've been rather ill, it is a great comfort to my nerves when I feel that fresh eyes are helping me with the proofs.

It was a great pleasure to have Miss Taylor[1] and you. Miss Bennett and I both enjoyed your visit.

Sincerely yours,

ELLEN GLASGOW

[1] Helen K. Taylor, then advertising and publicity director for Harcourt, Brace and Company.

TO ALFRED HARCOURT

Richmond, May 30th, 1935

Dear Mr. Harcourt:

One thing I neglected to ask you. Will you please let as few persons as possible read the uncorrected galleys, and positively no one who is to review the book, with the single exception of Stark Young. He sent me galleys of *So Red the Rose*.

Already, I have thought of several changes I wish to make. One will be to call the first part "Toward Life" instead of "The Will to Live." Also, will you notice again the punctuation of the quotation on the title page and have the commas put in exactly as they are in my manuscript.

You are a treasure to work with, and I suppose this is because you let nothing stand in your way when you wish to apply yourself.

Sincerely yours,

ELLEN GLASGOW

TO ALFRED HARCOURT

Richmond, June 6th, 1935

Dear Mr. Harcourt:

I have just returned to town and found Miss Taylor's interesting proofs of the book-flaps. There were one or two minor changes that I suggested in a telegram.

Two things have been in my mind while I was motoring through the mountains (If you will come in October with Mrs. Harcourt, we will take you over the Skyline Drive), and one of these things is a doubt whether it is really wise to push the book for this autumn when so many novels are crowding on the scene. I leave this entirely to your better judgment. Only I wish you to feel perfectly free to do as you think best. I shall accept either plan, and I promise not [to] discuss it again.

The other thought that kept coming was:—how long shall I have between galleys and page proofs? I cannot correct proofs anywhere else, but if the printer will take more than three weeks to make up the plates, after I return the galleys, I should like to go away for the latter half of June. Of course, nothing must stand in the way of my book, not even my health. I like particularly, in Miss Taylor's jacket proof, the explanation of the title, *Vein of Iron*.

As soon as the galleys are corrected finally, will you take up the question of the British and foreign rights?

Sincerely yours,

ELLEN GLASGOW

TO ALFRED HARCOURT

Richmond, June 8th, 1935

Dear Mr. Harcourt:

No, the galleys did not come until a day after I had received your letter. They reached me on the 6th, and I have worked steadily from six o'clock in the morning.

The type is excellent, and there are few typographical errors. But I dislike some of the forms supplied in the manuscript by your proof reader, and I am changing a number of these. For example, I cannot take out so many hyphens, and I do not like the verb "practise" spelled with a "c," as if it were the noun.

I shall do a good deal of revising, as usual, and more important than anything else to me is the care with which these corrections are followed. Would it be safer for me to see the corrected galleys? Or may I trust your proof reader to verify every correction in the proof? This is most important.

Sincerely yours,

E.G.

TO HELEN K. TAYLOR

Richmond, June 13th, 1935

Dear Miss Taylor:

Thank you for that nice clipping. No, I had not seen it. Look up an article by Howard Mumford Jones in the current *Virginia Quarterly*.[1] There is a timely remark about my work.

I suppose I shall have to subscribe to a clipping bureau. Three years ago I left off, and I see few notices. But forty dollars in a few weeks for reviews, many of them duplicates or mere lists of books, seemed more than publicity was worth

[1] "Social Notes on the South," July, 1935.

to me. Could you arrange with a clipping bureau for me? I had Romeike, and they offered me some special terms. Maybe you know what they are, but I've forgotten. Seven dollars for a hundred and fifty clippings, I think. The point I make is that I do not wish to pay for lists of books received. I wish reviews and articles. If you know a good bureau that does not use pink slips, I should prefer it—provided the work is thorough and discriminating. By discriminating, I mean merely discrimination against "Books Received."

I am working, a veritable galley-slave (forgive the pun) from dawn till dark.

Sincerely yours,
ELLEN GLASGOW

TO ALFRED HARCOURT

Richmond, June 17th, 1935

Dear Mr. Harcourt:

I am returning the proofs today by express. I have put so much work in these galleys that I shall be nervous until I know they are safe. Every correction is important to me, some vitally so, and if anything seems obscure, or appears to be an unconscious slip, will you instruct the proof reader to ask me what I meant. Please have every detail carefully verified before I see the page proofs. I hope they will not require changes.

There is something else I have wished to write you about— only I am so tired I can barely string words together. As soon as these corrections are made, could you send advance sheets to Dr. Edwin Mims, who is in Great Britain lecturing as the Carnegie Exchange professor.[1] He has a whole lecture on my work alone, and he is eager to see my new novel. You

---

[1] Dr. Mims was to spend a year in Europe on a Carnegie Traveling Lectureship, but he did not actually leave for England until several months later.

would have to find his address. I think Columbia University could tell you through Dr. Butler.[2]

But nobody must see my book until all the revisions are made in the plates.

Please forgive this rambling letter. I have been in my study since five o'clock, and the heat has been so intolerable that I scarcely know what I have written. However, I shall be ready and waiting for the plate proofs as soon as you can send them.

After I have finished them I expect to come to New York for a few days and talk things over.

Sincerely yours,

ELLEN GLASGOW

Will you tell the proof reader that I tried to delete all the quotation marks in thinking. I may have missed a few because I had to go back. There is no doubt in my mind that this is my best and biggest and truest novel! Now to the autobiography!

[2] Dr. Nicholas Murray Butler, president of Columbia University.

TO ALFRED HARCOURT

Richmond, June 18th, 1935

Dear Mr. Harcourt:

I approve heartily of your dropping the idea of serialization. Thirty thousand dollars would not compensate me for the mortification I should feel if I appeared in one of these magazines.

On the other hand, I rather favor the Book-of-the-Month club, and these are my reasons. You may take them for what they are worth. This book club has, I think, a perfectly undeserved reputation. When so many novels are coming out, it might be a help in a way. I know it was a help with Miss Cather's *Shadows on the Rock*. Alfred Knopf told me that, though he disliked book clubs, he was obliged to admit that the Book-of-the-Month had done a good deal for *Shadows*. The price they pay seems absurd, but all things considered, it may be advisable to consider their offer. My idea would be to let them take as small an edition as they would. The mistake Doubleday has always made is to urge the clubs to take large editions. They sold the Literary Guild seventy thousand of *They Stooped* [*to Folly*], and when a few thousand were left over from their subscribers, the Guild sold them to some magazine to give away as prizes. We stopped it (at least I did), but they said they always did this with books that were left on their hands!

At Doubleday's they worship numbers. But I should like the club to take as few as they will—and leave us a larger public outside. Of course, we shall have to make up by energetic advertising the loss suffered through the club, but I believe we can do this. Anyway, these are my reasons.

Sincerely yours,
ELLEN GLASGOW

TO IRITA VAN DOREN

Richmond, June 18th, 1935

Dear Irita,

I am sorry to say (how sorry only a reader who has suffered from the same misfortune can understand) that I have read every book I ever meant to read. It has always been a regret to me that more books—I mean good books—were not written. Some books I have deliberately avoided, and some other books I have left unfinished. But when your telegram came I was trying to decide whether to read over *The Martyrdom of Man*[1] or (for the fourth time) *The Chronicles of Barsetshire*. (For You).

At last—at last—at last my book in finished, and I feel that I must thank you again for your great help in selecting

[1] By Winwood Reade. Dutton, 1931; originally published in 1874.

a publisher. There is no doubt in my mind that this is my best and truest book. For many years (so many that I couldn't count them) I have had it in my mind to write of the Valley of Virginia, which I know quite as well as I know the Tidewater. I feel sure that you will like it. My father's earliest American ancestor of the Glasgow family settled in the Valley before the Revolution.

I hope Pat will not fail me, for I like the reviews she writes, and I would rather have her than anyone else. If, for any reason, she is unable to review *Vein of Iron,* could you ask Henry Commager. Though I have never met him, I have [a] feeling that he will understand this book, and I hope he is going to review Stark's short stories. I do not think it matters in the least whether a reviewer has ever before reviewed fiction or not. Insight is the one thing needed, and insight is given by God alone.

I hope to see you in July if you will still be in town.

Much love always, dear Irita,

ELLEN

TO EDWIN MIMS

Richmond, July 1st, 1935

Dear Doctor Mims;

Seldom has any letter given me such pleasure as yours! I am sure that only a writer who has striven as long and as hard as I have done to perfect an art and to win the kind of recognition I value, can understand how such generous and discriminating appreciation helps to round out the world. I have tried from the beginning to write truthfully and sincerely, to interpret life as I *know* it and have found it to be. Even in the years when only fiction in fancy dress (costume novels) could find readers, I looked always to throw off the falseness and the sentimentality which made most Southern history and the general Southern attitude of mind so untrue to itself. Sometimes I have felt discouraged and the struggle has seemed unavailing, but people are made more ready to listen now, I think, and there is a better understanding not only of what the South means in literature, but of what literature means in the South. Of course we are still in the childish stage of culture. Shaw's "infantilism" describes it, but we may finally grow up.

Yes, it would be a pleasure to talk with you. I am leaving Monday for Barnstable, Mass., care of Mrs. V. D. Bacon; but perhaps you will be in Richmond next Autumn. I am much interested in your book.[1]

Sincerely,

ELLEN GLASGOW

[1] Possibly Dr. Mims's biography, *Chancellor Kirkland of Vanderbilt,* Vanderbilt University Press, 1940.

TO HOWARD MUMFORD JONES

Richmond, July 8th, 1935

Dear Howard,

I am trying to find a copy of my poems[1] for you. They have been out of print for many years, if they were ever in print! Nine copies sold, my publishers said.

Well, they shocked an age of sweetness, and some of them (the first one at least) are good.

Why has Bessie never replied to my letter? I consider her the only eighteenth-century letter writer left in the world.

I am sorry to hear of your mother's illness. But don't give up your plan of coming to Virginia. I have much to show you.

As always,

ELLEN GLASGOW

Your article in the *V.Q.* brought forth a long leading editorial in the *Richmond Times-Dispatch.* Virginius Dabney[2] must have written it, and he held out his hand to you.

[1] *The Freeman and Other Poems.*
[2] Then chief editorial writer of the Richmond *Times-Dispatch.*

TO LEWIS GANNETT

Richmond, July 12th, 1935

Dear Lewis Gannett:

I expect to be at the Chatham in New York next week, and I am hoping to have a glimpse of you before you go away on your vacation. Could you run in to tea with Mrs. Duke and me on Tuesday, the sixteenth, or perhaps Thursday would suit you better. I should love to see Mrs. Gannett, but I suppose she stays out of town in this weather.

Thank you for the clipping.[1] I was interested in your point of view, and I hope to live long enough to be convinced or converted. For more years than I like to think of (a silly figure of speech, for I am not afraid of the years) I have battered my nerves against human cruelty. If I could believe that the present preoccupation with violence and obscenity springs, either in literature or in life, from compassion for suffering and a noble rage against social injustice, I should willingly offer thanks to any god ever invented, not excepting that strange deity worshipped by the Marquis de Sade.

It is difficult, I admit, to separate certain aspects of moral indignation from the pursuit or exploitation of horror for its own sake. But, it may be because I have lived so long in the South, I am unable to accept the comfortable theory that all the cruelty in this section is confined within the feeble bosoms of degenerate aristocrats. For one thing, there are not enough aristocrats left among us to make one first-class sadist. The few that are left seldom open a book, and too

---

[1] Mr. Gannett's column in the New York *Herald Tribune,* June 7, 1935. Miss Glasgow had said in her speech to the Friends of the Princeton Library, "The literature that crawls too long in the mire will lose at last the power of standing erect." Mr. Gannett gently took her to task for this remark on the grounds that her own career had been "a protest against refusal to look into the slums of a society and of the individual human nature."

many of these Southern horrors have a literary, not to say a theatrical, odour.

Still, I hope you are right, and that the dark obsession is not sensationalism pure and simple, but a fact "a fact of profound and hopeful significance." That is the encouraging view, and I should like to accept it. For you must admit that "to touch mire" is one thing, and "to crawl in slime" is another story. One may touch to destroy, but one crawls too long only for pleasure or profit.

But please do not imagine that I am defending human behaviour in the South or elsewhere. The senseless cruelty of it has cost me too many sleepless nights. It may be that we have more to torture the imagination in the South than we should find in let us say—New England. As the head of one of the very few humane societies in Virginia, I have sometimes asked myself if we are naturally more cruel than other Americans. Then I recall the laughing crowds at ghastly murder trials in the North, the throngs that press about the coffins of dead bandits and clamour to witness executions, the flocks of tourists that gape at the streaming entrails of old horses in the Spanish bull-ring. And I tell myself that we are all tarred with the same ugly brush. Experience has taught me that the only cruelties people condemn are those with which they do not happen to be familiar.

And so I remain to be convinced that our latest horror-mongers are all angels of light that have fallen by accident into the popular fashion. They may be torch bearers, but that is different.

I had intended to write only a note, and my typewriter has run away with me.

Will you call up the Chatham on Monday or Tuesday. It will be so nice to see you again. As for that little speech. Well, there isn't much that one can say, you know, in ten minutes. The truth is that I have never read a word that Erskine Caldwell has written, with the exception of a newspaper reprint containing what struck me as a pale survival of the Romulus and Remus legend. What I had in mind was Mr. Faulkner's Introduction to his *Sanctuary.*

Sincerely yours,

ELLEN GLASGOW

But, of course, nobody is obliged to mean anything that he writes. And this includes me.

TO DOUGLAS SOUTHALL FREEMAN

Richmond, July 22nd, 1935

Dear Dr. Freeman:

When I reached home I found your letter awaiting me. You are an angel to take this time from your busy life, and of course I consider it a high honor to have you write of me.

I shall be delighted to see you at any time if you will telephone me before I go out. The summer has been rather trying, and I try to stay out of doors as much as possible.

Affectionately yours,

ELLEN GLASGOW

TO STARK YOUNG

Richmond, Wednesday

[Probably in summer of 1935]

Dear Cousin:

I am distressed that you have hurt your hand. Surely, you have had more than your share of misfortunes. I hope your knee grows better.

The theme of my book, which I should like brought out, is easiest put in a question. What is it that has enabled human beings to endure life on the earth? One after another, I have considered and interpreted these answers. Religion? Philosophy? Love? Simple human relationships? Or merely the character that is fortitude? What is the vein of iron that has enabled not only families, but races, nations, strains, to survive and even to forge (or weave) some continuing tradition? In my book the vein of iron is of course this Scottish strain of fortitude that has come down from the earliest pioneers in the Valley. I have covered the whole way, in recollection, retrospection, and I link each step of the past with the long line before and afterwards. With John Fincastle, I treat of the fate, the isolation, of the scholar in America, of the thinker among the dynamos. Then, too, in "The Dying Age," [1] I analyze our very special form of disintegration.

I hope you will bring out the peculiar quality of the writing. I have tried to fit every sentence into the whole pattern, and I have used different rhythms for retrospection and for narrative or dialogue. For example, you noticed of course that in those five different reflections (or streams of consciousness), when my five characters were seated before the fire in the manse, I used varying cadences, from the long slow rhythm of age (I am very proud of that passage when Grandmother is dropping asleep) to the aimless staccato thinking of the child. I flatter myself that only a mature art could have dared do this, and I hope you will bring it out in its subtle distinctions.

All through the book, whenever there is retrospection, if even for a flash, I have employed a kind of inward rhythm.

I hope, too, you will bring out my analysis of our age and the modern tone of that section exceptionally. I mean the unsentimental and utterly unsoftened description of the 1930's in Queenborough—in a Southern city. I think my depiction of a single street, Mulberry Street, was a happy thought, and each of these minor characters in that street is as real, I think, as three-dimensional, as the major figures. But you must admit that I have made Ironside in the Valley as real as if it were a place on the map—more real, indeed, to me.

[1] The title of one part of *Vein of Iron*.

Will you let me know the date of your review.[2] I must order my copies ahead.

Bless your heart! Do you know I had a letter this morning speaking of my review of *S.R.R.* and it ended "Now that is a perfect novel."

Affectionately,

ELLEN

[2] Stark Young reviewed *Vein of Iron* in the *New Republic,* September 11, 1935.

TO EDWIN MIMS

Richmond, July 31st, 1935

Dear Dr. Mims,

Your letter gladdened my heart. I felt sure you would understand my book and read it with a responsive mind and imagination. It is beautiful to feel that you will interpret my work in Great Britain, and I shall think often of your first lecture at St. Andrews.

I enjoyed so much seeing you in New York. Good miracles do occasionally happen. Of course we might have had a longer time to talk—but then, it was only the treasure of a moment that we saw each other at all. I was very much pleased to have your attractive little daughter drop in to tea. She looked so fresh and pink and happy on that torrid day.

I wish for you a most successful and delightful year. When you come back you must stop in Richmond and tell me all about it. Or it may be that I shall see you in England next summer. . . .

TO ALFRED HARCOURT

Richmond, August 6th, 1935

Dear Mr. Harcourt:

The first copies of V. of I. have just come. I am delighted with everything, format, feeling, appearance,—everything. The paper is exactly what I wanted—a creamy tone that blends well with the not too heavy type. It weighs well, too, in the hand, and this is so important. Then the dustjacket is quite distinguished. Only a book of substance would take that rich, dark cover.

Please thank everybody. I have not read a line of it, but I am trusting to the accuracy of the printing.

Sincerely yours,

E.G.

TO BESSIE ZABAN JONES

Richmond, August 10th, 1935

Dear Bessie,

It was so nice to have a word from you after this long silence. Yes (to me at least) this is the most satisfying novel, from both a human and an artistic point of view, that I have ever written. As a comedy of manners, I feel (why should I pretend to false modesty?) that *The Romantic Comedians* has never been surpassed in the novel form. But this book strikes its root far down in the soil. It is, of course, far deeper than a study of the pioneer spirit in Virginian civilization. I have used as my theme:—what is the motive that enables human beings to endure life on the earth? One by one, I have tried to interpret these various motives:—religion, philosophy, love, simple human relationships, and the strain of fortitude that has held families and races and nations together. After all, human life has endured, when to a civilized mind, general self-destruction would have appeared at times the only logical choice. I have tried, too, to interpret the age in which we are living and our own special form of disintegration.

In a theme like this, placed in the Virginia Valley, that glancing wit would have sounded a false note. But I have never given more care to a style which I have deliberately subordinated to fidelity and characterization. For the first time, (in what I feel to be my last novel),[1] I have depended upon a mature art and dared to do what I wished. I have tried to make every sentence fit perfectly, without an extraneous edge, into the whole pattern. You will notice, when you read the book over very slowly, the various uses of rhythms in the thoughts of my five persons seated about the fire in the manse. There are the different cadences, caught from life and carefully sustained, from the long slow rhythms of age to the aimless staccato recollections of a child. Of all these things, I am justly proud. Then, too, I have never lived so completely in any of my other characters. For three years (I began this book before *The Sheltered Life* was published) I have lived night and day with these people. In John Fincastle (my favorite) I have written of the loneliness of the scholar in America, of the thinker among the dynamos.

But if I ever write another book, I think now that it will be my autobiography.

Affectionately yours,
ELLEN

[1] There would be one more novel, *In This Our Life*, Harcourt, Brace, 1941.

TO DOUGLAS SOUTHALL FREEMAN

Richmond, Monday
[Probably in August, 1935]

Dear Dr. Freeman:

The article[1] is very vivid and interesting, and I feel highly honoured. There are one or two small points I should like to discuss with you if you have time to stop by. For example, could you begin without the first two paragraphs, just with the house and the changed neighbourhood? For a quiet person the first paragraph seems to me a little too vehement in tone. I know, too, that it is silly beyond words to be sensitive about such a thing, but I can't help wincing when anyone speaks of my deafness. The later allusion comes in less noticeably, and should stand, I suppose.

All the description of my surroundings is excellent. I see the neighbourhood more vividly than I have ever done. And I particularly like the way you end the article.

I hope it won't put you to much trouble to stop by for a minute. It is always delightful to see you, and I think you are a perfect friend to do this for Dr. Canby.

Sincerely yours,

ELLEN GLASGOW

[1] Dr. Freeman's article "Ellen Glasgow, Idealist" appeared in the *Saturday Review of Literature*, August 31, 1935.

TO H. L. MENCKEN

Richmond, August 30th, 1935

Dear Mr. Mencken:

I am so glad to have your letter and to know that you think *Vein of Iron* my best work. I feel sure Sara would have loved this book.[1]

[1] Mrs. Sara Haardt Mencken died in 1935.

All summer I have been far from well. It looks now as if I should not be able to come to Baltimore. Perhaps some day in the autumn you will feel the wish to come to Richmond. I should love to talk with you of Sara, and I think she would have liked our talking of her. Any day that you can come for a week-end I shall be delighted to have you, and I know James Cabell will welcome you with open arms.

When you see Anne Duffy, will you tell her how happily I remember the afternoon Sara took me to her apartment. I have thought of her often since then.

Sincerely yours,

ELLEN GLASGOW

And I should like so much to see your sister again.

TO STARK YOUNG

Richmond, Thursday

[Probably in September, 1935]

Dear Cousin:

The Dallas review seems merely silly when I read it through. Probably written by some weary reporter who was lounging about the office.

I am enclosing a very sympathetic review from the Galveston paper; but the silly review was syndicated in about ten different papers, and I received only one copy of the more dignified Galveston piece.

I am glad you sent me Harry Hansen's[1] comment. Last week I discontinued the clipping service. It was too expensive, and there were too many duplicates.

Of course, I would rather you would not review that book[2] unless you say in a brief press notice that [it] is trivial gossip and not worth publishing. If there is any talent, or even

[1] Then literary editor of the New York *World*.

[2] It is not now clear what book or to whom Ellen Glasgow refers in these caustic paragraphs.

sense, shown in the book, it must have been supplied since it left the mind of the author. He is as clear a case of arrested mental development as I have ever encountered, and he is simply trying to exploit hospitality—or rather kindness to what appeared to be discouraged and unhappy youth. I hate that kind of thing.

But you know best what to do. The only reason that he was ever admitted inside a house in Richmond, or anywhere in Virginia, was that he seemed to be pathetic and well-intentioned, though so ignorant that everything he touched in print became common. I wasted several hours on him, and I was never able to convince him that he should learn to write and to record accurately before he tried to make a sensation.

I wish I could see you. Virginia is beautiful now in the Valley. We motored to the Skyline Drive a few days ago, and I wished for you all the time.

But the doctor is making me go away. I have taken a little house at Ventnor, New Jersey, and I expect to stay for four weeks. My letters will all be promptly forwarded, and I am not going until the middle of next week.

Affectionately,

ELLEN

This reviewer in Richmond is quite intelligent, but the other one—I mean the reviewer on the other paper—is hopelessly ordinary in his preferences. He was the one who didn't like *S.R.R.*, but delighted in something called "They Shoot Horses—" [3] Anyway that's as near as I can recall the title.

You must remember I have not seen this book you ask me about. I am judging by his other dreadful writing this young man brought to show me.

[3] *They Shoot Horses, Don't They?* by Horace McCoy. Simon & Schuster, 1935.

TO J. DONALD ADAMS

106 Sacramento Avenue
Ventnor, New Jersey
October 2nd, 1935

Dear Donald,

I was made happy by your letter this morning, for it over-flowed with good spirits and brought the good news of your coming—or at least of the hope.

The doctor sent me away for my first real vacation in four years, and I expect to be here until the end of October. Can you possibly come for the week-end of November the first? It would be such joy to have you bring my dear Alya—and I hope Mary. If you will let me know as soon as you can decide, Miss Bennett will have everything ready and we will plan for that day's motor trip through the Blue Ridge.

I am tremendously interested in the *Book Review,* and I hope I shall be able to write for it. Just now I am forbidden even to think or to put pen to paper.

I loved your review, and I see your point about Ralph's[1] coming slowly to life. Yet when he does begin to live, I think he is completely alive, as you say.

About the beginning I cannot feel that you are right. To me, the whole book grows and flowers from those child chapters and the expanding mind of the little Ada. I love her better even than the grown Ada. But it was all beautiful of you, and I appreciate everything that you wrote.

God bless the three of you. Let me know whenever you make your plans.

Affectionately yours,

ELLEN

[1] Character in *Vein of Iron.*

TO ARTHUR GRAHAM GLASGOW

Ventnor, October 5th [1935]

My dearest Brother:

It was splendid of you to have Dr. Mims and Mr. Cape[1] to lunch and to plan with them for the reception of *Vein of Iron*. I had a letter from Dr. Mims overflowing with appreciation of you and Marjorie and the house. He enjoyed every minute with you and everything that he heard and saw.

The doctor insisted on my having a change before winter, and I rented a cottage here for the month of October. I feel stronger, but my cough is no better.

We are eagerly awaiting your visit.

With dearest love to the three of you,

Your devoted sister,

ELLEN

I am glad you gave Dr. Mims the papers, and Anne Virginia will send you others.

[1] Jonathan Cape, London publisher of the novel.

TO H. L. MENCKEN

Richmond, November 25th, 1935

Dear Mr. Mencken:

It was a disappointment not to see you in New York, and a second disappointment that I was unable to stop in Baltimore on my way home. I am glad you are keeping that apartment. While you are still there, I shall feel that something of Sara is there too, some essential spirit of harmony, in the manner of living. All moved so smoothly and quietly that I can well understand how it still runs on of itself.

When the book is finished (and I hope that will be soon) do come down for a week-end. I shall love to have you at any time.

[*199*]

Will you give my regards to your sister. I shall always remember that last pleasant lunch when she was there, and Sara was looking so radiantly well.

Sincerely yours,

ELLEN GLASGOW

TO JOHN CHAMBERLAIN [1]

Richmond, December 2, 1935

Dear John Chamberlain:

May I make one correction in your recent kind comment on my *Vein of Iron.*[2]

The life at Ironside was village life, and the farm, or farm life, is not treated anywhere in my novel. My characters do not "find a way out of economic difficulties by going back to the subsistence farming of our ancestors."

In the end, it is true, the characters that survive are driven from the city into a smaller community; and, it is true also that the interdependence of human beings in a small community, or even in a single street, is one of the major themes in the book. But Ralph and Ada do not return to a farm. In Ironside their ancestors had lived, not as farmers, but as clergymen and, in one case, as a teacher. They go back to a simpler way of living; but their livelihood will depend, not only upon the good will of their neighbours, but upon the growing use of such industrial inventions as the motor car and the tractor plough in the Valleys of the James and the Shenandoah.

When one has written novels for more than thirty years, one should have learned, I suppose, with proper humility, that whatever a reader finds in a novel, it will certainly not be

[1] Author, lecturer, sometime associate editor of the *Saturday Review of Literature* and book critic for *Scribner's Magazine, Harper's Magazine,* and the New York *Times.*

[2] In *Current History,* October, 1935.

the exact meaning that was put into it. Nothing, for example, has astonished me more than to be told that *Vein of Iron* was a defense of the old order. For I still cling to the belief that the novel should illumine experience, not prescribe conduct. What I tried to do was to look through human nature and human behavior, and discover the motives, or qualities of endurance, that have enabled mankind to survive in any order under the sun. Through each individual in a family group, I have tried to trace this hidden motive, this vein of iron, which has held the generations together. Religion. Philosophy. Young love. Simple human relationships. Or the unbreakable will to live that we call fortitude. But nothing was farther from my purpose in this interpretation of the vital spirit beneath all orders and all systems than the implications the several reviewers have discovered to be "almost too obvious." *

It was charming to see Mrs. Chamberlain and you in New York. If you will come to Virginia in the spring, I shall be delighted to show you the laurel blooming in our Great Valley between the Blue Ridge and the Alleghanies.

Sincerely yours,
ELLEN GLASGOW

* And it was one of these reviewers, no doubt, who discovered that the Scotch-Irish, of the Valley, were not metaphysicians. You are my authority for this. I had never heard of the discovery. But I may ask and the converted reviewer may agree, though totally immersed in the Communist Manifesto, had he never looked into the Confession of Faith or the Larger Catechism?

TO MISS FORBES[1]

Richmond, December 3rd, 1935

My dear Miss Forbes:

I regret that I have nothing in the form of notes to contribute to your lecture on *Vein of Iron*.

This book did not require notes. Indeed, I cannot remember that I have ever referred to notes in writing a novel. *Vein of Iron* was torn up by the roots from the experience and observation and reflection of a lifetime. The background had sunk into my subconscious mind as a child, at the age when impressions are most vivid and lasting. Moreover, my memories were inherited as well as acquired, for my father's ancestors and family connections had helped to conquer and settle the Valley of Virginia. The novel had always existed below the surface of thought; and for the three years while I was actually writing it, I lived in a state of total immersion.

You may understand my amusement when a friend in New York told me that some reviewer had complained that it would be impossible to find a metaphysician in the Virginia mountains. Never having been there, except perhaps as a tourist (and I doubt even this) I suppose he imagined that the Valley of the James River was settled by an unlettered band of Scottish adventurers. As a matter of fact, these first settlers, called Scotch-Irish, were religious pioneers, and in some cases brought over their Presbyterian congregations. The history of the first John Fincastle was not unusual. And the truth is, of course, that the Scottish mind is incurably metaphysical. The doctrine of predestination, for example, is an excursion into pure metaphysics. All my life I have been familiar, though far from sympathetic, with my father's faith, which was of the Presbyterian church in Virginia. In

[1] It has not been possible to identify this correspondent.

order to refresh my mind, I read over again not only the Confession of Faith, but the Larger and the Shorter Catechisms.

But John Fincastle was far more than a sceptical philosopher. For twenty years, in my early youth, my chief interest was the study of philosophy; and all that I read and thought was embodied in my favorite character in *Vein of Iron*. I had read widely, and I might easily have filled pages with appropriate quotations. However, if there is one failing I dislike in a novel, it is the handing on of second-hand opinions and passages in the form of quotations. In more than thirty years of novel writing, I doubt if I have used as many as a dozen quotations. Knowledge, like experience, is valid in fiction only after it has dissolved and filtered down through the imagination into reality.

I wish I had time to write a longer letter. It seems to me that I have only begun, and I should like to correct several obvious misconceptions on the part of reviewers or readers. For instance, the very last thing I had in mind was the thought of writing an economic treatise or a defense of any social order, old or new or uninvented. I am more interested in human nature and in the springs of character than I am in any social system or theory of government. But it appears that economics has become the Banquo's ghost at every modern literary feast. What I tried to do in this novel was neither to defend nor condemn any social order, but to look through human behavior and discover the vein of iron that has enabled human beings to endure and survive in the struggle for life.

Now I must stop. I have written hastily but I hope clearly.

Sincerely yours,

ELLEN GLASGOW

TO ARTHUR GRAHAM GLASGOW

Richmond, December 10th, 1935

My dearest Brother;

I have thought of you so much since you left, and hoped that you were beginning to feel like yourself again. Both Josephine[1] and I thought we had never seen you looking so splendidly and so vigorously well as you looked in New York. It seems too bad that you should have had this cold—but everything is that way.

I am eager to hear how Margaret is and what the doctor says of her general condition. She has lived under a strain for so long.

Yesterday we sent you the papers for Mr. Cape; but I have not too great confidence in his way of publishing. People in Great Britain know little of American letters, and the little they know is confined to the shilling shockers of the New Barbarian school of fiction.

It would be nice if you yourself sent some copies to your friends, as you did with *The Sheltered Life*; but I shouldn't wish you to spend much money that way. I do not like to give away copies myself; but of course your sending some out in England is a different matter. If you should happen to know any editors or reviewers, it would be a help to speak to them and ask them to look after the book when it is sent to them for review. I know this is often done in England; but I do not know any reviewers over there and of course I could not speak to them. But Dr. Freeman told me that one at least of his friends had been very helpful about reviews.

Don't bother about this. These are merely suggestions that did not occur to me until you had gone away.

Once again, since it cannot be said too often, I must tell you how grateful I feel for all that you have done for me.

[1] Presumably Josephine Glasgow Clark, a niece.

But for you I could never have lived through the past fifteen or twenty years.

Dearest love to Margaret and to Marjorie when you see her.

Devotedly always,
ELLEN

TO H. L. MENCKEN

Richmond, Tuesday [1936]

Dear Mr. Mencken:

I should love to have my autographed books go to Goucher College. If you will let me know where to send it, I will give the College my new book in memory of Sara. There is no hurry about this. Wait until you return, and then let me see you.

Sara will always be living for me in all that lends dignity and beauty to life.

Sincerely yours,
ELLEN GLASGOW

TO H. L. MENCKEN

Richmond, February 16th, 1936

Dear Mr. Mencken:

I am so glad that you collected Sara's short stories into this volume.[1] Only a few of her earlier stories had come my way and I did not realize how her gift had ripened in the later years of her life. In these stories I am astonished by the depth of insight and the singular accuracy of observation. The South has lost, I think, one of its most promising writers. It is in "Dear Life" that she seems to me to give herself as I remember her and as I loved her.

Your preface seems to me to be a very nearly perfect thing

[1] *A Southern Album,* Doubleday, 1936.

of its kind. You said just enough, not too much, not too little, and you said it with the simplicity and serenity that belonged to Sara herself.

Thank you for remembering me. I shall treasure this book always.

Sincerely yours,

ELLEN GLASGOW

TO MISS PATTERSON [1]

Richmond, March 4th, 1936

My dear Miss Patterson:

Without second thought, I can tell you the names of six books you should select for your study.

The Novel of Character.

Vein of Iron, 1935
Barren Ground, 1925
Virginia, 1913

These three novels are concerned with the place and tragedy of the individual in the universal scheme. They treat of the perpetual conflict of character with fate, of the will with the world, of the dream with reality.

The Tragicomedy of Manners.

The Romantic Comedians, 1926
They Stooped to Folly, 1929
The Sheltered Life, 1932.

These depict the place and tragicomedy of the individual in an established society. They illustrate the struggle of personality against tradition and the social background.

Important Note. *The Romantic Comedians, Barren Ground* and *Virginia* should be read only in the *Old Dominion [Edition] of the Works of Ellen Glasgow,* published by Doubleday, Doran and Company. *Barren Ground,* in this definitive edition, is included in the Modern Library.

[1] It has not been possible to identify this correspondent.

Required reading. All the prefaces included in The Old Dominion Edition, especially the long preface to *The Miller of Old Church*.

"One Way to Write Novels," *The Saturday Review of Literature,* December 8th, 1934 (Christmas Number).
"What I Believe," *The Nation,* April 12th, 1933. This essay is reprinted in Mary A. Beard's *America through Women's Eyes*. Macmillan, 1933.

> With best wishes,
> Sincerely yours,
> [Not signed]

TO HELEN K. TAYLOR

Richmond, March 21st, 1936

Dear Miss Taylor:

Mr. Cape has sent me several very good advertisements. I think he is handling this book in a more intelligent manner than I am accustomed to from English publishers.

But the delay was so long, and I have been asked to the point of weariness why the book has never come out in England. For this reason, could you put in the press something about its reception in Great Britain, which appears to have been of the best kind. I am enclosing one or two quotations Mr. Cape sent me from his advertisements. They are, I think, very appreciative, and I notice that both Harper and Houghton Mifflin have a way of making the most of such a reception. I do not agree that English notices make no difference over here, because I see the impression they make on our reviewers. Of course this may not be done in an advertisement (though that is a good way) ; it may be brought out (as I see it so often done) in one of the book notes in *The Times* or *The Herald-Tribune*.

But I should like to have it known that at last V. of I. has been published in Great Britain and that it is receiving enthusiastic reviews.

I hope you understand and do not think me troublesome. You are very busy, I know, at this season.

I am looking forward to Virginia Woolf's novel,[1] and I am sorry that I had to decline to review it—for the present at least.

Sincerely yours,

ELLEN GLASGOW

The typewritten letter from Lowes Dickinson (page 230, [E.M.] Forster's Life of G.L.D., Harcourt, Brace) is very consoling to me. He appears to have been no better at typing than I am.

[1] *The Years,* Harcourt, Brace, was announced in 1936, but was not published until 1937.

TO EDWIN MIMS

Richmond, March 28th, 1936

. . . My brother also feels that Mr. Cape is inclined to be indifferent to quality in a novel—but then who cares for quality nowadays? That, I think, is what takes the heart out of the profession of letters. All my life, ever since I was eight years old I have lived in my work and struggled to perfect it, to achieve a happier union of style and substance. And the irony of it is that I go on writing better and better in an age when no one cares any longer for the standard of perfection —not even as an unattainable excellence. Violence commands both literature and life, and violence is always crude and distorted. Yet the whole outside world, including the British, prefer apparently to believe that the American horror-mongers portray the beginning and the end of the American scene. This is one special reason that your interpretation will be of lasting importance. These people have never before heard what you tell them.

My complaint, it is needless to explain, does not apply to the feeling for my work over there. This latest book has had a really remarkable reception and the response of Virginia has been genuinely moving. I have never written a book which made so wide and so deep an appeal. So far as I know there have been only two attacks. One (what else could you expect) in the communist paper, *The New Masses,* and the other, strangely enough, from the other extreme of intolerance in a magazine of the Deep South published at Baton Rouge.[1] The two points of view, so far apart and so violent, are amusing, I think, but *The New Masses* objected that I was not radical or proletarian in my economics, and the Baton Rouge paper declared that I was both too radical and too proletarian. I have seen neither paper, but I heard of them from my loving friends. The moral is that it is impossible to please two extremes.

Yes, I am much better. . . . After three years of total immersion in an imaginative scene (though for me it was more living than the actuality) I felt simply drained of vital interest. But at last the springs are slowly filling up and a new idea, which had been scarcely more than a phantom in the night, is assuming shape and animation. All I can do is wait and let the spirit renew itself. To try to hasten the process is, for me, the way to frustration.

I am eager to hear of your time in Great Britain and of your lectures and visits to places I love. Occasionally, I find myself planning to spend five weeks in England this summer. It is barely possible that I may come over for a brief visit. I haven't dared think of it seriously. There is so much that has to be done to my old house. . . .

[1] *The Southern Review,* Autumn, 1935. Review of *Vein of Iron* by Randall Jarrell.

TO DOUGLAS SOUTHALL FREEMAN

Richmond, April 15th, 1936

Dear Doctor Freeman:

Do you know of any traditions concerning Tom Moore's brief visit to Richmond in 1804? Was he influenced in his views of America by the Federalist group here? He appears to have visited John Wickham[1] and to have known the members of the Barbecue Club.[2]

Howard Mumford Jones is writing a life of Moore[3] and he has asked me these questions. I am unable to answer them. And if you do not know the answers, I am sure nobody does.[4]

I wish I could see you now and then.

Affectionately your friend,

ELLEN GLASGOW

[1] A distinguished lawyer.

[2] The Barbecue Club met on Saturdays at "Buchanan's Spring," near Richmond, for recreation and dinner. Chief Justice John Marshall was one of its members.

[3] *The Harp That Once—*, Holt, 1937.

[4] Apparently Dr. Freeman did not "know the answers." In the corner of this letter is inscribed "Not in Christian," which would indicate that he had vainly sought the information in Dr. Asbury Christian's history of Richmond.

TO J. DONALD ADAMS

Richmond, April 28th, 1936

Dear Donald:

I was so glad to have your telegram and Mary's attractive card on my birthday. It is lovely, when I forget all birthdays, including my own, to find that somebody remembers me. I have a deep and enduring affection for the three of you, and as time goes by, even though we see one another so seldom, I feel that the bond holds more firmly.

Virginia is at its best at this season, or a little later, and I wish that you could have come before I leave for the house at Ventnor, which I have taken again for a month. I shall be there (barring an Act of God) until the 18th of June, and then I expect to be in New York for ten days. By that time, I suppose, you will have gone to Woodstock, and how I shall miss you!

At last—at last, after this long Siberian winter of the soul is over, I feel that the springs are beginning to fill again and I hope the thaw will continue until I am able to start to work. You were right, however, for another novel [1] has pushed itself in front of the autobiography. It is a good idea, I think, full of meat, and it came in spite of my effort to keep it out and almost against my hostile resistance. I tried the memoirs, but, for some reason, they simply would not dissolve and change into a fluid. The form is all there, but it is still too stiff and solid in memory, and the pattern must break up in my imagination before it will flow easily. I suppose I am a born novelist, for the things I imagine are more vital and vivid to me than the things I remember. But to go on seeking perfection in any form nowadays is a forlorn enterprise. The art of fiction has become a lost cause, and nobody cares even for quality. No one in the modern world is more lonely than the writer with a literary conscience.

What are you doing, I wonder? How does the book go and are you better than you were in the winter? I hope with all my heart that fate is kind to you. Among the blessings of my life I count you and your unfailing sympathy and understanding.

With love to the Adams family, and the hope that Mary is becoming an author by this time,

Always affectionately yours,

ELLEN

[1] *In This Our Life.*

TO ANNE VIRGINIA BENNETT

Ventnor [N.J.]
June 1st [1936]

Dearest A.V.:

I am enclosing the check for Dugald Walker.[1] Tell him I feel that the book plate expresses me perfectly. "That is my tree," I said when I saw it, and the work is exquisite. I love the fern and mushrooms—and above all the long swift bird in the delicate leaves.

But please find out if the plates can be made to stick without paste. I could never have paste put on smoothly.

I am glad to hear that the policeman is so attentive.

If you would rather come on the 14th it will suit me perfectly. I will go in to Philadelphia on Monday and leave for New York on Tuesday. You can pack my Cornwall suitcases after I leave. But I thought a few days of sea air might do you good. There are proclamations on the lamp posts forbidding dogs to go without a leash—but one doesn't anyway. The law has just been passed. . . .

Love to all,
As ever, E.

[1] Dugald Stewart Walker, eminent Richmond artist, designer of Ellen Glasgow's bookplate.

TO JAMES SOUTHALL WILSON

West Cornwall, Connecticut
July 15th, 1936

Dear James:

It was delightful to receive a letter in longhand. I dislike typewriting, but it is much easier for me to play the keys, however badly, than it is to handle a pen—especially when everything blots, as it does in this weather.

I am looking forward with much pleasure to my visit,[1] and, as I wrote to Mr. Gay yesterday, I think July 30th would be most convenient. If it were only to see Julia[2] and you, I should not hesitate to accept. Your directions are very clear and I am sure that we shall have no trouble in following the road. I am sorry Miss Bennett cannot come, but my niece will be with me.

Yes, I know Dorothy Canfield and I am very fond of her. But she might prefer to have Bread Loaf to herself, as she can see me in New York.

This typing is even worse than my usual effort, but I have just returned from a trip that seemed to grind my intelligence to powder. I suppose it is even worse in Richmond, but our little hollow is holding its own.

With love to Julia,

Affectionately yours,

ELLEN GLASGOW

[1] To the Bread Loaf School of English, where Dr. Wilson was teaching.
[2] Mrs. Wilson.

TO J. DONALD ADAMS

West Cornwall,

Saturday, July 25th [1936]

Dear Don,

I was heartbroken yesterday when I thought that I should miss you and Alya. This is Carrie's last week-end here, and we had promised long ago to visit an old friend at Pawling.

But I have talked with Irita, and she says you will come next week instead. I am obliged to go to Bread Loaf on Thursday (30th), but I can easily come back by Friday night or Saturday afternoon. You mean far more than New Hampshire to me, and we can motor there just as well when you and Alya are in the Argentine.

So I have accepted Irita's invitation to dine with you Saturday next.

I am eager to talk with you. There are at least a thousand things I wish to discuss. Your review of *Gone with the Wind* [1] was excellent, but your article on Huxley's book [2] was a deeper piece of work because there you were dealing with elemental values, not with a stirring narrative of events. I cannot remember a better review of any book within the last year. I was glad I read your article before I got the novel, because you found more in it than I should have discovered without your interpretation. Something in Huxley's personality drops like a veil between me and his ideas, which are often brilliant and in *Eyeless in Gaza* really profound.

Love to dear Alya and Mary and to you,

ELLEN

[1] By Margaret Mitchell. Macmillan, 1936.
[2] Aldous Huxley, *Eyeless in Gaza,* Harper, 1936.

TO BESSIE ZABAN JONES

West Cornwall, September 9th, 1936

Dear Bessie:

If only I were nearer, I should love to see Howard receive his degree.[1] I have always wanted to know just how one should behave on such important occasions. But, unfortunately, I must go back to Richmond at the end of this week. My old house there is in the hands of painters, and I must hurry home before they begin to mix the wrong colors.

I am so glad you have sold your house and are not tied to the West any longer.[2] And I am simply delighted that you have a Springer spaniel. That is the perfect final touch to our friendship. Do you know there is always a barrier be-

[1] Howard Mumford Jones was about to receive the degree of Litt.D. from Harvard.
[2] Mr. Jones had been appointed professor of English at Harvard.

tween me and any man or woman who does not like dogs. . . .

The summer has passed almost before I felt that it was beginning. We have motored all through the Berkshires and they are beautiful beyond words, especially the Housatonic Valley, where we are staying. I spent a night and a day up at Bread Loaf, where I had the audacity to take over two classes in English and talk all the time. Though I had gone on the understanding that I should not be asked to speak, I was shocked to find that I enjoyed the sound of my own voice saying unorthodox things. . . .

Give my love and congratulations to Howard. Why is he so much more alive than most other professors? Are you to be thanked, or to be blamed, for that?

It will be lovely to have you in Richmond. Do you know the date of the Conference?[3] Write to me and let me hear all about Cambridge and how Howard looks in the fine new cap and gown. I wish I could see him and you.

Love always,

ELLEN

[3] The Modern Language Association meeting in Richmond, in December, 1936.

TO HAMILTON BASSO

Richmond, November 1st, 1936

Dear Mr. Basso:

I have just finished *Courthouse Square*,[1] and I send you my congratulations. It is a fine book, saturated with the feeling of things Southern. I like particularly the latter part, with the description of the night in the Square and the inflamed mob. The figure of Alcide is made very appealing.

With best wishes,

Sincerely yours,

ELLEN GLASGOW

[1] Scribner, 1936.

TO HARRY SCHERMAN [1]

Richmond, January 14th, 1937

My dear Mr. Scherman:

Thursday, the 28th, suits me perfectly. I regret that I cannot be present at the fellowship meeting.[2]

I regret, too, for literature, like life, seems to be full of regrets, that there is only one book in the final list, for which I am able to feel anything like enthusiasm. This book is *Theodore Parker,*[3] of course; and I believe that Mr. Commager may become one of the most important American biographers or historians.

For the rest, I must admit my total inadequacy as a judge. Promise of finer things is the quality I put first in such a contest of merit, and this is the very quality I find absent in almost all of these books. Nevertheless, I should not oppose any selection by the other members of the jury. I am too clearly aware of the force of personal preferences.

Flowering Judas[4] I might vote for with an easy conscience. The author has a sense of style and a delicate insight into obscure motives. Yet her work seems to me, as I wrote you before, to lack vitality, and I have an impression (perhaps mistaken) that she will never grow larger and stronger than she was at the beginning.

In Dubious Battle[5] has more promise, I think, than most of these novels. But there is an obvious proud disdain of all craftsmanship and even of good writing. After all, how does literature differ from life except that it is writing?

The central figure in *A Yankee Saint*[6] is made interesting.

[1] Then president of the Book-of-the-Month Club.

[2] Jury of Award for the Book-of-the-Month Club Fellowship (instituted in 1937), on which Ellen Glasgow served.

[3] By Henry Steele Commager. Little, Brown, 1936.

[4] By Katherine Anne Porter. Harcourt, Brace, 1930.

[5] By John Steinbeck. Viking, 1936.

[6] By Robert Allerton Parker. Putnam, 1935.

Still, I did not find myself asking hopefully: "What will this author do next?" And this seems to me to be the vital question in any award to a promising writer.

I am told, on authority that I respect, that Mr. Milburn has done better work than *Catalogue,*[7] and that an award would be helpful to him. It is a pity that one of his better books was not submitted.

Deserts on the March[8] is the kind of book I enjoy, yet I found it extremely hard reading. It was like ploughing through sand.

"Solstice" [9] is, in my judgment, the weakest and thinnest poem by Robinson Jeffers that has ever come my way. For all that, I should like to see him receive a fellowship.

I suppose *Mules and Men*[10] is good Negro folklore, but what does it promise except more and more of the thing?

Best in the Greenwood [11] is attractive but trivial. It is the only one of these books that my secretary enjoyed while she was suffering from influenza.

With warmest apologies,
Sincerely yours,
ELLEN GLASGOW

[7] By George Milburn. Harcourt, Brace, 1936.
[8] By P. B. Sears. University of Oklahoma Press, 1935.
[9] *Solstice and Other Poems,* Random House, 1935.
[10] By Zora Neale Hurston. Lippincott, 1935.
[11] By J. C. Titzell. Doubleday, 1936.

TO ALFRED HARCOURT

Richmond, February 3rd, 1937

Dear Alfred Harcourt:

I am delighted with *Paradise.*[1] Thank you for sending it to me. I always liked *A Mirror for Witches,*[2] but this later novel has a maturity, a ripe wisdom, which shows an enor-

[1] By Esther Forbes. Harcourt, Brace, 1937.
[2] By Esther Forbes. Houghton Mifflin, 1928.

mous advance on the earlier work. I both admired and enjoyed it from beginning to end. After so much spineless and flabby fiction, this vigorous and bracing revaluation of the past will help to clear the air in the present. American fiction is recovering its health when two such fine historical novels as *None Shall Look Back*[3] and *Paradise* appear from South and North in the same month.

Will you give Miss Forbes my warm congratulations.

As always sincerely yours,

E.G.

[3] By Caroline Gordon. Scribner, 1937.

TO HOWARD MUMFORD JONES

Richmond, February 6th, 1937

Dear Howard:

Why did you never tell me that you are a poet? You might have imparted this dark and guilty secret to me in all the years I have known you.

I like your book[1] very much. The sonnets, in spite of their modern emphasis, are really too good to be modern—or so it seems to me. I like particularly the last sonnet in The Forties—**XXXVI** and **XXXIV** and the Dedication, which seems to me entirely appropriate.

But my favorite, and I think the finest thing of all is the Heartbreak series. This verse is filled with the beauty and the sadness that make the illusion of memory. For, I suppose, memory is always more or less of an illusion.

Many thanks for the thought and the book. I wish I could talk to you. We have only skimmed the surface, but there is so much more—so very much more.

It is good to know that you are well again and that your natural relish for living has come back to you. I hope your life in Cambridge will be all that you expect and that Bessie

[1] *They Say the Forties—*, Holt, 1937.

and you will both feel at home there and enjoy the people.

I cannot tell you how grieved I was about Tommy.² Life is like that.

Affectionately,

ELLEN GLASGOW

² The Joneses' dog.

TO BESSIE ZABAN JONES

Richmond, May 9th, 1937

Bessie dear,

Just a word to tell you that I am sailing (if Providence does not intervene!) on the Conte di Savoia, May the fifteenth. I am going to visit a friend who has a beautiful villa at Fiesole, so you may think of me when June comes in Florence.

We have had such a very trying time here that I felt I had to escape into a different scene. You remember James, the prop of our house and our cook for the last thirty years? Well, he was taken desperately ill, and for three weeks hovered between life and death. Now, he is out of the hospital, but I doubt whether he will ever really recover. If you have ever tried a series of substitutes, you will know what we have suffered.

Love to Howard and you. Isn't it running true to life to find that I can now rent a place in New England, high up in the Berkshires, that I wanted last summer? But I cannot afford that and a trip to Italy too.

As always,

ELLEN

TO DOUGLAS SOUTHALL FREEMAN

Richmond, July 8, 1937

Dear Dr. Freeman,

How I wish it were possible for me to write that article! If I could bring myself to write anything, it would be an essay for you and the *News Leader*.

But I simply cannot force my mind to work in that way. My writing faculty is asleep, and I have not written a line for publication since I finished *Vein of Iron*. I envy you your fine discipline. It must be splendid to have command of one's gifts. But I have no such control. The power to write anything comes and goes like the winds of doctrine, and I am scarcely more than a medium. At present, I have no lack of ideas; yet I find it impossible to put these ideas into any form, appropriate or otherwise.

I am so sorry.

As always gratefully yours,

ELLEN GLASGOW

SECTION V

August 21, 1937—May 17, 1942

TO ALFRED HARCOURT

Richmond, August 21st, 1937

Dear Mr. Harcourt:

It is pleasant indeed to have word from you, and to know that Alfred is himself again.

Was it simply an accident, or a stroke of publisher's insight, that prompted you to write to me just as I was beginning a new novel? For it is true, and no novelist can be trusted. After vowing that I would never, never commit another novel, I am launched upon an adventure that is growing bigger and better.

Yes, your letter found me in too hot Richmond, and that describes it today and yesterday and tomorrow. No New England this summer. But I had a wonderful spring in Florence, where I visited in a paradise of flowers that belonged to a friend.

Have you heard of the subscription edition of my works that Scribner's [is] to bring out immediately? I hope there will be no difficulty about including *Vein of Iron* in this set. Please let them have it, for it is very important that all my best books should be gathered together. These books are to be sold only by subscription, and they are to cost ten dollars a volume. I am to do a preface for each volume, and so fine an edition ought to help rather than hurt the sale of a cheap *Vein of Iron* whenever it comes out.

I suppose Maxwell Perkins[1] has written to you. Nelson

[1] Mr. Perkins was working with Miss Glasgow on the Virginia Edition of her novels.

Doubleday told me he was glad to let them have all the other books.

I know it is agreeable to you to see my familiar typing once more, with all the friendly letters tumbling over one another.

As always sincerely,

ELLEN GLASGOW

And shan't we have a good time with the new novel!

TO AMELIE RIVES

Richmond, August 23rd, 1937

Darling Amelie,

I am sending this word of love to greet you on your birthday tomorrow. It will be a day of sorrow,[1] I know, and I am thinking of you with a heart filled to overflowing with tenderness. Though we never see each other, I have always the feeling that time has been scarcely more than an illusion between us. Only yesterday (or so it seems to me) I was with you in that dear room of yours, and we were reading your manuscript of "The Golden Rose."

"Always the painted apple,
Never the golden rose."

How many years ago that was. Yet I can see your deep eyes when I look up from the page, and beyond the nimbus of your hair, I can see the lacy green of the bush, and the flashing wings of the cardinals in the sunshine. Dear, dear Amelie! Is there not that moment that exists somewhere beyond time? Which is more sure for you, the lost happiness with Pierre or the present anguish of separation?

I know how you miss Pierre with every breath, every heartbeat. Yet you had so much, and when one has had per-

[1] Prince Troubetskoy had died on August 25, 1936.

[224]

fection, it is there forever, while the heart is alive and remembers.

And so I am with you in spirit on your birthday. Are you well enough to see me if I were to drive up some afternoon? If you could not, I should understand perfectly.

Blessings on you, my darling. How I wish I could comfort you,

ELLEN

TO J. DONALD ADAMS

Richmond, August 26th, 1937

Dear Don,

I was delighted to have your good letter this morning, and to know that you are entirely yourself again. Nothing has pleased me so much in a long time.

My visit to Italy was a joy and it did me a great deal of good. I was terribly disappointed not to find you in New York, but happy to hear that you were enjoying your vacation. The news of your book[1] is excellent, and I am very much interested in the course of lectures. You simply *must* arrange to make those speeches. Yet it will not mean a long absence, I hope, from the *Times*. When I come on to New York the first week in November, you will have a mountain of things to tell me.

I know you will understand when I tell you that I cannot become interested in any literary fellowship. I admire Elinor Wylie's gift and her high integrity as an artist. But I think her work is her best memorial. Any other memorial, indeed, appears to me to be superfluous. As for modern poetry, I am inclined to think that what it needs most is a little benevolent discouragement. It suffers nowadays, I think, from too much coddling.

[1] *The Shape of Books to Come*, Macmillan, 1944.

Love to Alya and Mary and the happy third. I am looking forward eagerly to seeing you in the autumn. At last—after two years of restless loafing, I have begun a new novel!!

Affectionately,

ELLEN

TO AMELIE RIVES

Richmond, Tuesday, [September 28, 1937]

My darling Amelie:

How precious you are! I cannot thank you enough for the dear inspired letter that came by special delivery, and now this morning brings me another in your beloved handwriting.

I have been working very hard over these prefaces,[1] or I should have written to you long before this. No. Scribner's are not my publishers, and I was astonished when they expressed the wish to bring out this sumptuous edition. I know they will lose money, and I am inclined to think they ought to postpone publication until the market improves. But all they respond is "Do not worry about us."

I like Harcourt, Brace very much, only it seems hard that I have to give one third of my royalty on this edition to the original publishers of the books. [. . .][2]

Early in October I hope to drive up to see you one afternoon. That *wish* makes "sunshine in the shadie places" of the present. Give my love to all the cardinals.

This very morning I am ordering those preparations. Do write me as soon as you can decide about that new cleansing cream. Since I have been using Woodbury's and your way of washing the face everyone tells me I look so well. There must be something in it. And it is so inexpensive compared with Valoze and Arden.

No, darling, those books are not to be reviewed or sent

[1] Prefaces to the Virginia Edition of her novels.
[2] Passage partly indecipherable.

anywhere. Never would I bring you anything you had to box or wrap up. There is nothing that exasperates me more than having to wrap things or get Anne Virginia to do it. They were light books for diversion. I'll bring more if you can read them. Doubleday sends me all they publish, and they send a lot of books I have no room for. Then I buy a great many more and still my bookcases are overflowing. I am always giving away piles. After you read them just hand on what you don't want and Landon[3] has no use for to anybody in the neighborhood.

Bless you, darling. I must go back to work.

Devotedly,

ELLEN

[3] Landon Rives, Princess Troubetskoy's sister.

TO ALFRED HARCOURT

Richmond, October 25th, 1937

Dear Mr. Harcourt:

I had meant to thank you for your letter about the Scribner edition, but I have been working day and night over twelve prefaces—and good long ones at that! It seemed only fair for me to warn Scribner's that they would lose every penny they invested in this series; but to this warning, they replied gallantly, "Don't worry about us!"

The sad part is that I had written the first chapter of my new novel, and when I got seriously to work on the prefaces, of course I had to put everything else out of my mind. If I ever return to the novel, however, it will be all the better, I believe, for a little absent treatment. I feel in the mood for it; it came unsolicited; and it will be as good as I am able to make it.

But it is all very disappointing. The statement this morning was naturally a blow, and I was shocked, too, to hear the other day that *Vein of Iron* could now be bought in the standard edition for ninety-eight cents. My understanding was that, at the end of two years, the book would go into a different cheap edition.

Well, life is like that. I had hoped when I put myself in your competent hands that my books might be kept going for a longer time. But novels are becoming more and more like newspapers. A work that is written in three years will live about three months—or, if that isn't exact, about six months and a half.

I hope, however, that this limited subscription edition may be preserved in Caslon Old Face type in somebody's library. But, I confess, that I am inclined to agree with Nelson Doubleday, who says he would not dare to bring out an autographed edition of the Bible and ask ten dollars a volume for it.

Sincerely yours,
ELLEN GLASGOW

TO MARION GAUSE CANBY [1]

Richmond, November 6th, 1937

Dearest Marion,

It was like seeing you again to open your book of poems.[2] These verses tell me so many things that I felt about you, but had never been able to put into words. They are eloquent not only of feeling but of thought, and that is rare in poetry written by women. It is a joy to me that you should have found your gift and your own right expression. When I see you again, and that, I hope, will be soon, we will talk of these poems.

I had planned to come to New York this month, but now I find that I must postpone my visit. Do stop when you go South in the spring.

[1] Wife of Dr. Henry Seidel Canby.
[2] *On My Way*, Houghton Mifflin, 1937.

Will you give my love to Henry. I hope he is well and happy after the summer.

Devotedly,
ELLEN GLASGOW

TO ALLEN TATE

Richmond, November 6th, 1937

Dear Allen,

When I returned from a month's absence, I was delighted to find a copy of your poems[1] awaiting me in my study. I read them immediately before plunging into a hard piece of work which had to be finished.

All my favorites are here, and I am glad indeed to have your poems in one volume. Few modern poems have moved me so deeply as your "Ode to the Confederate Dead." That is, I think, a great poem, because it strips away not only appearances but experience itself, and bares some dark and nameless quality of being. It seems to me that this is the true test for greatness in poetry:—that it should go beneath experience, as prose can never do, and awaken an apprehension of things we have never, and can never, know in the actuality.

This is put badly, but the experience I have in reading such poetry is obliged to be put badly in any language. It is a wordless state.

I like "Sonnets of the Blood" more than ever, and all the Mediterranean poems, especially "Aeneas at Washington." The three last lines seem to me to say everything of this present hour.

There are several questions I should like to ask, but I should wait for some happy meeting in the future.

Will you tell Caroline that Scribner's sent me *The Garden of Adonis,*[2] and I read it with much admiration. She has an extraordinary power of infusing life into a scene. But it

---

[1] *Selected Poems,* Scribner, 1937.
[2] By Caroline Gordon. Scribner, 1937.

does not take the place of *Penhally* in my mind because I feel that the people are, to me at least, less completely realized. I may be wrong, and I was greatly interested in it all. Still, I prefer both *Penhally* and *None Shall Look Back*³ which I feel have superb qualities. She gives me an impression of not having used her full strength. When she does that, she will be a great novelist.

Affectionately,

ELLEN GLASGOW

³ By Caroline Gordon. Scribner, 1937.

TO ALLEN TATE

Richmond, December 16th, 1937

Dear Allen:

Though I am working under great pressure, I must stop long enough to tell you how thoroughly I liked and enjoyed your article in the *Virginia Quarterly*.¹ For some reason, which eludes me when I pursue it, your image of the man at the gate of the Confederate graveyard was just what I needed to complete my impression. Until you put him there, I had never thought of a spectator at all, for I had identified the whole poem, not only with myself, but with some deeper subjective source of my mind. Why, I wonder, did the experience gain in power when you introduced an alien vision into the scene? For I fail entirely to merge my consciousness into the separate existence of the spectator at the gate. What I share in is the whole poem, with its background, its images, its emotional responses and recoils, and its tremendous conflict of memories.

All this is put very badly, but you may grasp what I mean. I wish I could talk with you about the poem and the essay.

¹ "Narcissus as Narcissus," Mr. Tate's explication of his "Ode to the Confederate Dead," Winter, 1938; later republished in *Reason in Madness,* Putnam, 1941.

Do stop in Richmond on your way North, and come to dine with me the first evening that you are in town. It will be lovely to see Caroline and you again and to have a chance to discuss many matters. Love to you both.

As always sincerely yours,

ELLEN GLASGOW

TO SAMUEL S. SLOAN [1]

Richmond, January 21st, 1938

Dear Mr. Sloan:

It is a pleasure to hear from you after so long a silence, and I am much interested in your letter. My first impulse is always to refuse an offer to dramatize one of my books. Several dramatists have wished to make a play of *The Romantic Comedians*; but they were all strangers to me, and apparently immature in their craftsmanship.

In the first place, and I hope you will put this clearly before Mr. Stange,[2] my work is not now, and has never been, in the fashion of its period. An audience that enjoys the humor of *Tobacco Road* [3] could scarcely be expected to enjoy the wit of *The Romantic Comedians,* or even to know what it is about. I am the last person on earth who could help anybody to achieve a popular success. I have been a novelist for forty years, and I have never been in the fashion of the moment. My first book *The Descendant,* published in 1897, was written in the mood and tone of 1930. It came exactly thirty years ahead of its time. But when the public began to be interested in that particular mood, I had escaped from it and passed on into another. This suggests to me, by the way, that there might be either a play or a moving picture in that first crude and vital story. Have you ever happened to read

[1] Then an editor at Harcourt, Brace.
[2] Hugh Stange, playwright.
[3] By Erskine Caldwell. Scribner, 1932.

[*231*]

The Descendant? Harper published it, and I imagine it has long been out of print.

But to return. Mr. Stange is absolutely right in demanding a free hand. Indeed, the paragraph you quote from his letter gives me an impression that he would be the right man to dramatize this particular book. *The Romantic Comedians* is so close to my heart that I should be distressed to have it cheapened and vulgarized. It is a slight novel, but, I think, very nearly perfect as a comedy of manners. As for any interference on my part, as an author, I can only say that I have no interest in the theatre, and know nothing about the writing of plays. It is doubtful whether I could be induced to read an acting play (I like plays that cannot be acted) or to attend a rehearsal. For myself, I could never feel an interest in writing anything with which a producer might tamper.

And so it appears:—You are free to make any arrangements that seem best to you, and Mr. Stange, if he makes the dramatization, is free to follow his own ideas, provided, of course, that the comedy is restrained to a delicate sophistication. But, in a country that prefers the tough guy as a popular hero, there is not the slightest possibility that such a play could succeed. If it falls through before it is written, I shall not be disappointed, but I should be sorry to have Mr. Stange waste subtle and delicate work. The appetite of modern audiences appears to demand only meat that is raw.

Sincerely yours,

ELLEN GLASGOW

I am so frightfully busy that I have had to dash this off without proper reflection. But let it stand.

TO CLIFTON FADIMAN [1]

Richmond, January 23rd, 1938

Dear Mr. Fadiman:

Your letter has interested me very much. The kind of essay you suggest is the only kind I enjoy writing. For many years, all my life indeed, I have thought on these subjects; and to be asked to express, without evasion, one's honest belief, or lack of belief, is as tempting an invitation as one could well receive.

But, unfortunately, it is impossible to "make time" except by a miracle. For the next few months, I shall be completely immersed in other work which I have promised to finish by the middle or end of April. I write very slowly, and of the twelve long critical prefaces I have agreed to do for the edition of my works to be published by Scribner's, I have at least half still left to write. Moreover, I have just begun a new novel which has been in my mind for the past three years, and in which I believe.

I am telling you these things, not because I imagine them to be interesting, but simply to explain why I am obliged to decline an invitation I appreciate so heartily.[2]

With best wishes for the success of the work.

Sincerely yours,

ELLEN GLASGOW

[1] Then book editor of the *New Yorker*.
[2] Ultimately Miss Glasgow did contribute to Mr. Fadiman's collection (*I Believe,* Simon & Schuster, 1938) a somewhat expanded and revised version of her essay "What I Believe," which had appeared in the *Nation,* April 12, 1933.

TO DOUGLAS SOUTHALL FREEMAN

Richmond, February 5th, 1938

Dear Dr. Freeman:

The honor to be conferred upon me by the University of Richmond[1] is doubly appreciated because I owe it to you. You are always goodness itself to me.

Dr. Boatwright[2] has fixed the twenty-ninth of April, and this suits me perfectly. As this is to be a private Convocation, I assume that I shall not have to bother about a cap and gown. Also, I shall trust to you to see that no loudspeakers and cameras are admitted. I never speak over the radio, and I hate, above all things, to be photographed.

I wonder if you saw a comment in *The Herald-Tribune Books* for tomorrow.[3] In speaking of my Virginia Edition, the reviewer said, "Surely she is entitled to realize—or, if she does not, then to be told—that she has given Virginia such a history in fiction as no other American state has had from a single writer." I liked that, and I like to think that Virginia recognizes what I have tried to do.

And what of you? Only the other day I was telling a fellow novelist that if any work written by an American was assured of immortality, it is your *Lee*. And there is no question in that.

Affectionately yours,

ELLEN GLASGOW

[1] Miss Glasgow was to receive an LL.D. degree on April 29, 1938.

[2] Dr. Frederic William Boatwright was then president of the University of Richmond.

[3] In "Reprints and New Editions," over the signature "Bookwright," February 6, 1938.

TO DOUGLAS SOUTHALL FREEMAN

Richmond, March 22nd, 1938

Dear Dr. Freeman:

It is unkind to bother a man who is busy with important matters; but past experience has taught me to take advantage of your characteristic generosity.

It has occurred to me that I should like to have my own cap and gown, provided that decorative costume is required on April the nineteenth. Can you tell me how and where I may order a cap and gown of my special size. The last time I wore a gown I could scarcely move in it, and the cap would not stay on my head because it was too small.

I confess that I am dreading an occasion which I might enjoy if it were not for this damnable deafness.

I have followed with much interest your comment upon the situation abroad. I wish you could talk to me on that exciting topic.

My blessings on the Washington.[1] I hope it goes as you wish.

Affectionately yours,

ELLEN GLASGOW

[1] Dr. Freeman was writing his *George Washington, a Biography*, six volumes, Scribner, 1948-54.

TO BESSIE ZABAN JONES

Richmond, April 11th, 1938

Dear Bessie,

Not for a long time have I enjoyed a letter so much. I wish I could arrange for a weekly column, but I shall never have that luck when I can send only scraps in reply.

Of course, as usual, you put your finger on the spot. It is perfectly true that the portrait is in slim profile, and shows only one angle; but that happens to be the view that J.B.C. seems to like best.

It will be lovely to see you and Howard in New York. I hope to be there by the fourteenth. Do let me know when I may keep the time free from engagements. It seems an age since I saw you and Howard.

Of course I should like to have him do something about me, and I am very eager for you both to read these prefaces. I have put so much of myself into them. Just now, I am in the middle of the last one. I had not expected the edition to be reviewed, but Maxwell Perkins, of Scribners, has written me that he expects excellent articles when the set is finished. I hope to Heaven he will not be disappointed.

What do you think of this suggestion? Don't pass it on to Howard unless you approve of it. I feel sure that George Stevens, the new editor of the *Saturday Review,* would be glad to have Howard write a review of this edition. In that way, George might get a set from Mr. Perkins, and then Howard and you would have it for your own. Does Howard ever suggest the books he would like to review? Anyway, George is a good friend of mine, and has a strong liking for my work.

No, the autobiography has been put aside, in the first rough draft. I have a chapter written on my novel, and I am very enthusiastic about it. I hope it will be one of my very best; but it is a big theme, and will take time. For the last six months I have been working on these prefaces. Love to Howard, and love to you.

ELLEN

There were so many things I did not say that I have had to tear open this envelope. I simply adore Vermont. It is in my opinion, the most satisfactory state in the Union, and the most beautiful in the way I like. If only I had a place there!

What you write of Cambridge seems almost incredible. I imagined that it was the one spot in this Republic where standards survived. But I haven't been there for twenty-five years, and then only for a few weeks. I should love to run over to see you if only I had time. But I am always pressed for time, and so is Carrie Duke, who will be with me. Certainly I agree with all that you say of most of the books Howard has to review. I can read very few modern novels. They are all unspeakably dull to me, and most of them badly written. Speaking of Standards!!

As always, E.

TO DOUGLAS SOUTHALL FREEMAN

Richmond, April 14th, 1938

Dear Dr. Freeman:

Why, I wonder, are you always so good to me. I suspect, however, that it is a part of your general benevolence of mind.

It is more than I dared hope for to have you deliver that address. Would it be possible for you to let me see it ahead, or tell me what you will say? This would be a help to me.

Will you let me know, too, just what I am expected to do or say? I understand that I am not expected to say a word in reply, simply to stand up and receive the diploma and hood. If anything else is required, please let me know in advance.

If it can be arranged without embarrassment, I would rather not walk in the academic procession, and I should appreciate your taking me to the Chapel instead. But I do not wish to make trouble. Only I do hope I shall not have to be photographed in cap and gown. They look very nice, by the way.

Before the time comes, will you please tell me whatever I need to know, and where I shall meet you.

Affectionately yours,
ELLEN GLASGOW

For several years I have had to decline all such honors, as I told you, but already, after accepting this degree, I have been unable to refuse another in June.[1] It was because of you and your kindness that I wished to accept this one, but I find it is not easy to refuse after one has begun.

[1] Miss Glasgow was awarded an LL.D. degree by Duke University in 1938.

TO BESSIE ZABAN JONES

Richmond, April 18th, 1938

Dear Bessie:

What a friend you are! The 16th of May will be perfect. That afternoon, I will ask some friends to a little party, among them my very special friends on the *Saturday Review,* and later we can have dinner together, and a good long talk. Carrie Duke will be with me. You remember her? I shall probably stay at the Weylin, but I have not decided.

I think that article may be arranged, and of course I should be delighted. Especially, I wish Howard to have this definitive edition because I have revised all my earlier books —or rather those we include in this set. Then he simply *must* read the prefaces. I think he will find them revealing. You can't imagine how amused I was to find that he had discovered the autobiographical basis of my New York novel, *The Wheel of Life.* Most people have thought I was writing of strange ground, but this was, in fact, the only one of my books that was taken directly from experience. That may be why it was so much less convincing than the Virginia books. I was too close; for the mystic phase, and even the incident of the little blue flower, really occurred. But that book was not a good novel, and I have long since disinherited it. All the work I wish to be judged by is in my Virginia Edition. And, in particular, the style I wish to be judged by is in that edition.

I have dashed this off in a rush of work.

Love to you,
ELLEN

TO BESSIE ZABAN JONES

Richmond, May 9th, 1938

Dear Bessie:

At last I am able to be explicit, though I am still obliged to be hurried. However, you have inspired me with such complete trust that I am going to write frankly and leave you to pass on to Howard as much or as little as you think best.

Now, Irita Van Doren has just spent the week-end with me. She told me that she wished to have a really fine critical, sympathetic and interpretative article on my Virginia Edition, not a review, she said, but a long analytical essay. She had someone else in mind, but without asking her directly, I led up to the fact that Howard had made a study of my work, that he was thoroughly sympathetic, and, as we agreed, brilliant and penetrating, though sometimes "difficult" in his reviews. I think, though she was not positive, that she is planning to ask him to write this article. Of course, I don't know that he cares to give the time, but you told me he had an article in mind and wished to do it. The *Herald Tribune* reaches a much wider public than the *Saturday Review*.

Will you do this for me? Find out if Howard really feels that he would like to write about me. I regard him as the most brilliant of the younger English scholars in America (I do not know just who the older scholars are!) and I should love to have him do it if—if he will do it with the sympathy and understanding you tell me he feels for my work. This edition means more to me than anything that I have ever had, and I am eager to have it well presented. I can forgive an affront to myself, but not an affront to my work. So will you put it gently, and with wifely tact, to Howard that if he has not the time and the sympathy, it would be better for him not to accept the offer. You will understand how I feel, and you will know, too, that I should like the article done from the new slant that Howard would bring to it. He knows what I have stood for from the beginning, and these prefaces will be, I think, very illuminating. Irita said that of course whoever wrote the article would have a set of this really lovely edition. And just the qualities that James Cabell omits in his portrait[1] are the qualities that I know Howard would bring out—not fastidiousness, but humanity. Humanity and distinction, reality and art—these are the special qualities for which I have striven throughout my work.

I have had to rush this letter, but I know you will understand in spite of the scrappy writing. Do come to New York while I am there. If you will let me know, I will keep any day between the 20th and the 31st.

Much love and tell Howard just what you think will be good for him to hear.

As always,

ELLEN

[1] Possibly Mr. Cabell's essay on Miss Glasgow in *Ellen Glasgow*, edited by Dorothea Lawrence Mann, Doubleday, 1927, or in Mr. Cabell's *Some of Us*, McBride, 1930.

TO EDWIN BALMER [1]

Richmond, May 14th, 1938

My dear Mr. Balmer:

Mr. Maule,[2] of Doubleday, Doran, has sent me your letter, and I like your sincere appreciation of *The Sheltered Life*. Certainly, you present the case from a new angle, and I am inclined to wonder why you became an editor instead of an advocate.

This does not mean that I have as yet reconsidered my

[1] Then editor of *Redbook Magazine*.
[2] Harry Edward Maule, then a director of Doubleday.

[*240*]

decision. What it does mean is that your letter is convincing. In any event, however, I prefer to deal directly with an editor, and not through an agent or a publisher, however friendly. Mr. Maule suggested as much to me in his first letter, because, in order to protect my work, I had retained entire control of all second serial rights.

The chief interest in my mind at present is the Virginia Edition of my works published by Scribner. I could make no final decision until I had asked the opinion of Mr. Maxwell Perkins, and it is entirely probable that I would abide by his judgment. Everything with me now is a question of how it might recoil upon this beautiful subscription edition, for which I have just written twelve critical prefaces.

But I am moved by your very real understanding of *The Sheltered Life.*[3]

Sincerely yours,

ELLEN GLASGOW

[3] Ultimately, *The Sheltered Life* did appear in a 50,000-word condensation in *Redbook Magazine,* October, 1938.

TO MAXWELL E. PERKINS

Richmond, June 25th, 1938

Dear Mr. Perkins:

The last three volumes of my Virginia Edition have reached me, and I am delighted with the edition in every detail. The format is both dignified and artistic, and typographically, I find the books very impressive.

So far, I have discovered only one slip, and I realize that this may have come from my changing the subject in a sentence and then neglecting to alter the verb in the galleys. If the books have all been printed, we shall just say nothing about the error, but if some copies still remain unset, perhaps the subject may be made plural, to agree with the verb. . . .

It was a great pleasure to meet Mrs. Perkins and you in New York, and I hope that we may make that visit to Williamsburg in the early autumn.

Sincerely yours,

ELLEN GLASGOW

TO HOWARD MUMFORD JONES

Richmond, July 22nd, 1938

Dear Howard:

I have just read the article in *Books*,[1] and I am so grateful to you for writing it. It is both interesting and dignified (not a usual combination), and I think the approach is exactly right.

I like especially what you say of these prefaces. Nothing could please me more than that, and I like, too, the paragraph about style and the flow of time. You saw there just what I was trying to do. My only regret is that the article could not be longer, and so you did not put in what you had said to me of Marmaduke in *They Stooped to Folly,* and the note of pity. But I am delighted to hear that you have agreed to an article on my work for the *Atlantic.*

With only one tiny point do I take issue. No, my friend, I have not, and have never had the Virginian "family complex." I don't care a continental about "family" in that sense. Did you find that idea in J.B.C.'s charming fairy tale?[2]

How I wish I could be with you and Bessie in Vermont. But I am hard at work, and enjoying the effort. I am a firm believer in the theory that the strongest motive, whether we

---

[1] Mr. Jones's review "The Virginia Edition of the Works of Ellen Glasgow," the *Herald Tribune Books,* July 24, 1938.

[2] James Branch Cabell had written of Ellen Glasgow in various books and periodicals.

are conscious of it or not, rules our conduct. Perhaps, as a reward of merit, I may see you both in the autumn.

Affectionately yours,

ELLEN

TO HOWARD MUMFORD JONES

Richmond, August 3rd, 1938

Dear Howard:

I looked up the July *Atlantic* (though I take it, I seldom glance over it), and read your essay[1] with a kind of sardonic merriment, especially the paragraphs about Mr. Faulkner and Mr. [James] Farrell.

It is a brilliant article. The part concerning the Gothic and neo-Gothic was delightful. I hope you will continue in that vein, and then do the series.

I had two letters today about the Tribune article,[2] and Irita sent me an enthusiastic letter she had had from Miss [Agnes] Repplier, who is so fine a writer that her praise always pleases me.

Love to Bessie.

Affectionately yours,

ELLEN

[1] "Relief from Murder," *Atlantic Monthly,* July, 1938.
[2] The review of the Virginia Edition.

TO BESSIE ZABAN JONES

Richmond, September 27th, 1938

Bessie dear,

Your letter has just come, and I am torn by the wish to visit Cambridge (and stay with you), and the fear that I might fall ill on your hands. If only I were well, I should love to spend several days with you and Howard. Carrie and

I always stay together when we go away, and I also have only one guest room. But this will have to be some other time, I think, possibly in the spring.

Now, I am going to New York for two reasons—to see my doctor and to give a rambling talk before Dr. Lyon's class at Columbia.[1] For years he has tried to make me come to one of his meetings and six months ago, in a moment of weakness, when I was feeling unusually well, I promised him to speak on October 12th. But I have not been able to write a speech (I simply *cannot* do it) and I do not know what to talk about. Will you ask Howard whether students are more interested in literature in general or in a personal experience. Please send me his advice.

And please, please, please, come over to New York. October 15th comes on Saturday, and I will stay over that Sunday if you will come. There are a thousand things I wish to discuss with you both, and I have had a genuine friendship and affection for you and Howard (my friendships run deep) ever since we first knew one another at the N. C. University, where you so gallantly came to my rescue.

Do let me know positively, and tell me how long you can stay, and exactly when I may expect you. I shall want to arrange some plans for you. Is there any one especially Howard would like to meet? I wonder whether he is entirely satisfied with his publishers? In his position, I think I would rather have Scribners than any other, and Maxwell Perkins is, in my opinion, the perfect publisher.

The reviews of the Virginia Edition start with Howard's. I like his much the best, and I think it showed the most penetrating insight. But we shall discuss this when I see you.

Only yesterday I was thinking of that sad visit you had in Richmond, when Howard, poor fellow, was down with influenza. Some day you must come again, in a good season,

[1] John Henry Hobart Lyon's English class.

not in Winter, and I will take you to Williamsburg and Jamestown and the other places. Spring is the best time, but autumn is usually beautiful until the end of November.

Isn't the state of the world simply fearful? I feel as if the universe had turned into a vast lunatic asylum, and the riot of emotionalism bears out my belief that human beings are driven to war by some blind destructive instinct, that the cause of war is deeper than any geographical boundary, and is rooted in the facts of biology, and in primitive impulse. . . .

Love to you both,

As always yours devotedly,

ELLEN

TO VAN WYCK BROOKS

Richmond, October 29th, 1938

Dear Mr. Brooks,

This is the first note I have tried to write since I went to the hospital, but I am home again, after a miserable month, and I cannot wait longer to thank you for your wholly delightful letter. I have always admired deeply your artistry and your wisdom.

Already I am looking ahead eagerly to your visit with Mrs. Brooks in the spring. Do let me know at least a week before you come. I should like to make some plans for you and to show you both something of the Virginia we still love and value. Charleston is far more charming, yet I think you will like it here.

When we meet I hope to talk with you of your work, but I am not yet equal to writing.

Sincerely and gratefully yours,

ELLEN GLASGOW

[*245*]

TO HUDSON STRODE [1]

Richmond, October 30th, 1938

Dear Hudson:

After twenty-two days in the Doctor's Hospital in New York, I am at last home again, and I feel rather as if I had been through a war on the wrong side. It wasn't a "serious accident," but I injured a muscle or two in my spine.

I have just looked over your Anthology,[2] and I find it unusually satisfying. My only criticism would be that the work should have been twice as long and have filled two such volumes. But J.B.C. and I agree that it is wholly delightful.

Do let me know ahead when you come to lecture in Richmond, and be sure to keep an evening or a lunch here for me. I hope Thérèse[3] will be with you.

Affectionately,

ELLEN GLASGOW

[1] Writer and professor of English at the University of Alabama.
[2] *Immortal Lyrics,* Random House, 1938.
[3] Mrs. Strode.

TO VAN WYCK BROOKS

Richmond, November 14th, 1938

Dear Mr. Brooks,

Yes, May is usually our loveliest month, though, of course, much depends on the season. It would be best to avoid the crowds in Garden Week, a dreadful affair which takes place the last week in April. The fourth or fifth of May would be a good time; and I could take Mrs. Brooks and you to the gardens you would wish to see without throngs of tourists about you. I am praying, as my father would have said, that I shall be well, but even if I am not able to go with you, my ever-helpful friend Mrs. Duke, who remembers you with pleasure, will be delighted to serve again in my place.

I wonder whether you will care for Virginia as much as I care for New England. Strangely enough I feel a closer kinship with the clear outlines, and with the green fields and ponds and the dreamy blue hills of Vermont, than I feel with any tropical splendor of bloom. But Virginia is not really Southern as the Deep South is Southern; and after all Virginians are (or were) a people within themselves and a border between two alien or hostile cultures.

My kind regards to Mrs. Brooks.

Sincerely yours,

ELLEN GLASGOW

TO MAXWELL E. PERKINS

Richmond, December 27th, 1938

Dear Mr. Perkins:

Thank you for your thoughtfulness in telling me of the review in the *Times*. It was unusually good, and I hope will help the Virginia Edition.

Just before I left for New York the first of October I had a call from Mr. Schiff, who appeared both competent and enthusiastic. He asked me to see Mr. Merritt at Scribner's, and I had intended to do so; but, unfortunately, my entire visit to New York was spent in the Doctor's Hospital. As I have had no further word from Mr. Schiff, I am afraid that he found book selling in Virginia as difficult as I have always believed it to be.

I am very much pleased by what you say of Marjorie Rawlings and her liking for my prefaces. Few books have ever moved me more deeply than *The Yearling*.[1] The tragedy of the end seemed to me almost too intense to be borne. It is a perfect thing of its kind, with the accent of inevitability

[1] Scribner, 1938.

that tempts me to use the word "genius." And genius as a term in literary criticism does not often appeal to me.

With my good wish for the coming year,

Sincerely yours,

ELLEN GLASGOW

TO H. L. MENCKEN

Richmond, January 10th, 1939

Dear Mr. Mencken:

It was lovely of you to write to me, and I am delighted to hear that Henry is himself again.

Yes, I had a rather hard time, and I spent three quiet weeks, with an injury to my back, in a hospital in New York. However, I have to live, more or less, as an invalid, and if only my capacity for work will last as long as I do, I shall feel that I am satisfied. I look upon those weeks in the hospital as the only complete rest of the nerves I ever had in my life.

You sound encouraging about the coming Battle of Washington. Why don't you decide to take a day off and come down to lunch with me?

As always,

ELLEN GLASGOW

I think so often of those perfect hours with Sara and you in the Victorian drawing-room in Cathedral Street. I have never felt that her loveliness was lost to us.

TO BESSIE ZABAN JONES

Richmond, February 5th, 1939

Dear Bessie:

So often I find myself thinking of you and Howard; but it is very difficult for me to write letters.

I hope your winter has been more satisfactory than mine.

Ever since I had that accident in the autumn, I have been obliged to live more or less by a schedule. After two hours work in the morning, I spend the rest of the day walking and resting; and nine o'clock usually sees me well on the way to bed. But the life suits me, for I ask almost nothing of fate except the strength and the time to work. Already I have given a year to this new novel, and I shall require still two other years before I come to the end. I shall be woefully disappointed if it does not turn out to be one of my best books —rich and full-bodied in character.

The first signs of spring were in the woods today. Birds were beginning to pipe and call, and we found snowballs blooming under the trees. Of course, there is always danger of a cold wave or even a blizzard—our worst one was in March. But it looks as if we should have an early spring, and I am hoping that you and Howard will be able to run down for a few days in April or May. Then you can see the Tidewater at its best, and the danger of influenza, which has invaded my house this winter, will be over.

Do let me hear from you. I wish we did not live so far apart, for you and Howard are among the limited group of persons I really enjoy.

With love to you both,
Affectionately yours,
ELLEN

TO WILLIAM H. F. LAMONT [1]

Richmond, February 15th, 1939

Dear Dr. Lamont:

Thank you for your interesting letter. I wish it were possible for me to visit your American novel class; but at present I am in a state of total immersion. I began a novel a year ago, and I have still other years ahead of me.

[1] Member of the English faculty at Rutgers University.

[249]

I am glad that you perceived the special uses of color in my books. Do you recall from *Barren Ground* the shadings of color in the broomsedge? These range from ivory to deep rust-color, and for me the whole book is suffused with the smothered glow.

With cordial regards,
Sincerely yours,
ELLEN GLASGOW

TO ERNEST E. LEISY [1]

Richmond, March 16th, 1939

My dear Dr. Leisy:

No, my Pedlar's Mill is not the Pedlar Mills that you may, or may not, find on the map. I cannot recall whether I had ever heard of this post-office, but I did not wish to confine my scene to a particular place. It interests me to portray the spirit of a country, but I have tried to avoid a photographic realism. When a character enters my mind, however, he usually wears his own name and countenance, and I have found it a mistake to try to change either the name or the appearance.

Thank you for the kind things you say of my work.

Sincerely yours,
ELLEN GLASGOW

[1] Author and professor of American literature at Southern Methodist University.

TO VAN WYCK BROOKS

Richmond, March 27th, 1939

Dear Mr. Brooks:

. . . It has been in my mind to tell you that April 17th ought to be the very best time for Williamsburg and lower James River. I hope nothing will prevent your coming, and

I am looking forward with the greatest pleasure to meeting Mrs. Brooks and you. . . .

I hope you will be able to spend several days in Richmond, and to see the James River places at their best. Mrs. Daniel [1] has asked me to bring you to lunch on the 19th, and I should like to take you on to Claremont Manor for tea, and if possible to Upper Brandon, which is a simpler place, but very charming and characteristic. Then you should certainly see Westover. The Cranes [2] are in mourning, but I saw Mrs. Crane yesterday, and she urged me to bring you there to lunch. That would take another day, because it is too exhausting to go across the river and back again.

Then, by all means, you should see Stratford, the Lee place, and if you have not been to the University in May, you should stop there on your way North.

I do not know how you would go back by the mountain way, but our mountains are very beautiful. Roanoke is modern and uninteresting. You could well miss that, but Lexington is attractive and interesting because of the Lee associations. I have a sister who lives there, and she would love to have you lunch with her on your way, and she could show you the Lee chapel and Washington and Lee University. By all means avoid the hotel at the Natural Bridge. You will find a charming inn called Forest Tavern a few miles beyond the Natural Bridge, on the road to Roanoke. There might be time for the Skyline Drive, and I think you would enjoy taking that.

If you reach Richmond in the afternoon of the 17th, I hope you will dine with me, or if not the 17th, any other evening you prefer. When you have decided, I will ask the Cabells and the Freemans, who look forward to meeting you both.

[1] Mr. and Mrs. Robert W. Daniel owned "Brandon," one of the finest of the James River estates.

[2] Mr. and Mrs. Richard Crane had purchased "Westover," the old Byrd estate.

But I have suddenly remembered that Dr. Freeman lectures at Columbia [University] every Tuesday.

With cordial regards to Mrs. Brooks,

Sincerely yours,

ELLEN GLASGOW

TO MARJORIE KINNAN RAWLINGS

Richmond, April 16th, 1939

Dear Mrs. Rawlings:

If you should go by Richmond on your way North, I hope you will let me know. I should love to talk with you, for I am watching your work with great interest. *The Yearling* seems to me to be a perfect thing of its kind. And this can be said of few modern works of fiction.

Sincerely yours,

ELLEN GLASGOW

TO VAN WYCK BROOKS

Richmond, July 4th, 1939

Dear Mr. Brooks,

What charming letters you write! It is so seldom nowadays that I receive an interesting letter written in the distinguished handwriting of the author that it is quite an event when I catch sight of an envelope addressed by you.

I was really touched—no, thrilled is the better word—by what you wrote of Edward Sheldon.[1] That for me is supreme heroism, an actual triumph over fate. Courage in battle appears so trivial beside that magnificent fortitude. Mary Albro, a very fine and remarkable woman, told me a great deal about him, and I have always felt that, in a way, I had

[1] Author of *Romance, The Boss,* and other plays. E. W. Barnes has written his story in *The Man Who Lived Twice.* Scribner, 1956.

known him. It was a kind of shyness, I think, that prevented my keeping my promise to Mary and going to see him. By "shyness" I mean that constant damnable fear that I may not hear what is said to me.

For the past few days Mrs. Brooks and you have been much in my mind as I have driven over the Virginia country-side. Your visit was quite the nicest thing that occurred in the spring. I am delighted to hear that you will certainly come again. Next time, you must talk with many more Virginians—or, as it will probably turn out, let them talk to you. The only art we have ever cultivated with enthusiasm is the art of conversation. But of talk, good, bad, or indifferent, we have never enough.

Day after tomorrow (God permitting, as Mr. Pickwick would prudently remark) we shall leave for a long vacation at Castine, Maine. I have taken a cottage there in the hope that I shall be able to go on with my work. Never before have I written away from this special room in this special old house;[2] but Castine will be very quiet and I have a little studio (the house belongs to a painter) out in the garden. . . .

I am wondering how your book goes.[3] Are you still confined to New England (how beautifully your imagination handles that scene!) or have you turned your thoughts to the South? The mockingbirds are still singing in the Tidewater. A few weeks ago when I went to Williamsburg (at last Mr. Bryan prevailed upon me to receive a degree)[4] the birds in the trees did so much better than the speakers that Miss Bennett said she blushed for the human voice. The exer-

[2] Miss Glasgow overlooked the fact that she wrote *Life and Gabriella* during her residence in New York from 1911 to 1916.

[3] *New England: Indian Summer,* Dutton, 1940.

[4] An LL.D. from the College of William and Mary. John Stewart Bryan was then president of the college.

cises were held out-of-doors, and every bird was in an ecstasy of excitement.

With affectionate greetings to Mrs. Brooks.

Sincerely yours,

ELLEN GLASGOW

TO VAN WYCK BROOKS

Littleplace
Castine, Maine
September 2nd, 1939

Dear Mr. Brooks,

Your letter gave me the greatest pleasure, and all summer I have set my heart on a visit to Mrs. Brooks and you in October. It is lovely of you both to want us, and there is nothing I can think of that I would rather do. But there are so many complications (what else is life?) that we shall be obliged to go back as we came, by the shortest route, spending only two nights on our way. It is impossible to tell you what a disappointment this is. I have thought so much of that hoped for visit, and it is the only real pleasure I looked forward to in this troubled season.

There is a bare chance that Carrie Duke and I may come to New York a little later in the autumn. If this is possible, we shall accept, with the greatest delight, the invitation to visit you.

I am tremendously interested in what you write of your new books. No, none of these persons has the appeal of Thoreau and Emerson (what a masterly interpretation you gave of them and their circle!), but I must confess to a secret sympathy with that malicious old demon, Henry Adams. His penetration was as narrow (and as fine) as a needle (and in matters Southern, a crooked needle); but the most irritating thing about him is that he was so often right in his malice. I shall be eager to see just what you make of his generation.

Yes, my "Littleplace" belongs to the widow of Allen Tucker, and, until the fog drove me into the house, I worked in his studio. The flowers were not many in the garden just outside but they were wonderful. Roses in August, and delphiniums as blue as the heavens and nearly seven feet high!

I have found this an excellent place for working—the only spot except Richmond in which writing comes naturally. Already I am nearing the end of my first draft, and until the world seemed to go deranged with war madness, I spent my days very peacefully. Work, walk, rest, drive, never anything else, and almost complete isolation. Every morning, after my working hours are over, I tramp over the Indian trails in the Maine woods. It is an ideal life for me, and if there were no fogs in Maine, this place would seem perfect. The country is beautiful, just the Northern part of "the country of the pointed firs." [1] It is green, fresh, with deep blue sky, sea, and mountains, and is all amazingly restful. I like the sturdy Maine folk, just as I liked the folk of Vermont. They have many advantages over us of the South. For one thing, they live in a thinly settled country, and, in Maine at least, they have the inestimable blessing of belonging to a single race. Unless you have lived in the South, I suppose you could never understand how thoroughly I enjoy the simple cleanliness of the Maine villages and farms and roadsides. In a few weeks now the autumn will have blazed a trail through the woods and over the glorious meadows. I hope to stay on until the first week in October, and by that time the autumn should be well on its way.

When you write, and I hope you will, give me more news of Ned Sheldon. I take a great interest in him and admire him, his work, and his spirit.

[1] A reference to the book by Sarah Orne Jewett bearing this title.

It is good indeed to know that your book will bring you again and again to Virginia. Then we shall have other trips to other places, and I should like Mrs. Brooks and you to know more Virginians. Some of them still live in the past, and they will bring tradition to life for you, some of these older ones. It is amusing about Mr. Macrae's bed—I mean the bed of Lee.[2] Well, I can credit that, but not the peg on that lofty head. But, after all, what is legend except, as the great Napoleon remarked of history, "a fable agreed upon."

And now I must stop and turn back to the radio. In a distracted world how close and dear human relationships may become. Knowing Mrs. Brooks and you is the very nicest thing that has happened to me this year.

My affectionate regards to you both,

ELLEN GLASGOW

[2] John Macrae, president of E. P. Dutton and Company, Mr. Brooks's publishers, had inherited the bed in which General Robert E. Lee was born.

TO VAN WYCK BROOKS

Castine, October 4th, 1939

Dear Mr. Brooks,

Summer has gone South, and we follow. It is a deep disappointment not to see Mrs. Brooks and you, but I am hoping to return for that pleasure. Even if that isn't till spring, it is something bright on the Northern horizon.

I enjoyed your letter immensely, and I am so much interested in all you say of your book. I did not realize that you are treating of Henry James on this occasion. Your book on James[1] is very suggestive, and, I think, a penetrating interpretation. Why was he so limited in emotional scope? What you say of his absence from America seems to me sound and logical, and you give a reason for the feeling one

[1] *The Pilgrimage of Henry James*, Dutton, 1925.

has that he was a cosmopolitan airplant. His work is that of the perpetual exile, and I feel that great novels must have roots. The time was when I read his books, as I did Meredith's novels, every year, but now both these authors irritate me. They seem so importantly earnest and sentimental about the wrong things. James gushes about Society and Meredith about Woman. Neither of these subjects appear to me to be worth a rhapsody. Yet I can still enjoy *The Turn of the Screw* and *The Ambassadors,* and I can enjoy, too, Meredith when he forgets to be sentimental as in *The Egoist* and *Evan Harrington.* But from *Richard Feverel* and *Diana,* good Lord deliver us!

When I was in London in the spring of 1914, I met Henry James several times, but only in the houses of my wealthiest and most important acquaintances. I thought of him then, as I did when I read his *Letters,* as the pluperfect snob. Not an offensive snob, for he was kind and cordial and rather pathetic in a ponderous way, but the kind of innocent snob who places extravagant value on worldliness. In his *Life and Letters* I sought in vain for a single letter that was addressed to a simple person, or even to one of moderate means. His personality, when I met him, and it is hardly fair to judge from so slight an acquaintance, seemed to me to ring hollow. And his work, for all its smooth and brilliant surface, rings hollow, except in a few novels. Even his literary criticism seems to me to lack depth—or is it simple humanity [?] I used to think it strange that in my ardent youth I felt no inclination to imitate him, as so many novelists were trying to do at the turn of the century. Of course, he is a great novelist in his special form, but, somehow, I feel that, even without Mrs. Wharton, one Henry James is enough for any country—or even for any two countries. And this does not mean that I fail to admire Mrs. Wharton.

That same spring of 1914 was made unforgettable to me by my meeting with Hardy—and, in a lesser degree by my meeting with Conrad, who was, as you know if you met him in England or over here, the most lovable of human beings. But Hardy was to me the most sympathetic Englishman, and one of the most sympathetic persons I have ever known. Nothing rang hollow in his nature.

Well, my pen has run away with me. I should hate to think I had reached the age of reminiscences, when all one can do is to sit down and remember.

This has been an active, and a satisfactory summer, too, for I have finished the first draft of my novel. This is only the beginning, but the work after this will be easier because I shall have at least a foundation to build on and a framework to follow. I have spent a year and a little more on this novel, and I shall have still two years of work before it is finished. Did you ever stop to think that a writer will spend three years, or many more, on a book that the average reader will skim through in a few hours? A sobering reflection, dear confrere.

Please remember me to Ned Sheldon and tell me about him. And do—oh, *do* tell me of your book and when you may finish it. Will the war put off publication? Another senseless catastrophe, with nothing to be done about it. I hate war anywhere, and I hope we will stay out of it, yet I believe there is a subconscious urge to conflict in most human beings.

My affectionate regards to you both, and the hope that you will soon turn to Virginia.

As always sincerely,

ELLEN GLASGOW

TO EDWIN MIMS

Castine, October 4th, 1939

Dear Dr. Mims,

I take my brightest paper to tell you how pleased I was to have your letter and to hear the good news of your happy summer. So many pleasant things appear to happen to you, and I know why that is, you are so friendly to the universe that the universe is obliged to reciprocate.

I have had a little house in this enchanting place for the summer and it has been a miracle of freshness and greenness. No one who has not lived in the South can possibly realize the joy that one feels in New England cleanliness. No waste paper, no offensive billboards, no refuse heaps, no unsightly trash by the roadside. And, best of all, no miserable ill-treated animals. Many times I have thought, "If only when they conquered us, they had civilized us as well." Certainly, the Maine people have many advantages over us Southerners. They are independent and thrifty and self-respecting. They keep their places neat, even the poorest. They plant flowers about their houses, and they take a pride in their well-kept horses and their happy dogs. It all comes back, I suppose, to the climate—or does it? And they have too the incalculable advantage of belonging to a single race—at least up in Maine, where the Polacks have not yet penetrated. For, of course, all this does not apply to Massachusetts and the border of Connecticut. There, in places, the Polacks have made a desert and call it peace.

Are you ever coming to Richmond again? It seems another epoch in history since that "bright interlude" at Duke University.[1] Why not go on with the book you had planned and leave war to take care of itself?

This has been a fine place for work. I have finished the first draft of my novel, but that is only the beginning, which represents a year's work. Two more years are still ahead of me, and I go as slowly as possible because the only part of a novel I care for is the actual atmosphere of writing. After one is published I feel that it is no longer mine.

Yes, the war haunts me in the shape of a nightmare. I feel not only saddened but outraged, and it all seems to me so

[1] A reference to the degree received by Miss Glasgow in 1938.

utterly unnecessary. But never, never, never again shall I surrender to the contagion of war hysteria. I suffered that once and once is enough—or too much. Even the trumpet of the Lord will not awaken me this time; I have lost my faith in salvation through violence, and I do not believe that anything can be saved by murder in masses. I think the grave error, as I see it according to humanity, was when England and France pledged to Poland and encouraged her to fight Germany instead of giving up in the beginning. Wouldn't it have been better by far for Poland to have yielded the Polish Corridor than to have lost everything? And when the war is finally over and Poland destroyed what country will the Poles hate most heartily, the country of the enemy or the countries of the friends that failed them? But, like you, I love England and long to see her victorious. . . .

TO DOUGLAS SOUTHALL FREEMAN

Richmond, December 21, 1939

Dear Douglas,

I am sitting up for the first time after a painful illness, and my thoughts turn to you, in gratitude, for your enlightening book.[1] I read it with deep interest, and I am the richer by two copies, for I had ordered one for myself before the beautifully inscribed copies came from your generous hands. The work is of great value to the South, for it brings fresh illumination to several dim passages of history.

Affectionately and gratefully yours,

ELLEN GLASGOW

[1] *The South to Posterity,* Scribner, 1939.

TO VAN WYCK BROOKS

Richmond, January 6th, 1940

Dear Mr. Brooks,

How good you were to send me the Emerson Essays,[1] and how delighted I was to receive this charming copy, with its inscription, to place among my treasures in a very special bookcase. Many thanks for your thought of me. I can scarcely wait for the promised book next September.

I should have written to you before this, but I have been far from well this Christmas, and I am now in the listless stage of convalescence when everything in the world seems too much. I have taken time, however, to read Carl Sandburg's *Lincoln,*[2] and I have been overwhelmed by the power and vivid truth of the work. This is the only book of Sandburg's I have ever read, and I can understand just how and why he has impressed you profoundly. If his name does come up before the Academy,[3] and you have not asked anyone else in my place, I should consider it an honor to act as one of the five sponsors.

When I spoke as I did, by the way, of the too far-reaching influence of the Middle West, I was thinking not of space or numbers, but rather of that amazing conquest of the flat pedestrian style in fiction. Even the South has surrendered to it and tried to imitate the Dust-Bowl atmosphere, and I think that much of the South is now as arid as Kansas or Oklahoma. And while it is in my mind I must tell you that the vital spring and freshness and living warmth in your style drew me first to your work as a critic of life.

[1] Probably Mr. Brooks's *Emerson and Others,* Dutton, 1927.

[2] *Abraham Lincoln: The War Years,* four volumes, Harcourt, Brace, 1939.

[3] The American Academy of Arts and Letters.

You must have known how happy your praise of *The Sheltered Life* would make me. I sent you a copy of the first edition, and in the second edition I had added a sentence of three words because one or two reviewers I respected seemed to assume that George had killed himself. This would of course give the book a false ending in my mind. The two overlapping themes are, as you no doubt perceived, we cannot put up a shelter against life and we kill what we love too much. Not always in Mrs. Birdsong's way, but in some other less obvious way. But how I loved what you said of my book!

I was deeply touched to have the telegram from Edward Sheldon on Christmas Day. When I think of his courage I feel as humble as a sparrow.

With affectionate greetings to Mrs. Brooks, and good wishes for all the years to come,

ELLEN GLASGOW

TO ETOLIA AND HAMILTON BASSO

Richmond, March 15th, 1940

Dear Mr. and Mrs. Basso:

In clearing off my desk after a long illness, I was shocked to find that I had not thanked you for the lovely flowers you sent me last autumn. It was charming of you to think of me, and I was much disappointed to miss your promised visit.

Do come in the spring (this is a blustering winter day) and let me know a little ahead. I wanted to tell you how much I like *Days Beyond Lent*,[1] though I think *Courthouse Square*[2] is still my favorite.

Sincerely yours,
ELLEN GLASGOW

[1] Scribner, 1939.
[2] Scribner, 1936.

TO VAN WYCK BROOKS

Richmond, April 11th, 1940

My dear Mr. Brooks,

I have waited to answer your letter until I felt that I was not breaking in on your book. Is it really and truly finished? I gathered that from a note in the *Herald-Tribune* (I think), and I am eager to hear that you are happy and satisfied. Or is it that you are feeling completely lost and unreal, as I feel whenever I have written a final page?

The spring is coming rapidly now. We can see the green creeping over the woods and the tiny leaves growing larger. I am hoping that, with your book out of the way, you and Mrs. Brooks will come again to Virginia. And I am hoping it all the more earnestly because my doctor has just said "no" to my plans for New York in May. Of course, if I feel surprisingly well, I may defy his advice, but it is too dreary to be in New York and yet unable to go about and have the kind of pleasure I miss and need after a long shut-in winter. Heaven be praised that I could still work, and my book has gone very well in spite of every impediment. But I have a theory that one's best work is done in such periods of illness or depression.

How I envy you your New England spring! Here, our summer comes too quickly, but I am playing with the hope of another summer in Castine. Do let me hear that you and Mrs. Brooks are coming South.

My love to you both,

ELLEN GLASGOW

TO ALFRED HARCOURT

Richmond, May 8th, 1940

Dear Alfred:

The doctor has said "no" to my New York visit. He is willing for me to go and sit in a hotel, but not to rush about as I should wish to do. I am saving myself for the long trip to Castine in June.

Meanwhile, I am wondering if you could come down the first of June, and read two thirds of my book before it goes to the bank for the summer. The second draft has gone very well. Strangely enough, I seem to write better when I am not in bounding physical health.

I hope to finish the third part by autumn; but I should like you, and Miss Taylor, if she can come, to know something about it and talk over plans with me. Of course I should not wish to publish a novel just at election time, and I remember you asked me to give you six months to prepare. We might plan for the spring, though I should prefer August as usual.

The book is long, full, and rich, but it is sailing against the stream. My mind always does that, and nothing could be more boring to me than the popular idiot psychology of the present literary fashion.

I shall have to change the name, because the word "tomorrow" has been used too often of late. How does "The Age of Unreason" strike you? What I am trying to do is an analysis of the modern temper, a cross section of American life as it is lived today. The scene runs from April 1938 to September 1939, just to the beginning of the new world war.

Sincerely yours,

ELLEN

Another title I have thought of is "Yesterday is not Today." Will you let these names sink into your mind.[1]

[1] *In This Our Life* was the final choice of title.

TO VAN WYCK BROOKS

Doctor's Hospital, New York
July 11th, 1940

Dear Mr. Brooks,

How glad I was to have your letter this morning! But this was as far as I came on my way to Castine. The doctors have, assisted by X-rays and cardiograms, discovered that my heart is entirely inadequate to do the work I expect of it. Of course I had known in Richmond that I felt like the Wrath of God, but I had refused to bother with X-rays, because, to tell the truth, I really had not cared one way or the other. By the time I had run about New York, however, I was feeling so miserable that everything was taken out of my hands.

This is a pleasant retreat from life, as hospitals go, but a whole month of inaction seems a little too much. The doctor says I am improving steadily, but I have been here for two weeks, and he has not allowed me to have any visitors, or to talk to anyone, not even my nurse. The result is that I am finding the days intolerably tedious, and the nights even worse. Thank Heaven, I am planning to leave for Castine on the 24th of July.

Do come to see me as soon as I am settled.[1] Miss Bennett is there already, and I shall be ready to see you any day after the 27th. Only let me know a day ahead, and I hope Mrs. Brooks and you can arrange to come over for lunch— or whenever you would find most convenient. Here comes the nurse!

My affectionate greetings to you both.

As always,

ELLEN GLASGOW

[1] The Brookses were spending the summer at Boothbay Harbor, Maine.

TO CHARLES HANSON TOWNE [1]

Castine, July 30th, 1940

Dear Charley:

This is the first note I have written since I left the hospital in New York; but I must tell you how much I appreciate your letter. It was dear of Leonora and you to think and speak of me and to try to find me in the Doctor's Hospital in that intolerable weather. I love you both, and so often in those last five days there (when the doctor said I might have a few visitors) I was on the point of telephoning Leonora Speyer and asking her to come with you for a little visit before I left. But the heat was so intense that it seemed cruel to ask either of you to make so great an effort and come such a long distance.

Will you tell her what I have written you, and give her at the same time my love and admiration. I have always thought her an adorable person who looks and lives her enchanting poetry.

How exciting it is to hear that you [are] turning into an actor! [2] I can scarcely believe that you would ever prefer plays to poems, but I shall say my little prayer for your success, and I hope that I shall be able to see your part on the stage. Shall you go on the road or keep close to New York?

After a month of utter tedium on a bed in the Doctors' Hospital the X-ray showed that the organic trouble with my heart had not improved in the slightest degree. However, the muscular action is stronger, and I am still convinced that nothing except an Act of God will ever kill me.

Affectionately yours,

ELLEN

[1] Poet, essayist, and former editor.
[2] Mr. Towne was appearing in *Life with Father*.

The only thing that really matters to me is finishing my novel, and, thank Heaven, the first draft was written in the past five years and I have only some of the final writing to do. . . .

TO JAMES SOUTHALL WILSON

Castine, August 2nd, 1940

Dear James,

Your letter came to me in the hospital just when I needed it, and it did me a world of good to know you were thinking of me at Bread Loaf. It was a bitter disappointment that I was not able to go up for the degree in August. But I am not yet strong enough for a long drive or even a short walk. The latest X-ray in New York, after a whole tedious month in the Doctor's Hospital (and I am certainly not made for hospital life) showed no organic improvement, though the muscular action of my heart is stronger and steadier. However, that does not bother me. My only fear is that I should be the last creature left alive on this planet to fight a losing battle with mine ancient enemy, the cockroach! Life has taught me that the greatest tragedy is not to die too soon but to live too long. And there is a theory that only the insect will inherit the earth.

Your letter brought back to me a glowing memory of that happy visit to Bread Loaf. I could see you sitting there, in the midst of my chosen friends, the birds, large and small, under the green shadows of leaves, with the deep blue chain of mountains beyond; and I could hear above the song of birds that distant rippling sound of the brook. I remember it all vividly, and I wish with all my heart that I were with you.

But I must stop, because I am allowed to write each day a very little. The only thing that makes me careful is the need to save my strength for my book, which (Heaven be praised!) has already been written once and twice over, and requires nothing more than a summer's work on the last quarter. It is a very good book, and I have spent the past four years writing it. Since my only conscience is the literary conscience I could not bear to leave a good piece of work with the end unfinished.

My love to Julia and my warmest greetings to all my other friends at Bread Loaf. There is so much more I should like to say, for Bread Loaf will always have a very special place in my mind and heart.

Affectionately yours,

ELLEN

TO BESSIE ZABAN JONES

Castine, September 25th, 1940

Dearest Bessie:

I have thought often of you and Howard, but it has been impossible for me to write. You have not heard, I know, that I was desperately ill after I left the hospital and came to Castine. On the 9th of August I had a severe heart attack, and the doctor did not know whether or not I should come through. To me, the interesting part of it was that I was entirely conscious, except when I fainted for a few minutes, and though I was too weak to do more than flutter my eyelids, I knew and remembered everything that I thought and felt. While the doctor sat for an hour with his stethoscope on my heart and his finger on my pulse, afraid to do anything more, lest, as he said, it would "push me over the ragged edge," I really thought I was dying, and I felt not the faintest fear or reluctance, or even a wish to hold back a moment. My philosophy held firm, for that I was thankful, and I knew then that there was nothing to cling to in life and nothing, or less than nothing, to fear in death. Afterwards, I was tremendously interested, and even at the time, Anne Virginia said she believed my only sensation was one of curiosity. Anyway, I remember thinking, while they thought I was dying, "As long as I can't finish my book, I hope I can go quickly."

WELL, I came through, and I had an excellent doctor. He kept me in bed, without letting me stir for weeks, and all I saw of Maine was a tall pointed fir outside my window. I have become much attached to this tree, and I feel that it has a kinship with something deep down in myself. Or, maybe, this is vanity. Illness is apt to give one extravagant values.

Even now, I am permitted to go downstairs only once a day. I have been for four short drives, but no walks, which I loved best of all. Ten days ago, the doctor told me I might work fifteen minutes a day, and now I work half an hour every morning. But what a life! What a world! The horrors in Europe hang over me like vultures of darkness. I cannot put them out of my mind, and I can do nothing.

Do let me hear from you. I expect to go home on October 20th, but I shall not be able to motor down.

That was a dear visit from Howard when I was in the hospital. He looked so well and seemed so interested in this sorry world. How I should love to see you both again; but I do not know whether I shall ever be any better than an exasperating invalid. I have just told the doctor that I prefer death to a neurosis. It was refusing to live safely, however, that brought on my unpleasant, yet not unenlightening, match with fate on August the 9th. So I shall have to go either too slowly, or too fast and make a clean end of it.

My love to you both. You have been near me through all this dreary summer, while I lay in my room and watched the fir tree against a blue or gray sky. It is stormy and wild today. This has been an unhappy September, gray and rainy, with only a few glorious days now and then. . . .

Devotedly,

ELLEN

[*269*]

I do not like this letter. It has an egotistical tone, and I have been obliged to tap it out hurriedly. But if I tear it up, I may not be able to write another for weeks. So please make excuses for me and my general inadequacy.

But the book marches on!

TO VAN WYCK BROOKS

Castine, October 7th, 1940

Dear Mr. Brooks,

For the past few weeks I have lived with your *New England: Indian Summer,* and the latter half of the book (which I had not read when I wrote to you) has swept me out of myself and my long illness. The closing in of the book, and of New England's decline, will become a part of my consciousness. The book branches out into space until it reminds me of one of the splendid New England elms; and I think it grows in strength as it reaches out. The end is the finest part, as it should be with all books, large or small. How I wish I might talk with you instead of trying to write when my strength falters. I like immensely the chapters on Henry James, and I would change nothing you have written of Henry Adams. Something in both of these men has had a hollow ring, much as I admire and enjoy their books—or some of their books. . . .

The weeks go by, and no one who has not seen Maine in October can appreciate the full beauty of hills and fields and forests and harbors. I go for short drives when it is fair, but I have had no walks in my beloved woods. My tall pointed fir is filled with goldfinches and I have become deeply attached to the tree and the birds. I can see nothing else but the sky from my bed.

When I said "the end of your book," I meant the whole latter half, beginning with the chapter on Howells and James. This includes the chapter on Emily Dickinson—and

[*270*]

I like, too, all you write of Mary E. Wilkins. No better or truer stories have been written, I think, in America, but there's too little understanding of her at present.

But it is all a gorgeous book, bless you! My love to Mrs. Brooks and you,

E.G.

TO ALFRED HARCOURT

Richmond, November 27th, 1940

Dear Alfred:

Lying there in bed, several things have bothered my mind. Now, before trying to work, I should like to pass these worries on into your capable hands.

First of all, whenever this book is published (and we are not sure of the spring) will you please, please, please, promise me that it will be printed in large, clear, open type. Certainly no smaller print than *Vein of Iron,* and, if possible larger. But the important thing is to have it open. I like a long novel, so please do not let the printers try to make the book appear shorter. My eyes have not yet recovered from the small, close, glaring type of the new Virginia Woolf book.[1] Will you take this up with the other members of the firm.

I am noting these points merely because you may be in Florida when some questions come up, and you alone know what this book has cost me and how much I have put into it in these long months of illness. Could you let me see samples of type?

Then, in case you should be on your vacation, will you have all the new members read our contract. Will you make them understand how much is to be spent in advertisement, and all the other parts of our agreement. For example, you gave me and Irita, too, the most positive assurance that my

[1] *Roger Fry: A Biography,* Harcourt, Brace, 1940.

[*271*]

book, whenever it was published should be the leading and outstanding book on your list; and then your publicity department rushed ahead to put the Lindbergh book[2] in front. Of course, I am not implying that you yourself did this. I mean simply that the other departments were not aware, or had forgotten the clear outlines of our contract. Many persons have spoken of this.

Other points may be taken up later, including the way the book clubs got hold of the book weeks too soon.

I am writing very frankly, because, in the past few years, you have been so much more to me than a publisher. You and your Ellen are numbered among my close and dear friends; and I feel that you both understand the struggle of these weary months better than anyone else is able to do. For this reason, among others, I want you to keep this book in your hands and treat it as if it were your own.

I look forward eagerly to having you read the manuscript, and I shall so enjoy seeing Ellen and you.

Affectionately yours,
[No signature]

[2] Anne Morrow Lindbergh's *North to the Orient*, 1935.

TO ALFRED HARCOURT

Richmond, Thursday [No other date]

Dear Alfred:

I neglected to sign my letter yesterday, because the doctor stopped me, so this is merely a postscript. Also, I may mention in the beginning, I am writing it in bed and in a state of irritation, two things I try to avoid.

But I have just glanced at the announcement of my new book, and I very decidedly object! I stood this kind of thing with *Vein of Iron,* and I shall not submit so quietly this time. I refuse absolutely to be included in groups of popular piffle, or to play an "also" to anything so trivial as *Mrs.*

Miniver.[1] If your publicity department is headed this way, then please treat me as generously as you treated Sinclair Lewis, and *Let Me Go.*

This is the first time I have ever written to you when I was angry, and I hope you will make a note of it for your memory-book.

As always,

ELLEN GLASGOW

It is not too late even now to break contracts if anybody in your firm wishes to do so, and prefers "ping pong balls" as you observed. Anyway, I am not amused.

[1] By Jan Struther. Harcourt, Brace, 1940.

TO HELEN K. TAYLOR

[Richmond,] December 17th, 1940

Dear Miss Taylor:

Thank you for your letter. I enjoyed your visit very much —that day was a bright spot in my illness—and I wish you would come again. Has Mr. Harcourt gone to Florida? I am just finishing my book, and I hope to send the four last chapters by the first of next week. Will it be possible to publish the book the end of February. I am eager to do this. After all, the novel is not so long, only 510 pages of Miss Bennett's typing.

The first part of this description is very good. I think, however, that there is too much detail, and the description of the characters does not give, to me, the right impression. Why do publishers feel obliged to go into detail? Nowhere is there suggested the chief theme of the novel: an analysis of the modern mind and temperament in a single community. The word "background" must not be used for the Negroes. That sounds too familiar. The colored figures present a theme in themselves—a minor theme, perhaps, but still a theme which is closely woven into the major theme of the book. And (how

I hate to pick flaws, but you asked me to be frank!) the quality of evasive idealism was confined to the earlier generation, and passed away with it. Also, Roy is not "tough." I think "stronger" a better word for her. Toughness is my abomination. With these changes, I think the descriptions may stand, if we have to have definite portraits in the announcement.

As always sincerely,
E.G.

I have dashed this off before going to work. The doctor gives me only an hour and a half. . . .

TO HELEN K. TAYLOR

[Richmond,] December 19th, 1940

Dear Miss Taylor:

Many thanks for your understanding letter. I had hoped to see Alfred and Ellen when they went South; but it is good news indeed to know that you and Frank Morley[1] will come down after the New Year. Even if the doctors will not let me get up, I shall love to talk with you both.

You will be glad, I know, to hear that I have finished my book. I shall send the last four chapters as soon as I have had time to revise them.

Your ideas about the jacket seem to me right. This design is very attractive, but it has too much the look of a country scene or a village. It should give the outline of a city, with houses closer together, not separated by so many trees. There are far too many birds, and the birds are not city birds. The wings are too long for pigeons, and the shape is not what it should be. I think, also, that so much white on the jacket is rather too startling. However, I do not see how this can be entirely avoided. On the whole, I think it is not right—I mean, the design. If I saw the jacket in a shop, I should

---

[1] Member of Harcourt, Brace firm and later named as one of Miss Glasgow's literary executors.

assume that the novel was about the country, or perhaps a village; but we wish to convey the idea of a city scene, even if it is a small city.

As always sincerely yours,

E.G.

. . . The jacket design grows on me, and I think it is both striking and attractive. Still, it will not do for this book unless it is made to look like a city. The birds, too, must be changed.

TO ELEANOR AND VAN WYCK BROOKS

Richmond, December 22nd, 1940

Dear Eleanor and Van Wyck,

You have been much in my thoughts, and I send you my affectionate greeting and a blessing for each separate day in the New Year.

After reaching home, I had another collapse, and the doctors have made me stay in bed since the twenty-first of October! But I sit up an hour or a little more every morning, and, at last, I have been able to finish my book. I think it is good, and I hope you will like it. Alfred Harcourt says it is my best work. I cannot tell about this, but Heaven and I alone know what it has cost me!

Are you coming South again? How I should love to see you! That afternoon in New York makes a bright place in my thoughts.

I am so deeply interested in Van Wyck's next book. Not long ago, propped up in bed, I read over again both *The Flowering* and *Indian Summer*.[1] How superb they are when read together!

Have I told you that the title I finally chose for my novel is the first that ever occurred to me? I put it aside, forgot it,

[1] *The Flowering of New England*, 1936, and *New England: Indian Summer*, 1940, both published by Dutton.

[*275*]

and then found it again—"In This Our Life." You remember Meredith's "When hot for certainties in this our life." [2]

My love to you both,

ELLEN

[2] George Meredith's *Modern Love,* sonnet 50.

TO HELEN K. TAYLOR

[Richmond,] December 25th, 1940

Dear Miss Taylor:

I am wishing for you the very happiest Christmas, and a special blessing for every day in the year.

The jacket and the description are both exactly right. I could make no improvements, and do not think, please, that I changed a word of it. It happened, however, that James Branch Cabell came to say good-bye before leaving for Florida, and he arrived when I was reading your letter. He had just read the galleys, and he was very enthusiastic. So he insisted upon changing "culmination" to "masterpiece," because, he said, the culmination of a life work sounded too much as if I had ended. I think I *have* ended, or am ending, but he is convinced there is more creative effort still alive in me. Anyway, accept the change or not, as you think best. It is all very good, and I am perfectly satisfied.

The jacket is perfect for this novel, and exactly what I had in mind when I spoke to you and Alfred.

The final chapters go off tomorrow, by registered post. I am proud of this ending and of my own too. . . .

I am looking for you and Frank Morley after the first of the year.

As always sincerely yours,

E.G.

I am obliged to go slowly with the galleys. Will you see that corrected page proofs are sent to me. I am sending my only revised copy of the last chapters.

TO CHARLES HANSON TOWNE

Richmond, December 30th, 1940

Dear Charley,

You will never know how much I appreciated and loved your letter, written from Boston, about *Barren Ground*. It came while I was quite ill, and at the very time, too, when I was repeating to myself your verses to England. I saw them in a paper, and I liked to say them to myself when I was too weak to talk.

The trip from Castine was very hard on me. I have been kept in bed ever since, though, for the past six weeks the doctor has allowed me to sit up for an hour or a little longer each morning. It is not easy for me to work in bed, but I have been able to finish my book, and I am now submerged in galleys. . . . My heart has gone into it, and I know it is good. Don't you have sometimes this simply inevitable sense of what you are doing?

I am so much interested in your play—or your part in the *Life with Father*. If you should come to Richmond, do not fail to send me word a little ahead of your coming.

I am so glad that you should have selected the pages in *Barren Ground* that I like best. It amazes me how few persons saw what I was doing when the book was published. The reviewers praised it, but they did not understand what they were praising. It had, too, an unusual success in England. But only in later years has the novel really come into its own place.

When you see my dearest Leonora, will you give her my unchanging love and admiration.

And to you, dear Charley, a special blessing for every day in the new year.

Affectionately yours,

ELLEN

[277]

TO J. DONALD ADAMS

Richmond, January 20th, 1941

Dear Don,

. . . Since October I have not been allowed to go down-stairs or to stay up more than two hours a day. My heart has not improved, but I am still convinced that only an Act of God will really kill me. However, dying day by day, with the mind still enkindled with light is not an agreeable proc-ess. The doctors say I may get better, but not well or strong.

I know you will be glad to know that my book is at last finished, and I am now working, under tremendous diffi-culties, on the last proofs. I have put all my strength into it, and I think I have done nothing more vital, or, strange as it may sound at the end of life, more emotional. I am eager to have you read it, and I am eager, too, to see you again. . . .

Affectionately always, dear Don,

ELLEN

I wish so much that Charles Poore[1] could review my book in the daily column, instead of Ralph Thompson,[1] but I sup-pose this could not be arranged.

What I look forward to most expectantly is your review in the Sunday *Times* [*Book*] *Review*. I know you will like the book.

I kept this back, thinking I would rewrite it, and leave out the part about the reviews—but I have not been able to write.

Anyway, you will understand, for some weeks I have had a curious feeling that you were (or are) troubled, and I should like to hear that you are still happy and well.

[1] Book reviewers for the daily New York *Times*.

TO BESSIE ZABAN JONES

Richmond, February 25th, 1941

Dearest Bessie:

I was so glad to have your letter and to feel in touch with you again. How often I have wished that you were nearer and were helping me over those proofs. I had to do them in bed, with my mind all confused, and when at last I was through with galleys and page proofs, I felt that they had very nearly, if not quite, put an end to me. But in a few days I shall have my advance copies, and one of the earliest will go off to Howard and you.

I hope you will like it. After keeping alive to finish this book, I felt, after dealing with it in print, that I might, with far less trouble, have passed on in August. This, I suppose, is the inevitable recoil from driving myself while I was ill. Since I came home in October the doctor has not allowed me to go downstairs. . . . But no more of complaining.

How I should love to see you both. Do write to me.

Devotedly,

ELLEN

TO STANLEY YOUNG [1]

Richmond, March 13th, 1941

Dear Mr. Young:

It is always a pleasure to hear from you, for I have by no means forgotten your visit to Richmond. I hope you may come again soon.

I cannot trust my judgment about this broadcasting matter.[2] You have handled the moving picture rights so splen-

---

[1] An editor at Harcourt, Brace.
[2] A reference to Warner Brothers' request for inclusion of limited broadcasting rights in their motion-picture contract for *In This Our Life*.

didly that I would rather leave it to you and do what you decide.

However, it has occurred to me that this right to broadcast has no beginning or end in the matter of time. Heaven knows I should not wish the movie people to go on the air until the book is established! Might we say, "after three months from publication"? Or something like that?

I suppose it is futile to suggest that the movie shall make a kind of "Mr. Chips" picture, treating Asa Timberlake as the major figure, instead of playing up the subject of callow youth or broken marriages?

As soon as I hear from you, I shall sign the agreements according to your advice.

You have been wonderful.

Sincerely yours,

ELLEN GLASGOW

I confess that I shrink from a photoplay, without acting, written in Hollywood. Is it possible to avoid that?

TO VAN WYCK BROOKS

Richmond, March 15th, 1941

Dear Van Wyck,

You and Eleanor will never know how much your visit meant, and means, to me. It was perfect; nothing to compare with it has happened in this winter of gloom and illness. I was tremendously cheered and helped.

All of us surrendered to Eleanor's charm. She is lovely in every way, and (unlike so many other lovely women) she has that hard, fine grain of intelligence which I value so highly in women and so seldom find in the South, where, I sometimes feel, there is more sweetness than sense.

As for you—everything you said of my book was a tonic. I had felt wilted and drooping, but immediately I began to bloom and pick up. There is no one whose opinion I value so much, for I regard it as praise from the master.

Now I am hoping to see you in New York or in Maine.

My love to you both. This is just a word to welcome you home.

As always,
ELLEN GLASGOW

But I did not hear half as much of your own book as I wanted to hear. I seemed to have talked too much of myself.

TO STANLEY YOUNG

Richmond, March 18th, 1941

Dear Mr. Young:

It was a pleasure to have your understanding letter Saturday, and now there is another note from you this morning. I sent the agreements to you by Helen because I was not able to write on Sunday.

It is good news that you may make a suggestion to Warner Brothers. If only they will emphasize the father and daughter theme, and bring out the character of Asa with some subtle handling. An artistic, and certainly a more unusual, picture could be made from this angle.

But a cold chill ran down my spine when I read in some newspaper that Errol Flynn would take the leading part. Lord deliver us!

Anyway, you have been splendid. I am so glad you really like this book, and I appreciate all that you tell me.

Do come again.

Sincerely yours,
ELLEN GLASGOW

TO HELEN K. TAYLOR

Richmond, March 28th, 1941

Dear Helen:

If you should quote from that hotchpotch piece in *Time,* will you use one phrase that I like very much.

"Her novels are no more provincially Virginian than *The Trojan Women* is Trojan. Their major theme is human struggle."

And, oddly enough, this writer is almost the only reviewer to perceive that the major theme of *I.T.O.L.* is that "tragedy is never in defeat but in surrender."

But I chuckled at the bland pronouncement that, in spite of "unconventional thinking" . . . "she has lived a thoroughly conventional spinster's life in the big grey, brick, Georgian house."

If this is true, how does the reviewer know it? And as a matter of verity, the one experience I have never had is the life of a conventional spinster, whatever that is. Or a conventional life of any other nature.

This reminds me, as our orators would say, of an obliging friend of my own generation (in Richmond), who, when he was sixteen years old, went into court and swore that to his "own personal knowledge a certain Southern gentleman had wilfully deserted his wife's bed and board." And for nearly another generation the husband's family refused to speak to the too obliging witness, who was telling what everybody suspected and nobody knew.

Affectionately yours,

E.G.

TO VAN WYCK BROOKS

Richmond, March 28th, 1941

Dear Van Wyck:

My book was published yesterday, and I must tell you again how proud and pleased I was to see your comment at the head of the announcement. It was so good of you, and it is all a part of the happiness you and Eleanor have given me. I feel, strangely enough, as if this friendship contained the element, not of time, but of eternity—yet I do not believe in any eternity of the conscious ego—or, rather, in any continuing identity. Still the feeling is here.

But knowing you two dear persons has brought an awareness of happiness into a life that has known little but sadness —except in my friendships.

It is queer how few reviewers ever see what one regards as the chief, or only, meaning in a work of the imagination. Charles Poore thinks *In This Our Life* has "hope alone" at the end. Lewis Gannett thinks "the end is without hope." But you understood, through insight, that the meaning was (or is) failure lies not in defeat but in surrender to life. And no one, probably, but you and Eleanor will see that the whole theme was condensed into Roy's cry in the last paragraph. "I want something to hold by! I want something good!" All through her confusion and blind groping she was moving toward that search for "something good," and all through the book I was writing with that cry in my mind.

I hope you have been able to settle down, but I know it takes time to find a cleared space after research into history.

I never thanked you for selecting *The Sheltered Life* for translation. But I meant to thank you, and I do now.

My love to you both—

Affectionately yours,

ELLEN GLASGOW

[*283*]

TO CARL VAN VECHTEN

Richmond, April 3rd, 1941

Dear Carlo:

Your letter did me a world of good. I send my affectionate greetings to Fania and to you. How I wish I might see you soon!

As always affectionately,

ELLEN

I am so glad you feel about my book as you do. My life and all my will power went into it, and after rewriting most of it in proof, while I was ill in bed, I thought I was really finished forever. You may be interested to know that the Negro family was taken very nearly from life. You remember that distinguished old lady in a lace cape at my party a few years ago. She and her sister between them made my Minerva, and her grandmother, who died long before I was born, was my mother's Mammy. I was sorry you could not get a photograph of Aunt Roberta. She did not live with me, but she always came to help me with my parties.

TO HUDSON STRODE

Richmond, May 22nd, 1941

Dear Hudson:

If only I could tell you how much I enjoyed your letter! All winter I have been ill, as you know, and a letter like yours made me feel as if I were really out in the sunshine. I like everything you say of my book.

In a few days now we are leaving for our usual summer in Maine. (I forgot to say "if nothing prevents," but so many things have prevented of late, that I apologize to the Fates and the Furies together.) I have taken my same house at Castine, and I am longing for the green cleanliness of Maine.

My address, after a week or ten days in New York, will be simply Castine, Maine.

Yes, I feel as you do about the latest Cather story.[1] It was a bitter disappointment, for I love *Shadows on the Rock*[2] and several others. But I simply could not accept her Virginian background. It was all wrong and artificial, and so many details were false to the customs of the valley. Only the mountains were true. And, like you, I thought the technique was inadequate to the subject; but, unlike you, I considered the reviews absurdly laudatory. Please let this go no further. I make a rule not to say what I think about my contemporaries—not until I am dead, anyway, and can speak from the grave.

My love to Thérèse.

Affectionately yours,

ELLEN GLASGOW

[1] Willa Cather, *Sapphira and the Slave Girl*, Knopf, 1940.
[2] Knopf, 1931.

TO VAN WYCK BROOKS

Castine, June 16th, 1941

Dear Van Wyck:

This is just a word to tell you how much it meant to me to see you and dear Eleanor in New York. Every time I am with the two of you beloved friends, you come closer into the warm and loving circle of the people who matter most. I shall miss the thought of your being in Maine, but I understand that you must keep in your garden this summer.

The trip was rather hard on me, and I have had little strength since I reached here, in spite of the glorious air and the lovely views from my sun porch and my front windows. This cottage is lifted above the town and the bay, but we look down on blue water and across blue water to still bluer hills.

Of all the seasons, June is the month for Maine. The

country is so fresh that it might have been created at dawn, and blessed by its Creator. The lilacs are in full bloom, white and purple, and the big bush at my back door is covered with purple fragrance.

The world news weighs more heavily in the midst of this peace and loveliness of the earth. If only Man the Killer could cease from his killings and his lust for destruction.

Carrie and I agreed that you spoke more clearly and convincingly of the war than anyone we had heard, and when you have a free moment I wish you would try to make us understand why our attitude appears to be changing. Why have we given so little help after promising so much? The Lend-Lease bill, which seemed to us a mountain, begins to look like a molehill.

Well, I have given out—or my hand has. Do not stop your work to answer this, but think of me—you and Eleanor—when you are in your garden, among all the new flowers and the old. I hope Eleanor's transplanted plants have thrived beautifully.

My love to you both as always,

ELLEN

TO MARJORIE KINNAN RAWLINGS

Castine, July 24th, 1941

My very dear Marjorie:

I cannot tell you how much your letter meant to me—and still means. It came last night after a trying day, and it brought a thrilling sense of friendship and sympathy.

That was an extraordinary dream, and it was the more extraordinary because you have been so frequently in my mind since I have been at Castine. It was singular that the cold, and my cutting ice in geometrical patterns, should have come in. Ever since I finished *In This Our Life* I have felt as if I were drifting in an icy vacuum toward something—or

[*286*]

nothing. I wonder whether other writers have this sense of being drained and lost and surrounded by emptiness whenever they have finished a book. Of course, my illness and five years of work that was like pushing against a physical obstacle may have intensified this feeling of being swallowed up in the void.

But the dearest part of your dream was the way you brought me in and told me I must do no more cutting of ice in the roadway. And the warmth of the red curtains and the valance! Even the way James popped in and asked what we were up to had the accent of reality. I am so glad you wrote me about it.

Ever since you came to see me, so strong and warm and vital, I have felt very near to you, and you have had your own chosen place in my life, just as I had in the house of your dream. I am tremendously interested in the new book,[1] and I know it will be good when you let it go away from you. But there is a kind of slow agony, after the first rush of impulse, in bringing a book into the world. I shall send my helpful wishes to you every day, with the hope that you may feel them. You must keep well and not have a return of the hospital.

No, there is not a great chance of my ever seeing Florida. I, too, went into the hospital when I came through New York, and I heard yet once again that I had "absolutely no cardiac reserve strength." Well, no matter. My heart has served me hard and long, and I think a rest has been earned.

My love to you, dear Marjorie,

ELLEN

[1] *Cross Creek,* Scribner, 1942.

TO VAN WYCK BROOKS

Castine, August 23rd, 1941

Dear Van Wyck:

Ever since I read "Primary Literature and Coterie Literature" [1]—and I read it carefully three times—my mind has been full of it. It is amazing to me how you are able to carry your learning without the slightest appearance of effort or heaviness. The criticism is superb, and it has come at the exact moment when it is needed. I hope and believe that your challenge to futility in so much contemporary writing will alter the whole tone, and the direction, of American criticism.

As you know, I am not sanguine about our destiny, for I have not, like Margaret Fuller, made the great acceptance.[2] But I believe in a gallant endeavor, whether or not we are ever to come into a finer inheritance. I agree with everything you said, and I trust in the Lord of battles to give you the victory over the little thinkers and the destroyers of Milton. How I wish I could have written an adequate comment upon your masterly study! But I have been ill again, and utterly incapable of organizing my work. It looks now as if I were over and done with for good and all. . . .

The comment I sent Dr. [Louis] Finkelstein was so inadequate I almost threw it away. But you will see from it how heartily I appreciated your paper. I am ashamed, too, that I did not know he is the president of the Jewish Theological Seminary. My excuse is that I live in the provinces.

My love to Eleanor and to you. I cannot tell you how much you have both meant to me, and how happy I have been in your friendship.

As always,

ELLEN

[1] An article published later, in somewhat altered form, in Mr. Brooks's *Opinions of Oliver Allston*. Dutton, 1941.

[2] Margaret Fuller is reported to have said that she accepted the Universe.

You were angelic to write that long interesting letter in the midst of your work. But do not let me break in on the book.

TO ALFRED HARCOURT

Richmond, October 29th, 1941

Dear Alfred:

The answer to Mr. Madden's[1] pleasant letter is emphatically:—NO.

I have never thought that *The Sheltered Life* could be made into a play without destroying the subtle values of the novel. After a year's pressure, I yielded to Miss Turney's[2] wish to make a dramatization; but I yielded with a most definite understanding that the play should be submitted *only to Miss [Katherine] Cornell.* I urged Miss Turney not to undertake so difficult a task. For my part, I have never wished to turn the book into a play. I think novels and plays are two separate forms of art.

Since I came home I have had a rather bad relapse, and the doctor here thinks I overplayed my hand in New York. But I am trying to look up a few things for *A Certain Measure,*[3] and I hope to send the final proofs back to you in a day or two. Of course, I had no reference books in Castine, and equally of course, I find all my references were correct.

You will recall your promise not to bring out any other book of mine in the spring. If we cannot release this book by the first of February, please hold it over until early autumn —when the world may be even more overturned than it is at this season.

I find in going over the proofs that I ought to have put *The Sheltered Life* before *The Romantic Comedians.* If this

[1] Richard Madden, play agent.

[2] Catherine Turney, playwright.

[3] Miss Glasgow's volume of literary criticism (Harcourt, Brace, 1943), for which she rewrote the prefaces to the Virginia Edition of her novels and added a chapter on *In This Our Life.*

change does not make much extra work, I should like to have it made in the final proofs. If it does mean extra work, just let it stand as it is. All the other changes improve the text, and I hope they can be made. I have tried hard, and worked my mind, to keep within the space of the lines.

It was good seeing you, and I wish you and Ellen could have been at the gay lunch at Robert's.

Affectionately,

ELLEN

Will you please have somebody return to me the manuscript of *In This Our Life*. I have promised it to a collector, though I fail to see why anyone should wish to keep typed copies.

TO BLAIR ROUSE

Richmond, December 29th, 1941

My dear Mr. Rouse:

Your visit was a pleasure I should not like to have missed. Indeed, I enjoyed so much our discussion of books and things in general that I neglected to ask you please not to quote directly anything I may have said in admiration of (or in lack of admiration of) living writers. This sounds trivial, I know, but one or two incidents in the past have made me a little shy of repeated words.

A part of the tree in this bookplate, the twisted bole, perhaps, was drawn from the old "Blair tree" of your ancestors.[1]

I hope you had a pleasant Christmas, and I hope, too, that the coming year will bring you many rewards.

Sincerely yours,

ELLEN GLASGOW

[1] The tree in Miss Glasgow's bookplate was probably modeled on the tree growing between the graves of Commissary James Blair and his wife in the churchyard at Jamestown, Virginia.

TO FANIA MARINOFF VAN VECHTEN

Richmond, December 31st, 1941

Dearest Fania:

In spite of the war and the world and the universe, your charming card brought me a happy moment. How dear it was of you to remember me!

I send you and Carlo a very special blessing for each day and hour of the coming year.

With love always,

ELLEN

Will you tell Carlo I have had this old house searched, and we found nothing worth sending him. My manuscripts, all in long hand, were burned, I suppose, in 1911, when I left Richmond, as I thought for good, after a tragic experience. I can give him books, but not first editions. Even the manuscript of *In This Our Life* is a copy made by Miss Bennett. Not a correction was made in my handwriting. I asked Harcourt to return it, thinking I might send it to Carlo, but I found it was not worth keeping. It is a mystery where all my original writing in long hand has gone. The time has come when I regret that I was so careless.

TO FRANK MORLEY

Richmond, February 7th, 1942

Dear Frank:

Could you or Stanley Young gently remind Warner Brothers that my second payment on the movie was to be paid in January. I thought this was the agreement, and I have depended on that amount to meet my income tax. Taxes will take every penny I receive, and, without this sum, I shall have to sell my best securities.

It is a hard world, isn't it? Yet all the pictures from England are smiling. For my part, I think they rather overdo the cheerful grin.

As always,

E.G.

I fear I am not finished yet. Another book has been trying to push out of the depths, and I am trying, just as hard to keep it submerged.

TO ELLEN AND ALFRED HARCOURT

Richmond, February 13th, 1942

Dear Ellen and Alfred:

It was good of you to write to me, and I appreciate your letters. . . .

Certainly, I feel that you have chosen wisely.[1] If I had the choice of a farm or a publishing house, I should choose the farm, and I am sure I should never look back. For you and yours, I am glad, and I believe you both will be happier with that future ahead of you.

The hardest thing for me is the sense of impermanence. All passes; nothing returns. With my own future so uncertain, I suppose, I should feel it less; but I had come to depend upon Alfred, and I find it difficult to adjust myself to a sudden change. However, this is only in keeping with a world in upheaval.

You have both been lovely to me always, and I value your friendship more than I can tell you.

Devotedly,

ELLEN GLASGOW

I enjoyed so heartily Ellen's beautiful letters, and I hope she will write to me when she is not too busy. Florida is the place for you now. How I envy you the golf course by the sea!

---

[1] The reference is to Mr. Harcourt's then recent withdrawal from active participation in Harcourt, Brace and Company.

TO ALFRED HARCOURT

Richmond, March 1st, 1942

Dear Alfred:

You will never know how much your visit meant to me. Ellen and you were both so sympathetic and understanding, and my talk with you stimulated my drooping creative faculty. Before you left, I began to feel that the new book was really worth while, even in this terrible world; and I am now letting it grow and ripen in my imagination. You have always had that special influence.

Your notes to the firm were just right—right in what you said and in what you did not say.

My love to you both, and thank you for coming to see me.

Devotedly,

ELLEN GLASGOW

TO MARJORIE KINNAN RAWLINGS

Richmond, April 20th, 1942

My very dear Marjorie:

I have just finished *Cross Creek,* and I am overwhelmed by the sheer breath-taking magic of the book. The writing seems less a vehicle of expression than a luminous web, which captures and holds some vital essence of a particular place and moment in time: heat, light, color, scents, and sounds. Even the primitive enjoyment of killing, from which my inadequately covered nerves are inclined to flinch, I recognize as an essential part of the truth. Too well I know the cruelty that runs through the beauty of all things Southern —perhaps, though I am less sure of this, through the beauty of all things human.

But, as an interpretation of a special aspect of life, *Cross*

[*293*]

Creek appears to me to be flawless. Not that this, or any other book, can ever take, for me, the place of *The Yearling.* There is no Jody in *Cross Creek,* and no Flag. For the rest, I would add nothing, and take nothing away. You have up-rooted a landscape, with its tendrils still living, and you have made it over into a book that would bleed if you tore it apart. How could you keep up the rhythm, page after page, without a pause or a break?

My favorite chapters, I think, are "For This Is an En-chanted Land" and "The Magnolia Tree." I, too, am a tree worshipper, and after that heart failure in Maine, when I was thought to be dying, I lay for weeks gazing at the top of a single tall pointed fir.

I wish I were able to write more—or, better still, to talk with you for a whole long day. But, after all, what could I say but the same thing, over and over? You have written a gorgeous book.

With my love and admiration,

ELLEN GLASGOW

Oh, one incident did hurt me. With your deep sympathy for the human species, even for the utterly undeserving, like Leroy, how could you bring yourself to betray the confidence and the good-will of the yellow catch-dog? After reading that passage, I laid the book aside for a few hours, but you write so vividly that, even then, I could not put the story out of my mind. I suppose he is dead now, and it is too late to make amends in his old age. But so much good will to be wasted in a world where other beings have so little!

TO DONALD C. BRACE [1]

Richmond, May 4th, 1942

My dear Mr. Brace:

Thank you for telephoning me this afternoon. It was thoughtful of you, for I had not heard of the award.[2]

But I forgot the important part of my message to you. Please print and sell more copies. Publishers tell me that this prize is excellent for advertising purposes. I think it was Eugene Saxton[3] who said they sold fifty thousand copies of some novel on the strength of this award. It seems silly to me, but I hope you will follow that example. I could never understand why *I.T.O.L.* should have sold less well than any of my other books, and I confessed to you that I did *not* think a superlative job was done with the publicity part.

Except for this one complaint, my publishers are perfect.

As always sincerely yours,

E.G.

[1] Cofounder of Harcourt, Brace and Company.
[2] Apparently the first news Miss Glasgow received of the Pulitzer Prize award for *In This Our Life*.
[3] Editor in chief at Harper and Brothers.

TO VAN WYCK BROOKS

Richmond, May 7th, 1942

Dear Van Wyck,

All this dreary winter my dear Eleanor and you have been in my affectionate thoughts, but I have not felt equal to writing. Now, it is a joy to have your letter. The response of my friends is the one thing that makes me feel this award is not "too little and too late" for me.

It is good news indeed to hear that all goes well with you.

This means, I know, that Eleanor has had no return of pneumonia.

I had hoped for a glimpse of you in New York; but the conditions are so disturbed that Castine appears to be out of bounds for this summer. I have rented a house there, though the place is thirty-five miles from the station; and without a car living would be difficult. So the chances are that, like Brer Terrypin, I shall be "lounjun 'roun' en' suffer'n'" in Richmond all summer. The worst of it is that I shall miss my brief stay in New York. That is the only chance I have of seeing my friends there, and it means a great deal to me to have Eleanor and you and a few others come in for an afternoon.

With more love to you both than this scrawl can possibly convey,

As always,

ELLEN GLASGOW

TO DONALD C. BRACE

Richmond, May 9th, 1942

Dear Mr. Brace:

Will you give this suggestion your best attention, and if you agree with the idea, act upon it immediately.

In order to correct a rather general misconception, I think it would be well to give the last chapter of *A Certain Measure* to *The Saturday Review* for one of the next numbers. If you approve of the plan, will you or Frank call up Miss Loveman, or one of the other editors, and make the arrangement. It ought to be printed immediately, and I mention *The Saturday Review* because that paper has always been my best friend.

Will you, if this idea is worked out, *send me* a proof of that last chapter. I have no copy, and I wish to add several paragraphs *before sending it to* the *S.R.L.* Would it be possible to include these additional paragraphs in the pages of the book? I confess I am irritated by the way the minor character of Stanley is allowed to take the dominant place; and I suppose the movie will encourage this misconception.

In speaking of the book, we must not call it a book of prefaces, which it is not. It is really a volume of literary criticism. The prefaces have been rewritten, and a last chapter added. It is this chapter on *In This Our Life* that I wish published, and of course, since Scribner does not include this book, we should not infringe upon any copyright.

I hope I may add these extra paragraphs. It might mean adding a page to the book. This messy letter is a disgrace, but I am having a bad day.

As always,

E.G.

TO MARGARET MITCHELL

Richmond, May 17th, 1942

Dear Margaret Mitchell:

You were twice a dear to telegraph me, and I appreciate your message. Only the response of my friends (you are among them) has made me feel that this award is not too little and too late.

I have a charming recollection of your flitting in and spending an hour by my bedside. Now, praised be the Lord, I am up again; but the winter was far from a good season.

With you, I hope, life has not been so difficult. You looked happy, and that means more than one ever imagines.

Affectionately,

ELLEN GLASGOW

SECTION VI

June 26, 1942—November 5, 1945

TO BESSIE ZABAN JONES

Castine, June 26th, 1942

Dearest Bessie:

Your letter came just as I was leaving Richmond, and how delighted I was to have news of you and Howard! My winter had been very painful, and the intolerable heat of summer in Richmond is something one must feel in order to understand what it means. That about finished me, and I put myself in the place of all the other ill persons who ought to escape, and cannot.

How strong you are to look so small and childlike—yes, and innocent of the world. After your service with the strange and the lost on our shores, I cannot help feeling that anything else is too much to ask of you. I am not in the least reconciled to your being a nurse's aid. That sounds even worse than being a nurse; and the nursing profession, however noble in act, has never appealed to me. Even if, as you say, the bed pan has not changed its shape, it has remained for me an abomination. In the hospital, it was the one thing I successfully rebelled against; for it seemed to me to put the ultimate degradation upon human dignity, if there exists such a state. But, then, I wasn't born noble. I can only stand and gasp, and admire and envy nobility in others.

And you, lovely and prim-looking and eager-hearted little creature, why can't you stop doing good for a season, and sit back and let the mad world be damned if it wants to be damned?

How I wish I could see you. An eternity of change has come and gone since the Christmas week with the long talks and the egg-nog in Richmond. Life goes its own way in spite of us.

[*301*]

No, I did not see the movie of *I.T.O.L.*[1] The advertisements were enough to make me understand that Hollywood had filmed a different book, not mine at all, and had entirely missed the point of my novel. I hated the whole thing, but there were practical reasons why I had to let it be done. The sister conflict was, of course, a minor theme, and the character of Stanley a minor figure, who was treated objectively, from the first page to the last. The major theme, as I meant it, and you must have understood, was the conflict of human beings with human nature. In Asa and in Roy, I probed into this, but how brutally obvious one has to be in print to be comprehended. And how I dislike the obvious in any and in every form! Yet was the question too subtle? What is the essence, what is the spiritual quality, that will hold a man together after he has lost everything else?

Dearest love to you and to Howard when you write to him. If only you were both here in this sparkling blue air of Castine! After the intense heat, we entered the Arctic Circle, and the first night, with the stove on and a log fire in my bedroom, I slept under two blankets and two quilts. We came a day ahead and the house was just opened.

Do write again.

Devotedly,

ELLEN

[1] Released by Warner Brothers in May, 1942.

TO BESSIE ZABAN JONES

Castine, July 20th, 1942

Dear Bessie:

Your letter was delightful, and I cannot tell you how much I enjoyed it. As it happened, your comments on that maternity ward helped me to round out a paragraph I was writing. It was all so amusing, and your insight was so perversely acute.

What you tell me of Howard's study of my work makes me feel immensely proud and pleased and gratified all together. I only wish it were possible for me to go to Columbia and listen to his lecture. Do you think he might send me a copy?

All my life, or so it seems, something, usually frail health, has kept me from doing anything I really wanted to do. My one eager desire, as far back as I remember, has been to start out, quite alone, and go round the world by myself. Yet, though I have travelled a great deal, I have always been shielded and looked after, and advised and warned and retarded. For years, I was so sensitive about my deafness that I would not go into a shop unless someone was with me, and in earlier years I would not even see a caller alone. . . . I suffered from a morbid sensitiveness that was a kind of tepid Hell, and even now, I have not entirely got over it. My whole life has been a struggle not to be helped.

I don't know why I am writing you this. Your letter, which I have just reread, started a train of reflection; and I felt an impulse to assure you that there are more serious impediments to happiness than an enlarged conscience. I doubt, moreover, whether your analysis has not left out the chief element. You are, I think, singularly unselfish, and your sense of responsibility for the universe is probably an inherited misfortune. Didn't you have a righteous father or an over-righteous mother somewhere in the background? I had a father who believed that to disbelieve in Hell was the Great Refusal; but his orthodoxy merely sent me off on a new departure of heresy. Even as a child, I suspected that he *might* be to blame for my being one of ten children, but I certainly wasn't. Eight children before me had drained the vitality of my adorable mother, and in the years before I came the Reconstruction Acts combined with the struggle to rebuild a devastated region had worn her to a beautiful

[*303*]

shadow. So, whatever I brought into the world with me, it wasn't a conscience, and it wasn't enlarged.

Your letters invariably start an idea scampering out of its hole. Do write again, and tell me more of your hospital days. I hope with all my heart that I may see you and Howard before I turn back to Richmond. Everything is so upset nowadays that I cannot look ahead or make a sensible plan.

My love to you both,

ELLEN

I forgot to tell you that I am trying my hand [at] a short sequel to *In This Our Life*. So many readers missed the point of that book that I should like to do a less subtle approach. The broad pattern was meant to include the whole group consciousness of a community, using the ebb and flow, in a somewhat rambling stream, through different minds. My coloured people were very nearly, if not quite actual portraits of a family that had belonged to my mother's ancestors for over a hundred and fifty years. I particularly liked Minerva, who was a collective portrait of several sisters. But, of course, the theme holding the various elements together was the perpetual conflict of human beings with human nature. In Asa, I was depicting, not a failure in life, but a man in whom character, not success, was an end in itself.

But I am not sure that this sequel will ever be published.[1]

[1] This book, called *Beyond Defeat,* was not brought to completion.

TO FRANK MORLEY

Castine, August 11th, 1942

Dear Frank:

Thank you for the Forster lecture,[1] which I heartily enjoyed, and thank you, too, for the amusing book on the

[1] E. M. Forster's Rede lecture on Virginia Woolf, delivered in the Senate House, Cambridge, in May, 1941, and published (with a few additions) as a book by Harcourt, Brace in 1942.

"Pre-Raphaelite Tragedy." [2] The Lytton Strachey tradition in biography appears to be holding its own; and if it did nothing else, at least it punctured solemnity.

I should have written to you before this, but I had an annoying accident to my hand. A window fell on it, and I had to have three X-rays taken to prove no bones were broken. So this is an exercise with one finger. Fortunately, it was my left hand, but oddly enough, wearing a sling appears to make me lose my balance in walking. That sounds like Miss Fanny Squeers,[3] though it is a curious truth.

Castine is as lovely as ever, and the air is usually fine and bracing. The village seems to be inhabited entirely by old ladies, and I doubt whether I should recognize a man if I were to meet such a strange animal in the road. But the war fever burns. Old ladies are notoriously militant.

As ever sincerely,

E.G.

[2] *The Pre-Raphaelite Tragedy,* by William Gaunt. Harcourt, Brace, 1942.
[3] A character in *Nicholas Nickleby* by Charles Dickens.

TO FRANK MORLEY

Castine, August 26th, 1942

Dear Frank:

Your letter was sent to Richmond, but I am still at Castine, and I expect to stay here until September 27th.

Thank you for the book you sent with your letter. That has not been forwarded, and, I confess, I would rather have had the essays of Virginia Woolf.[1] Nevertheless, I am obliged.

This is one of those perfect autumn days that come only in Maine. The air is like chilled wine, sparkling with a blue haze of sunshine. Beyond our blue, rippling bay the hills are

[1] *The Death of the Moth and Other Essays,* Harcourt, Brace, 1942.

like crystal. I wished for you on our long walk in the woods this morning. It was my longest walk since my illness—two hours of peace and beauty in a war-maddened world. If only man had never been created, what a glorious earth there might have been. Or, having created man, if the Good God had chosen to leave out the anthromorphic delusion of grandeur.

I wrote you of the accident to my hand, which still troubles me. What could be more needless than having a window fall on one's fingers?

Unless my plans are changed by God or Hitler or another silly accident, I hope to see you in New York between September 28th and October 5th.

Affectionately yours,

E.G.

Yes, I love Dorothy Canfield.

TO ELLEN KNOWLES HARCOURT

Castine, September 15th, 1942

Dear Ellen:

It was delightful to have your intensely interesting letter telling me so many things I wished to know, and had been wondering about. I waited to answer it until I knew definitely where I should be in New York.

Now, after much uncertainty, I am planning to spend a week in New York, from September 28th until October 5th. I expect to stay at my old home, the Weylin, so will you telephone me what day will be convenient for you. Be sure to call up ahead, because, in spite of the doctors, I appear to be better; and though I am as thin as a shadow, I have recovered at least a part of my natural energy. I shall be out a good deal, I hope, on this visit.

You will never know how much I miss the knowledge that Alfred is an active member of the Harcourt, Brace firm.

Just knowing he was there and could be trusted to look out for me, meant a very great deal. But I am happy that he has found work he can enjoy, though I should rather imagine you both on the lovely farm, in the midst of that rolling country with the enchanted lights. When I see you I shall ask many questions, and I shall plead with you not to take a course in practical nursing. It seems to me that every friend I have is doing that, and it appears to me, too, to be about the most uninspiring job in the world. But, then anything that has to do with epidemics is a waking nightmare to me. I hate to think of your giving up your music. Why not keep your own private world of beauty and spirituality? Surely, not only the world, but the universe, will need both beauty and the spirit to be kept alive in the midst of "a darkling plain."

My love to Alfred, and to you as much as you can hold in your heart.

Devotedly,

ELLEN GLASGOW

TO BLAIR ROUSE

Richmond, October 14th, 1942

Dear Blair,

I was very glad to have your letter, and I meant to answer it before I left Castine and all the heavenly peace of that rippling bay. But autumn in the Maine woods kept me away from my desk. I wish you could have been brought there, by some miracle, to walk with me on the Indian trails, and to share that golden enchantment.

I hope you are happy—or as happy as the state of the world permits—in the Naval Training School. But I know you miss your other work, and I am hoping that the Navy will return you, in peace, to the profession of letters.

Meanwhile, keep in touch with me, and let me know when

[*307*]

you leave Cornell, and how you fare in the months of your training.

Blessings on you.

Sincerely yours,
ELLEN GLASGOW

TO BESSIE ZABAN JONES

Richmond, October 19th, 1942

Dear Bessie:

I am so sorry to hear of your brother's death, and I wish I had known you were in Richmond. About ten days ago I came home in a state of utter exhaustion, and I have been trying ever since to recover at least a degree of my Maine spirit.

This is just a hurried line to send you my sympathy. . . . But I understand how it is when a large family begins to break up. We were ten children, there were seven when I grew out of childhood, and now only three of us are still living.[1]

Tell Howard I share his anxiety over the defeat of the humanities. I suppose war and culture are eternally hostile; yet Jane Austen could write her quiet novels in the Napoleonic era and never so much as mention "the Corsican Monster."

The world, it appears, has become too small. We feel the nations closing in on us. What is the use? Must we wait in the hope of a joyful resurrection which may never come?

Thank you for telling me of the Kazin book.[2] Henry Canby is enthusiastic about it.

Always affectionately yours,
ELLEN

[1] Ellen, Rebe, and Arthur.
[2] Alfred Kazin, *On Native Grounds*, Reynal & Hitchcock, 1942.

TO VAN WYCK BROOKS

Richmond, November 5th, 1942

Dear Van Wyck:

I am grieved to hear of your loss, yet the end, after a life so well fulfilled, must come as naturally as the closing in of an autumn day. You will miss your stepfather's "keen and delightful mind," but those we mourn for and regret are the unfulfilled—are the lives that are broken off before they have really lived. From what you write, I can imagine no happier fate than that of "an innocent and guileless human being," who dies, at eighty-seven, without pain, in the midst of a war-torn world. Even so, there will be a vacancy in your world, which is not war torn.

I am still missing the invigorating tonic of a visit from Eleanor and you in New York. Why did that have to happen when I needed you both? After seeing you, I am always braced for the more or less tedious struggle with the empty mechanism of living. You will frown at this, because you have been able to keep a belief in the goodness and truth, and even in the beauty, of our lot on the earth. I admire you for your triumph, and I envy you whatever it is—a thing of priceless value—that gives you your serene fortitude, which is so close to happiness. But to think that I could not have that visit to Eleanor and you on your hilltop. And now, I may never again even see the skyline of New York!

I had not thought of going to Long Island, but, on a beautiful day, Nelson [Doubleday] sent for me, and I went to his place for lunch. I am very fond of him. Still, that, as you say of Dr. Mims's week-end, was ironical. For the one visit I had set my heart on making when I grew well enough was the visit to Eleanor and you. But, even if I did not see you,

[*309*]

I have just had the pleasure of writing your name for the gold medal of the Institute,[1] not that you care a fig for any medal.

I am reading the Kazin book, and I like very much his piece about me. He has told some of the truth, though not the whole truth—for who ever does that? Do you know the brave young man? I am tempted to send a note to him, but I have been so long acclimatized to the chill air of neglect that I have never learned how to behave properly in the milder climate of appreciation. Yes, Kazin has a brilliant insight. He proves this by making you his leading critical figure (and historian, too) even when he tries not to agree with you.

I rejoice to hear that you are at work on your new book, and I am eagerly awaiting it. Do you find it possible to write easily in New York? Anyhow, I am hoping that you may come South for a part of the winter. But the crowds and the military surroundings are making it hard for the natives, and for all of peaceful pursuits.

Will you thank Eleanor for her charming note. I always think of the word "charm" when I write of her, and it gladdens my heart to hear that she is well again.

Much love to you both. If only you knew how much better you make the world by simply being in it.

As always affectionately,

ELLEN GLASGOW

[1] American Institute of Arts and Letters.

TO FRANK MORLEY

Richmond, February 28th, 1943

Dear Frank:

It was angelic of you to write that long interesting letter, and I enjoyed every word of it. I had intended to answer it before this, but the setback with that inadequate organ, my heart, was sharper than I realized at the time. The doctor

[*310*]

made me give up everything, though I was really too weak even to give up, and finally I came through and began trying to put in fifteen minutes a day at my work. But the sequel goes on slowly and I may not feel, if it is ever finished, that it is worth publishing. So much for what I euphemistically call my life. . . .

At the moment, I must confess, any serious writing appears to me to be wasted. First of all, the only writing of the moment—the only writing that finds a reader—is war reporting, and the greater part of it I find pretty hopeless. But, from my point of view, writing that approaches an art has been successfully liquidated, at least "for the duration." The wave of the present will break at last, I suppose, but when that happens, probably I shall be no longer interested. If I could feel that the fashion helped our side in the war, it would be easy to endure the contemporary cult of rawness, and even the fascination of the repulsive, which is so much harder to understand than the fascination of sheer horror or of attractive immorality. But I have no belief that the sacrifice of standards in literature will be of the slightest help in winning the war.

But I am running away, and I have not the faintest idea where I may end. Do come down when you find it convenient, after the spring has made our country less forbidding. The terrible sleet storm simply slaughtered our trees.

Thank you for the books. Your niece has written a clever mystery.[1] I hope she will do others. As for *The Human Comedy*.[2] Well, we are an incredible people. There is no station, apparently, between "Tobacco Road" and "Pollyanna Junction." It was Samuel Butler, I think, who said, "Only extremes are logical, and extremes are always absurd." That remark sounds so modern that it is almost American.

[1] *Murder by Inches* by Stanley Hopkins, Jr., the pen name of Blythe Morley. Harcourt, Brace, 1943.
[2] By William Saroyan, Harcourt, Brace, 1943.

The Walter de la Mare story is delightful. Yes, my bears are seldom real bears, but they are the more dangerous for that.

I rejoice with you over the return of your nephew.

Thank you so very much for the set of proofsheets. Even if I do nothing else, I shall have left two good books to come after me—my autobiography, even if it requires rather drastic editing in certain chapters, may be the best that was in me. . . .

As always,

E.G.

TO HENRY SEIDEL CANBY

Richmond, March 2nd, 1943

Dear Henry:

I have just read your fine address[1] . . . and it has given me a rare sense of exhilaration. At last, to my delight, a scholar has taken part with the depressed humanities, and has refused to apologize for their defense. I agree with everything you say of an age that is governed by what we call "exact science" alone. There is no monster more destructive than the inventive mind that has outstripped philosophy.

My love to dear Lady, and to you. I was especially sorry to miss you both in New York, because it will be long, I regret to say, before I pass that way again. With the new year, my inadequate heart failed me again, and I have had to put aside the greater part of my pleasures in life.

I hope you have both kept well. Marjorie Rawlings wrote me of your happy visit to St. Augustine.

Sincerely yours,

ELLEN GLASGOW

[1] Printed as "The American Scholar and the War" in the *Saturday Review of Literature,* January 16, 1943.

June 26, 1942—November 5, 1945

TO VAN WYCK BROOKS

Richmond, March 22nd, 1943

Dear Van Wyck:

Twice in the past three days I have tried to write to you. . . .

Dear Eleanor and you have been much in my thoughts, and I have hoped all was well with you both. You can never know how your letter helped me in this dreary winter. It takes a stout heart to keep faith with life, but you have that blend of courage with hope, and your letters always lift up my more despondent spirit. . . .

But with you, I hope, the winter has not been so burdensome. I wonder if you are still in the country, and I trust you have the best possible news of your sons. . . . I have thought of your work so many times, and that is one reason I have hesitated to break in with a letter that was not cheerful in tone. For me, however, two world wars in one frail lifetime are overwhelming. An Englishwoman wrote me a few weeks ago that this seemed to her the saddest of all wars; and that may be true, I suppose, in the sense that we had believed war, as the last argument, had been left behind us in "the dark Backward and Abysm of Time." Do you, by the way, know a book I love bearing that title? It is a collection of essays by Henry W. Nevinson,[1] but you may know it.

Because the writing of the moment is unbearable to me, I have gone back to books I had loved before this madness broke over the world—or over our immediate part of the world. I have just reread *Oliver Allston,* and I found that it stood up superbly. All your work has that timeless quality which is, for me, the true test of literature. In an age like this, dedicated, in writing at least, to the glorification of the submental and the study, in fiction, of idiot psychology, the

[1] *In the Dark Backward,* Harcourt, Brace, 1934.

[*313*]

hope of the serious novel, as well as the hope of the liberal arts, must lie, I imagine, in the past or the future. For the first time in my long life, I feel that it does not matter whether or not one writes novels. I spent more than forty years believing that it mattered greatly, but the contemporary scene and contemporary standards of craftsmanship have destroyed, for me, the faith and the work of a lifetime. Nothing in the war has appalled me more than the victory of the inventive mind over the intellect, which is, really, the victory of what we call "exact science" over philosophy. It may appear a small thing in a physical conflict, but a world in which all intellectual standards have fallen has turned into a nightmare. In order to conquer the German cruelty must we first become like Germans? Or do we feast upon horrors because cruelty is an ineradicable instinct in all humanity? After this, it seems an anticlimax to return to the novel in modern life. But as far back as I can remember, or certainly from the age of seven, when I began to write, the novel has been, for me, an art or it has been nothing—and now, in my present mood, which of course may change, all such writing of the immediate moment has become less than nothing.

I am ashamed to send this confused and scrappy letter. My typewriter has run away with me, and you would not believe from this that I am still gay and still laughing at life —at everything, indeed, except cruelty. . . .

What you said of my work in your letter has been one of the bright spots, almost the only one, in this long winter. I am trying to do a short sequel to *In This Our Life* . . . but when one is too frail to fight, does anything else matter?

Tell me what you are writing. Has the war hurt you in spirit as it has hurt me? Or do you keep your high heart and Eleanor her angelic serenity?

My warm love to you both,

ELLEN GLASGOW

TO SIGNE TOKSVIG [1]

Richmond, March 26th, 1943

Dear Miss Toksvig:

It was kind of you to write to me, and I heartily enjoyed your letter. I feel as you do about the "dreadful callousness" and the cheapness of most contemporary standards, and I may confess that I resent the lack of a subtle sense of quality in current fiction.

This is modern, I suppose, but it is not, really, so new as one might imagine. I have done the work I wanted to do for the sake of that work alone; but always I have felt that I was pushing against the stream, and against immovable obstacles. If I had cared more for popularity than for craftmanship and simple truth telling, I should have given up long ago. But I held on, and I smile to think that it has taken me more than forty years to win my place in American letters.

I do not often write about myself, and I am telling you this because your letter is unusual, and, I think, extraordinarily sympathetic to my point of view.

No, I feel sure your friend is mistaken in what he says of the older residents in Newham. I know Virginia better than I know Connecticut, but I am positive that not one American of an older generation, or, for that matter, of any generation, would rather have Hitler than Roosevelt. I believe all Americans are determined to win this war, but some of them dislike the effort to introduce national politics into a world conflict.

I am slowly recovering from a long illness, and I may have to give up my usual summer in Maine and miss, also, my

[1] Danish-born writer and wife of the critic and historian Francis Hackett.

brief spring visit to New York, but if you should come to Virginia, I hope you will let me know.

Sincerely yours,

ELLEN GLASGOW

TO DOUGLAS SOUTHALL FREEMAN

Richmond, April 2nd, 1943

Dear Douglas:

By what miracle do you achieve this effortless mastery? Ever since Volume Two of *Lee's Lieutenants*[1] reached me, I have been completely absorbed. The terrible war of the present has reached into another, and it seems to me (I may be wrong) a less terrible war of the past. I may feel this because science, with the inventive mind, was not then in command.

But the amazing thing is that you have superbly reconstructed a period and the soul of a people. The Jackson of your book is more real than any general in our two modern world wars. Every figure comes to life, and is portrayed vividly. When that war was fought the superman still directed the battles. Each engagement in the field became a conflict of personalities.

I wish I could write more, but I have had a dreary winter, and after a sharp set back at the new year, I have felt unequal to the daily round of existence. I think so often of dear Inez[2] and of you with your splendid life, and I wish I might see you and be refreshed by your unfailing enthusiasm for work.

By the way, I wonder whether I may ask of you a very trivial thing. Have you still, and in a place that does not require search, that little picture of me, as a child, which Julia Sully gave you? I can't find another, and one is needed

[1] Three volumes, Scribner, 1942, 1944.
[2] Mrs. Freeman.

for [a] loan collection of photographs. If it is mislaid, just put this odd request out of your mind.

Affectionately yours,

ELLEN GLASGOW

I had meant to tell you how deeply moved I was by your description of Jackson's death. I seemed to be living through the scene and the anguish. You give just enough, and not one word too much of the inward struggle and of the subjective flow of time.

TO DONALD C. BRACE

Richmond, May 4th, 1943

Dear Mr. Brace:

Well, the winter has been a kind of nightmare; but at last, working not more than twenty minutes at a time, I have finished the rough draft of this sequel. Whether it will be worth publishing or not, I cannot say. But when I am not writing something, which means that I am existing, not living, in a vacuum, I might as well be dead in reality.

I was so glad to have your letter, and I have wished to answer it before this—only—only I have not been equal to more than those few minutes at the desk or the typewriter. But I have missed seeing my publishers. . . .

What do you think of publishing in this turmoil—I mean of publishing anything except war books, which have lost every remotest connection with letters? Should we attempt to bring out *A Certain Measure* next autumn? Or would it be merely a wasted effort? Does anybody read serious literary criticism, when literature, with the liberal arts and the humanities, cannot hold a place in modern society?—I have ceased to call the thing we have made, "civilization."

Or should we hold off from publishing for "the duration"?

I do not know what to think or say. I seem to be standing upon a crust so thin that it may break suddenly and send us all down into an abyss of primitive barbarism. What a world! Yet Mr. [Wendell] Willkie surveys with delight a world so small that it reminds me of the saddest of Negro Spirituals:

"There is no hiding place on earth . . . Oh, my Lawd,
    There is no hiding place on earth."

Well, this is a fine example of the kind of letter one should not write in war or in peace.

As always,

E.G.

TO DONALD C. BRACE

Richmond, May 10th, 1943

Dear Mr. Brace:

I was delighted to have your letter this morning. . . .

I am interested in what you say of publication prospects. I have a reason for wishing to bring out *A Certain Measure* before this short sequel appears. So many readers, perhaps careless readers, missed the point of *In This Our Life,* and a chapter, the last, in *A Certain Measure* clears up this misunderstanding. But I cannot really feel that any writing in this distracted period makes any difference. However that may be, the sequel would not be ready for next autumn. As for the book of criticism, I asked for no advance royalty on that, because of its uncertain sale, but I should have to have some advance on the fiction, though never, never until it is finished. Taxes have eaten well into my modest substance, and they are increasing daily.

I wish there were a chance of my being in New York this spring, or even in the autumn; but it looks now as if that were the vainest of hopes.

As always,

E.G.

By the way, there was an agreement with Alfred, when I

changed publishers, that my book should be the leading one on your list in any season—I mean, of course, in any season when one of my books is published.

TO SIGNE TOKSVIG

Richmond, May 21st, 1943

Dear Signe Toksvig:

Your letter gave me much pleasure, and you have been in my thoughts, though this wretched illness has prevented my writing. It is a sharp disappointment that you were not able to come to Richmond. I admire Francis Hackett; I know his work well; and it would be a delight to welcome you both to Virginia.

But the summer here is intolerable, and if I am sufficiently well, the doctors will make me leave for Maine before the middle of June. . . .

How I should enjoy reading your biography of Hans Andersen![1] I adored his fairyland as far back as I can remember, and I still love his stories, long after the fairy element has vanished from life. No, I am utterly ignorant of Swedenborg, but I shall look forward to your book[2] with great interest. Though I am not in the least "psychic," I have had always a deep interest in mysticism. For many years, I studied transcendental philosophies, and, oddly enough, in spite of a firm foundation of realism in my attitude toward life, I still turn to Plotinus when I seek wisdom and need consolation. Just here, I break off to remind you that materials for bindings will return after the war, and I shall expect, when peace, or what we call peace, has come, a copy of your life of Hans Andersen.

If the world holds together, my publishers are planning to

[1] *Life of Hans Christian Andersen*, Macmillan, 1940.
[2] *Emanuel Swedenborg, Scientist and Mystic*, Yale University Press, 1948.

bring out a new book of mine in the autumn. It seems to me a bad time, but one of the Harcourt, Brace firm came down yesterday, and almost persuaded me that all times are equally bad, mad, and sad for books, especially for a book that is not fiction, and has nothing to do with fighting. This is a work of literary criticism, personal and impersonal, and I shall hope to send you one of the early copies. I hope, too, that you will not find it unsympathetic. . . .

I have said—and this is true—that I am not in the least psychic; yet I have had in my life, very occasionally, the sense of a beginning friendship so strong that it seemed to hold the quality of recognition. Your first letter brought this to me, and I feel that we shall grow to understand each other, as if we had always been friends.

Sincerely yours,
ELLEN GLASGOW

TO CLARA CLAASEN [1]

Richmond, May 30, 1943

. . . I had already bought George Washington Carver's biography,[2] so I passed on my copy where I thought it would be appreciated. The book moved me deeply, for it revealed a great spirit. When I read of those early struggles, and followed the making of that simple and lofty character, I felt ashamed of an age so soft that all moral values have decayed at the roots. . . .

Affectionately yours
E.G.

[1] An editor at Doubleday, Doran.
[2] By M. V. S. Holt. Doubleday, 1943.

TO SIGNE TOKSVIG

Richmond, June 8th, 1943

Dear Signe Toksvig:

Your *Hans Christian Andersen* has meant a great deal to me! Not only has it brought both you and Hans Christian near to me, but it has given me a vivid impression of the world when it appeared (whether or not this could be true) younger and more vital and hopeful. Even when people were unhappy, they seemed still to keep faith in life, and in dreams too. Much in your little lonely Hans Christian reminded me of the time when I dreamed dreams, and was little and lonely.

Are you like me, I wonder, about books. When you take a book in your hands and open the covers and read the first paragraph, does something tell you whether the book will come alive in your grasp or remain merely inanimate matter? Well, your Hans Christian came to life in the very beginning, and he stayed alive until—no, he did not die, really, for he stays on, with the breath of life in your beautiful work. For the art with which he is presented is all that it should be; it is sympathetic, sincere, candid, and singularly revealing in character. That your words should be so naturally the *right* words came rather as a surprise to me. One would assume that English is your native speech, but, I suppose it is not.

I wish I could go on and on. There is so much I should like to say to you. The memory of certain pages or paragraphs in your work flows in my mind as a stream of impressions. One of these is the beginning of, I think, Chapter IX, when Hans Christian looks out of the dormer window in his attic and sees the bright view of Copenhagen, with the red-tiled roofs slanting in all directions. This is only one picture, and there are many others, and underneath, of course, is the deeper subjective current of being. But I must stop.

[*321*]

An intolerable wave of heat prostrated me, and the doctors are trying to send me away on the fifteenth. For the past two years my daily living has been at the mercy of a wholly inadequate heart. If nothing prevents, however, I hope to leave for Maine next Tuesday, and we ought to reach Castine on Thursday, the 17th. Usually, I spend a week in New York, for the pleasure of seeing my friends there, but this year I am not strong enough. Yes, Castine is enchanting, and so cool and bracing. Do write to me there.

I must tell you how much I like the illustrations of Hans Christian, especially those charming little scenes inside the bindings. If I have to send back this copy (and I am leaving it wrapped and addressed to Chilmark), I hope I shall find my exchange copy exactly like it. Macmillan did very well by you. So often the outside of a book is inappropriate.

It is disagreeable having to sue for plagiarism. I know just how you feel. This happened to me once, years ago. An Englishman boldly plagiarized my book, *The Battle-Ground,* but he disappeared and could not be traced. It was all done under an assumed name.

I hope you will have a satisfactory summer—one dares not wish happiness in a war-torn world. Oh, yes, I have, or had, Mackenna's translation of Plotinus. That had a beauty of its own, but my worn-out copy, heavily marked, after a bad habit of mine, is one of the old Thomas Taylor's translations. His were the earliest translations, were they not?

Since I know you better, there is an essay of mine I should be glad to have you read, and I regret that I haven't a copy to send you. You could find it in a large library, but perhaps not in a small place. This is in a collection of essays entitled *I Believe.* It is published by Simon and Schuster, and edited, oddly enough, by Clifton Fadiman, who, probably, did not suspect what he was doing. Some other time, when you are in New York and have an idle hour, you might drop into the library and look up this volume. I put a good deal of myself into this confession of faith.

Now that I really know you, as always,

ELLEN GLASGOW

TO FRANK MORLEY

Castine, June 25th, 1943

Dear Frank:

The Fall Catalogue has just reached me, by way of Richmond. I like the description extremely, and I am particularly glad that you make the price of the book $3.50, instead of $2.50. This is all to the good, I think. Would there be a chance of the Book-of-the-Month combining this volume with another offering? I think I suggested this to Donald Brace, because, though usually I should not grasp the notion, in such a world one must reach after shadows.

Yes, the heat in Richmond was too much for me, and here I am, safe and sound, after an exhausting trip, on my hill-top, which the friendly folk in Maine call the "Head." What it is the Head of, I do not know, but that also is in character with the country.

For the first time, this morning, we found the sun hot on our walk, but we have had a week of nearly perfect weather, as cool as an English spring, and as exhilarating as wine. From my window I look out on three splendid copper beeches, where a multitude of new leaves are coming out against the dark flame of the branches. A stormy day scattered the last blossoms of the lilacs, but the upper meadow, which no one will cut, is sprinkled with the green and gold bloom of grasses and flowers.

It is so restful here that one imagines a war on some less serene planet. The stars appear so near and so beautiful, and two years ago the Northern Lights made a new heaven and

[*323*]

a new earth in space. I cannot bear to think of your spending July in Washington[1]—of all intolerable places to be in that worst month of the year! For us in the South it is surely the worst month, but, then, I sometimes think I am, in reality, a child of the north, and I grew better with every mile of the distance that brought me toward Maine. . . .

As always yours,
E.G.

Do keep well wherever you are. I have grown to depend on you.

[1] Mr. Morley served on the War Labor Board during the war.

TO VAN WYCK BROOKS

Castine, June 26, 1943

Dear Van Wyck:

A letter from you is always a lift to my spirit, and I enjoyed, very especially, the one that came just before you went back to Westport. I was so much interested in what you told me of your winter in New York. I wish I could have been there at that time. You had the kind of winter I always wanted, and you met the special group of writers I should like to know better. But, somehow, I appear so often to do exactly the opposite of what I should choose, if I had any choice. Yes, I was much interested in the book *Writers in Crisis*.[1] Is that the title or have I confused it with something else? Anyway, you will know the book I mean, for you told me about it, and I bought it immediately. It is a brilliant book. I am glad, too, that you came to know Hamilton Basso. He is one of the very few younger Southern novelists whose prose has distinction, and in an age that scorns superiority in any form, distinction is the quality I prize most in literature.

In this group, however, Alfred Kazin is, to me, the most

[1] By Maxwell Geismar. Houghton Mifflin, 1942.

interesting. The quality of his mind impresses me, with its singularly living evocation of past and present moods, and I like, too, his gift of sensitive penetration. But enough of other writers. What I wish to hear is good news of dear Eleanor and you on your Connecticut hill. How I should love to send a message from a hill in Castine to that dreamed of hill near Westport! I think of you both in your garden, and of you at work in your library, and then of the distant view you described to me. Are you working now on the age of Jefferson? And do you find it possible to work in a world gone distraught? Yet, even in this unsettled state, nothing could give me greater pleasure than the hope of soon having a new book of yours.

After a dreary winter, the frightful heat in Richmond was almost too much for me, and the doctors insisted that I must return to my old habit of a summer in Maine. Scarcely more living than dead, I left the murky atmosphere of Main Street, but I began to pick up and show some faint animation with every mile of the distance that brought me farther north. When, at last, we reached Castine, late on Thursday, the 17th, it seemed to me that I had come to an earthly heaven. The weather was as cool as an English spring; the air sparkled like wine; the hills were crystal blue beyond the rippling waves of the bay. Around my house all the white and purple lilacs (real lilacs of New England) were still in masses of bloom. As I look down from my window, I see a multitude of new bright red leaves budding on the dark branches of three superb copper beeches. But you have beauty as heartening as this, and that beauty is all your own. What a difference that makes, to feel that beauty in earth and sky is one's own!

Well, we had a week of those perfect days, and I seemed to be made over, and made differently. Then a storm came and scattered the lilacs, and for two days now we have had the kind of soft, warm, oppressive atmosphere that is so unlike Maine. Still, I know I have gained strength, because I am able to walk in the woods, and just to be away from Richmond in the summer is more than enough!

Now, for my one bit of news. It had not entered my mind to publish a book until the war is well over; but Frank Morley, of Harcourt, came to Richmond and persuaded me to bring out my book of prefaces this autumn. This is not fiction but a mingling of autobiography and literary criticism. The book has been in print for a year, waiting for the right moment; but nothing in letters appears to be so rare as the exact right moment. The essays were first written as prefaces to the Scribner edition of my works—the Virginia Edition, but I have written them over, added many passages, and written one entirely new preface to *In This Our Life*. Unless the fall season looks disastrous, I hope to send an early copy to you in October. It is, I think, a good book, and I hope you will be interested, though it has no bearing upon any external conflict.

My love to Eleanor and you. If only you were at Boothbay Harbor, and one might still use one's car. And the hill at Westport still shines so far away. There is little chance of my being in New York until journeys become less difficult.

As always yours,

ELLEN GLASGOW

TO VAN WYCK BROOKS

Castine, July 27th, 1943

Dear Van Wyck:

Your letters do me a world of good, for they bring Eleanor and you to this hilltop, and I remember the summer you spent at Boothbay Harbor, while my inadequate heart kept me in bed, week after week, and I lay watching the goldfinches fly in and out of the solitary tall fir-tree. My life has been so shut in by circumstances, and has been lived so apart from people who speak my own language, that you cannot imagine what it means to discover in the actual world, not in a book, a mind that is really of the first order. When this happens, as it does so infrequently, I feel a wonderful sense of renewal and exhilaration. This is what you have meant to me. Eleanor and you have given me a feeling of intellectual integrity, of a certain rightness of mind and heart, which you describe, in writers, as breadth, depth, and elevation. And so I thank you for your friendship and for your unfailing sympathy and insight.

The news of your book heartens me. I like your talk of moods, because that means your subject is alive and kicking. Your books are among the very few I await with impatience and eagerness. You may belong, in sympathy, with "the century of the common man," but you stand head and shoulders above it. After all, there is so much of the vast average in American writing, and so little that is true superiority. And it is at least amusing, if not encouraging, to us whose natural sympathies are with the dispossessed of the earth, that, in years of trial, the common man turns to the uncommon man for inspiration and leadership. Who, for example, are today the chosen leaders of our proletarian multitudes? Two inheritors of superiority, Churchill and Roosevelt . . . and, by tradition, Jefferson, who made his home on a mountain. But tell me what you can of your book.[1] I am tremendously interested. So long as you write with your own special quality of distinction, it is safe to leave your understanding heart with the crowd.

Yes, I am writing, or trying to write, a little every morning, before my vitality ebbs. Though typing, poor as it is, hurts me less than the effort of holding a pen, something queer happens to my back after tapping keys for half an hour. I am writing a short sequel to *In This Our Life,* partly because I wish to bring my work to the present mo-

[1] *The World of Washington Irving,* Dutton, 1944.

ment in history, and partly because I felt that my latest book came to a pause rather than to an end. So I carry it on for a few additional chapters, running in all to a short, a very short novel. Whether it will be good or bad, I cannot say. But my book based on the prefaces to my Virginia Edition is, I feel sure, a good book. I hope you will like it. Much of myself went into that writing. It gave me an opportunity to ramble over my mental universe. Of course, nobody will read it at this time. It will be lost and swept away in the rising flood of war books. But that has always been my unhappy fate as a writer: to swim against the flood or the stream, and, almost invariably, to publish a book at the wrong literary moment. Why, I do not know, but this makes me remember one of the two books I have found deeply impressive—I mean, in the past year or two. Have you read *Pioneer to the Past,* the biography of James Henry Breasted, by his son, Charles?[2] Superb as his work on Egypt was, and is, the man's fortitude, his greatness of character and his intellectual integrity, should stand as a monument to the old American dream. If what we call, or miscall, democracy can produce that quality of human being, then, surely, it is worth every sacrifice we have made. Imagine a clerk, hidden in some small drug-store in a western town, who, burning with some inner flame, was able to become the world's greatest Egyptologist.

Well, the post goes, and I must break off. My warm love to Eleanor. If only I thought I might see you both in the autumn! But the War, among other deprivations, will keep me from that visit. I shall have to go straight back to Richmond, and remain there, I sadly fear, for the duration.

Always affectionately yours,

ELLEN GLASGOW

[2] Scribner, 1943.

TO SIGNE TOKSVIG

Castine, August 14th, 1943

Dear Signe (that is how I think of you) :

Your letter meant, and still means, so much to me, for it is a rare pleasure indeed to find a writer or a friend who speaks my own language and who, stranger even than that, has approached life by the road I travelled long ago, when I was very young. Yes, oh, yes, like you, I was, in youth, brought up against the ugly side of Christian dogmatism, against its cruelty, its narrowness, its blindness. My father, who sprang from that stalwart breed, the Scotch-Irish, so-called, was an elder in the Presbyterian church, and, in my childhood, I revolted from the creed, as well as from the severe conscience, of Calvinism. Like you, also, I had an early antipathy to Christianity, and I loved the broad humanity and the respect for the intellect I found in original Buddhism. But the teaching was too lofty for the human mind, and the metaphysical doctrine too profound for the human heart which craves a future of unbroken identity.

I had the misfortune, for I regard it, in my special case, as a misfortune, to inherit a long conflict of types, for my father was a descendant of Scottish Calvinists and my mother was a perfect flower of the Tidewater, in Virginia. Her ancestors had been broad Church of England and later agnostics. This conflict began in my soul as far back as I can remember. I adored my mother, and, even today, I cannot read Browning's "My Last Duchess" without seeing her luminous image.

But I think (and I am speaking now of my earliest youth) that the quality I disliked most in orthodox Christianity was its arrogant self-righteousness, that state of mind or soul which a great student of the animal world has called, "the anthropomorphic delusion of grandeur." In my childhood,

[*329*]

animals were very close to me. They were among my best friends, and after my mother, I loved best my dog. It was the Christian attitude toward animals that estranged me then, and turned me, in later years, toward more humane religions. My father was a sterling character and a zealous Calvinist; but he was without feeling for any creatures other than human beings, and among human beings, he firmly believed that the vast majority would be condemned to eternal torments. It appears incredible now, and appalling, but that was the creed my elders tried to teach me in my impressionable infancy. Because my mother believed none of this, I found a way of escape. . . . But, of course, I hasten to explain, I soon discovered that only original Buddhism was really merciful. We see, in later years, an almost fanatical Catholic, such as the wife of Richard Burton, carrying the gospel of humanity to India, the home of Gautama. Life, as I have lived it and observed it, has taught me that a man's humanity, as well as a man's goodness, bears no very close connection with a man's abstract belief. I have known gentle human beings who believed that if one died without the sacrament of baptism or even without extreme unction, one would spend an eternity in physical or spiritual torment, and I have known, too, or known of, simple monsters of cruelty, who accepted the rule of reason and every theory of science. Is there a spirit above and beyond any belief, any conviction? "O Thou Who dost take the shapes imagined by Thy worshippers!" [1]

No, I have not read Eckhart. I wish I could read your translation.[2] Yes, by inhumanity, I mean cruelty. Cruelty, I truly believe, is the one and only sin. It is the sin against the

[1] A Saiva saying from southern India which Signe Toksvig had quoted to Miss Glasgow.

[2] Signe Toksvig translated, but did not publish, part of the sermons of Meister Eckhart (1260?-?1327), German Dominican theologian, mystic, and preacher.

Holy Ghost. There is another Hindu invocation that I treasure. I found it in Schopenhauer, who was bitter because he was too humane to enjoy life as he found it. This, he says, was the prayer with which the ancient Hindu closed his athletic games, and Schopenhauer calls it the noblest of all invocations: "May all that have life be delivered from suffering." . . .

Tell me more of yourself. I am tremendously interested in all that concerns you. . . .

Yours,

ELLEN GLASGOW

TO SIGNE TOKSVIG

Castine, Sunday, August 15th, 1943

[No salutation]

Is it true, as I said, yesterday, in my letter, that a man's abstract belief has no close relation to a man's humanity? You recall Voltaire's illuminating comment on his age: "Men will commit atrocities as long as they believe absurdities." Surely, that is an admonitory truism. Yet it is true, also, that I have known kindly and gentle natures, as I said before, human beings with goodness of soul, who clung to the most terrible doctrines in morality and religion. Well, as my colored mammy used to say, "Well, well, the Lord made us all, and He must bear with us!"

Some other Sunday morning, when I have time and freedom, I shall tell you more of that golden August afternoon in the Alps,[1] and more, too, of a wonderful adventure I began, and did not finish, three years ago, in Castine. It was my severest heart attack. The doctor thought I was dying, and I came as near death as one may come and return. Yet I was completely conscious until the last glorious moment, when I felt that I was lifted up, on the crest of a wave, and

[1] It is described in *The Woman Within.*

[*331*]

swept out into some perfect fulfilment. I am not, as I told you before, in the least psychic, nor am I a believer in super-natural manifestations. Most of these occurrences, as they are reported to me, appear insincere, and simple examples, deliberate or otherwise, of morbid self-consciousness.

But I have known these two moments of vision, though I do not write of them, or even speak of them except in cir-cumstances that are remote from the ordinary surface of living.

Another interruption— Here is my morning cup of hot milk. Then, after a little, a very little work, I shall go for a short walk, and, on this walk, I take bird-seed and honey and water to the empty cottage of a friend who could not come back this summer. The birds near her porch are quite tame, and they return every year from the South. The humming-birds (we have only one species, the ruby-throated) come back from their long and far migration, to the same spot in the woods. At our first whistle, they darted out of the fir-trees, and circled about us, waiting until we put out the small bottles of honey-and-water. Few forms of life are so engag-ing as birds.

Yours,

E.G.

TO SIGNE TOKSVIG

Castine, September 4th, 1943

Dear Signe:

As soon as I had finished *Port of Refuge,*[1] I felt that I must write to you. But my heart had been giving a little trouble, and I was obliged to sink back and rest idly for a few days. Not to be strong is an unbearable nuisance—yet one can only bear it—and pretend not to mind it.

[1] Signe Toksvig's novel. Faber, London, 1938.

The book—a young book, it seems to me—is singularly living. The factory part, all of it, has a pulse of its own. I felt and heard those machines, and that terrible noise, roaring into space. And then that amazing, that miraculous vision of a world beyond sense and beyond matter. I was interested and thrilled and excited to know that it was true, that you had actually lived through it, and that the visitation had saved you. Otherwise, how could you have survived that particular horror? And yet the meaning. What was the inner truth of it all? Ever since I read of that miracle, I have been haunted, and I have tried to find the cause and the reason. Was it merely a revolt of exhausted nerves that turned, for sanctuary, to the secret province of imagination? Or was it a reality deeper than other realities? What puzzles me is the power you found to invoke and sustain the vision. That golden afternoon in the Alps came to me in the light and the air, and it passed on into the wind and the moving grass. But I could never recall, for so much as an instant, a glimmer of that ineffable sense beyond sense. Only when I seemed to be dying did I have the faintest return of the ecstasy, and this was so different, though, in some way, a part of it. But I never write of this, except to you, and I cannot speak of that moment. The nature of it has always been, and is still, indescribable. I have almost persuaded my mind that it was an escape for tormented nerves, after "a dark night of the soul."

But your profound release for the spirit has seemed to cast light on the obscure border of dreams.

I wish I were able to write on and on. There are so many subjects that I should like to discuss with you. But this is the poorest excuse for a letter. The warning tremor begins, and I must give way to it.

I shall send the book to you, for you may have no other copy. But shall I return it to your Connecticut address? The whole story has a moving quality, so vital and ardent with youth, and with delight in the entire range of experience. Your personality shines through the pages.

As ever yours,

ELLEN GLASGOW

. . . And you love the *Bhagavad-Gita.* Some other day, when I feel no warning, I shall tell you how much that has meant in my life. Not now, but when I was young, and when I was searching for a truth that I could not find. Like you, I doubt if higher ethical spheres have ever been reached than in that revelation.

TO HAMILTON BASSO

Richmond, October 24th, 1943

Dear Hamilton Basso:

Never, I think, has one writer written with more generous insight of another. Though I have not met you, I feel as if we had been close friends from the beginning. I am grateful to you first of all, for understanding (the rarest of all blessings to a writer) and after understanding, I am grateful, too, for the many fine points you have brought out in your splendid review.[1] And, especially, I thank you for making it plain that it is "wrong to think of Ellen Glasgow as a 'Southern' novelist." Well, for this, and for everything else. . . .

Recently, I have heard of you from my friend, Van Wyck Brooks. I envied him his winter in New York, because he appeared to have met the very writers (you among them) I wished to see. Unfortunately, I have had to give up my visits to New York, and most other things, since my long illness. Now, I have just returned, by slow stages, to Richmond. The trip down from Maine covered five days and four nights.

Some years ago, I remember, you came to Richmond, and

[1] Mr. Basso's review of *A Certain Measure,* the New York *Times Book Review,* October 17, 1943.

I have always regretted that I was away at the time, and missed seeing Mrs. Basso and you. Do come again.

Yesterday, I saw a notice of your new book,² and immediately, I ordered a copy from the Holliday Bookshop in New York. I am looking forward to it with a great deal of pleasure.

Sincerely yours,

ELLEN GLASGOW

I meant to tell you that nothing written of my work could gratify me more keenly than the last fine paragraph in your article. Here, you sum up, with distinction, the purpose (whether or not it was achieved) of my whole career as a novelist.

² *Mainstream,* Reynal & Hitchcock, 1943.

TO HOWARD MUMFORD JONES

Richmond, October 24th, 1943

Dear Howard:

How can I thank you for that admirable criticism?¹ I appreciate every [thing] you say, because I know you speak straight from the mind and heart, with complete fidelity to the high standards you hold. That you should believe in my work, with so fine and clear a comprehension, has been one of the greatest comforts in my ironic career as a novelist.

And thank you for saying: "She has not written of Virginia life, but of human life in Virginia."

Bessie and you are often in my mind, and always in my heart; but I find the effort of writing almost too much. My summer in Maine, at Castine, was wholly satisfactory, and I returned to Richmond only three days ago. But I was obliged to give up my visit to New York, and this I keenly regretted.

¹ Professor Jones's review of *A Certain Measure,* the *Saturday Review of Literature,* October 16, 1943.

How I should enjoy seeing you! My love to you both,

ELLEN

TO FRANK MORLEY

Richmond, October 24th, 1943

Dear Frank:

My drooping wings soared when I entered the house and saw the red roses. "Better times!" I exclaimed.

You were an angel to think of me, and to have this crimson glow to greet me at the end of my trip. We were five days and four nights on the road, and I reached here barely more living than dead. First of all, we left in a torrential downpour, which had kept up for two days and nights. In Maine, our road was washed away in several places, and once we had to wait while the wheels of a truck were dug out of the mud in front of us. But, oh, the autumn landscape, seen through a silver veil, was lovely beyond words! And, below Baltimore, after the frightful drought of last summer, the whole country looks as if it had been accursed by God, and never forgiven.

Thank you, too, for sending the reviews. All I have seen are good. I liked best Hamilton Basso's, and the article by Howard Mumford Jones, an able critic. What I hope we may achieve is a long, if limited, demand; and I trust you to keep this book always in stock. I am having trouble about my other novels, because, of course the Scribner edition is too expensive, and Doubleday, Doran let the other editions go down. Then people write to me and ask where they can find my books . . . and I do not know. But Nelson is very nice.

I have, so far, seen only two advertisements, but I suppose there will be others. Not splashes, but dignified quotations in small spaces.

[336]

As soon as I gather a little strength I am planning to take out the sequel and look it over.

As always,

E.G.

TO DORIS SCHNEIDER[1]

Richmond, November 3rd, 1943

Dear Doris Schneider:

Thank you for your letter and for the advertisements you enclose. . . .

Yes, I think the reviews are unusually good and serious. I liked Stark Young's article in *The New Republic,* and I wish you had had an advertisement there. Some people must read the paper, I suppose, though I stopped when the critics all were cheering the proletarian novel. How dull they were! As Herschel Brickell remarked while the fashion was in: "To write even a proletarian novel requires a little talent for novel writing."

Sincerely yours,

E.G.

[1] Member of the Harcourt, Brace staff.

TO DORIS SCHNEIDER

Richmond, November 9th, 1943

Dear Doris Schneider:

James Thurber has never failed to delight me, and I am captivated by *Many Moons* and *Men, Women and Dogs.*[1]

I enjoy Thurber's distracted human beings, and I enjoy and respect his philosophic dogs.

Thank you very much.

[1] Both published by Harcourt, Brace in 1943.

I am working now on my sequel. It is good, I feel, but it may be too short to stand alone.

As always,

E.G.

TO VAN WYCK BROOKS

Richmond, November 21st, 1943

Dear Van Wyck:

It was a keen disappointment that I could not come home by way of New York. An afternoon with dear Eleanor and you would have given me a fresh impulse toward living. So often you have been in my mind, and I have wondered whether you had moved into the city. Do let me have your New York address.

I am deeply interested to know how your book has come on since you wrote to me. Shall you finish it in town? Or have you stayed on in the country to write? I am awaiting two books with eagerness: yours[1] and Santayana's.[2]

There are at least a hundred subjects I wish to discuss with Eleanor and you; but it looks now as if I were chained here "for the duration" . . . and this particular duration seems to be longer than time. I hope you have good news of your boys, and that life has been, and will continue to be, kind to the family. . . .

What you wrote of London Terrace[3] interested and amused me. I shall always remember that part of town, because I haunted it while I was writing *Life and Gabriella.* The number of the house has slipped from my mind in so many years, but Gabriella's house may well have been the place where you lived in that year. I like to think I was

[1] *The World of Washington Irving.*

[2] George Santayana, *Persons and Places,* two volumes, Scribner, 1944-45.

[3] In the old Chelsea section of New York.

writing about your special house. That book of mine was the end, or conclusion, of what I thought of as a history of manners, and it was entirely accurate in scene. Later, with *Barren Ground,* one of my two best novels, I think, I broke away from social history, and allowed my creative impulse to take flight. But, oddly enough, these later books are more living and more true, I feel, than my earlier novels.

My warm love to Eleanor, and the hope that we may soon be together again, if only for one happy afternoon in New York. Is there any chance that you may come South? Do come to me if you are going to Florida or California.

With much affection,

ELLEN GLASGOW

I meant to tell you how astonished I was to find, in the midst of war, that my book of literary criticism could be so heartily welcomed. Never, I think, have I had reviews that were so understanding. Of course, the book will not sell, but it was not written to sell. If I had written to be popular, I should have taken a different road in the beginning. But I am pleased with this reception, and with the thoughtful treatment the book has won.

TO FRANK MORLEY

Richmond, December 7th, 1943

Dear Frank:

What a delightful letter! Thank you for the clipping. I should like to meet Harry Sylvester[1] if I am ever again in New York. But isn't it amusing the way phrases travel? He quotes my phrase "evasive idealism," which I coined, when I began to write, to describe the mental attitude of the Southern mind. And he appears to think that Joyce Kilmer invented it, and applied it to me. J.K. quoted the words in an

---

[1] A young writer who had reviewed *A Certain Measure* in the *Commonweal.*

interview he had with me for (I think) the *New York Times*. He never thought of me as evasive—or, I imagine, as an idealist of the period. Anyhow, he was a nice young man, but by no means as deep as a well.

Yes, the early part of January would be best for me. Any day before the fifteenth or sixteenth. I think this story could be made into a book as long (or perhaps a little longer than) *Of Mice and Men.*[2] However, I never know about the number of pages. I write what I have to say, and then I stop.

This sequel has developed, somewhat, into the nature of a modern parable, with symbolic overtones.

You will recall that *In This Our Life* interpreted the group consciousness of a community hesitating, undecided and unthinking, on the verge of war, living in the immediate moment, and pushing the idea of conflict and the act of decision, farther and farther away, in the search after happiness.

The sequel deals with the major figures in this earlier novel. The scene is placed in the autumn of 1942, more than three years after the close of I.T.O.L. The whole drama occurs in a single day, in the town of Queenborough, and on James River. The two older women embody the dying or dead past, so deeply planted in tradition, and in a declining social order, that they are unable to adjust themselves to a changing world, or to accept the unknown future, of which Roy's child by an unknown father is the living symbol.

Asa and Kate, on the farm, rooted, not in a decaying tradition, but in nature and in simple goodness of life, represent the part of tradition that lives on, by adjustment, that does not repudiate the unknown and the untried.

This is the roughest kind of outline, just to give you a bare idea of the symbolical *motif*. In the book, all is clearly brought out, or perhaps only implied. Even now, until I have gone over it from a little distance, I am not sure whether I should publish it, because it gathers all the threads of my

[2] By John Steinbeck. Viking, 1937.

work into a single firm pattern, or whether I should leave my career resting on *A Certain Measure* and my coming memoirs, of which more anon. . . .

Bless you.

As always,
E.G.

TO SIGNE TOKSVIG

Richmond, February 4th, 1944

Dearest Signe:

Your letter has just gladdened my heart, and I feel that I must send you a very small word of grateful appreciation. Some weeks ago (that time is no longer divided) a "mild" attack of influenza proved almost too strong an antagonist, and I have not yet recovered sufficiently to tap out a whole letter. . . .

How serene you appear in these little pictures, and how victorious over fate—or over circumstances! I love them, and I thank you for sending them to me. I am enclosing a passport picture taken before my long illness, in 1937, when I was sailing for my last—my very last—trip to Italy. I looked younger than my years then; but since these years of physical suffering, I am more broken and I appear frail, instead of vital.

All you write of *Barren Ground* touches me deeply. That book was torn out of myself, and it was written in one of those blessed pauses that fall between the "dark wood" of the soul and the light on the horizon. Yes, it is true, as you understand, the land and the sky, time and space, are the great harmonies. The moment of madness in which Dorinda had the impulse to kill Jason is true, psychologically, I feel, of her nature. The dark wood was there as well as the distant light on the hills.

There is so much I wish to say to you, but, even after so

brief a note, my touch has begun to grow more uncertain. The reason, I suppose, that your husband missed *Barren Ground* is not far to seek. It came out in 1925, and, in the decade of the lost generation, most American novels (all the popular fiction, in fact) were rooted, not in the American soil, but in the boulevards of Paris. Francis Hackett and you had both left America before my book was published, and in some way you must have missed reading it in Denmark.

The two books of mine I like best are *Barren Ground* and *The Sheltered Life.* They are very different, but equally true to experience. For sheer craftsmanship, and for more than craftsmanship, for swiftness of vision, and for penetration into the hidden truth of life—I value the second section of *The Sheltered Life,* the part called "The Deep Past." But that whole book interprets a dying age and a slowly disintegrating world of tradition.

I rejoice, with you, to hear that your two dear brothers in Denmark are unharmed. That has been in my mind constantly. Whenever I see the name Denmark, I remember you and your anxiety. But I am thankful for your refuge of work, and I look eagerly forward to the biography you are writing.

Now, my fingers have refused to go on. No, I could not send you a dictated note. I have a secretary, but she copies, she does not write any but business letters. Since my illness she has been overworked, and she is not well. How I wish I had known you in other and happier days, when this old house was gay, at times, with visitors. War has made living conditions very hard in Richmond. It is true that I have a Fluvanna,[1] but "she" is a man, who has been in our family for nearly thirty-five years. He used to be a remarkable cook, but now he is old and decrepit, though still faithful. There

[1] Dorinda Oakley's Negro assistant and friend in *Barren Ground.*

are few of his generation left anywhere, and least of all, I believe, among the colored younger servants in the South.

We are living without adjustments, in a broken world. The pattern has changed so utterly that we have almost forgotten it. But what I regret most will always be the lost harmonies of the spirit, as one regrets the great music in a period of jazz or swing. Will the people who set the tone and dictate the manners of today ever prefer the greater harmonies, or ever . . . ever like all the little lost graces that made life so much easier? Then I ask myself whether more good may not come to the many? After all, I suppose, the little graces, as well as the great harmonies, had their part in a smaller world. Has the world of the spirit, or of the inner life, ever held many seekers of truth?

Devotedly,
ELLEN

TO MARION GAUSE CANBY

Richmond, February 24th, 1944

Dearest Marion,

Even when we do not write, I have a happy sense of companionship. It takes more than space really to separate us.

Your dear and lovely visit has been the one bright recollection in a nightmare of winter. A few weeks after you went away, I came down with this wretched influenza, and my wholly inadequate strength has suffered from my heart, which was weak before, to my head, which has felt weak ever since. I have not yet been out of the house, and I have been downstairs only once in the past four or five weeks. When your card reached me, I was feeling that I should never need a street dress again. But it was dear of you to attend to it, and if I am well, or fairly well again, I know I shall regret not ordering it. But can you, in your glowing health, imagine a state of mind when so simple an exertion as taking one's measure seems entirely too much?

And now no more about illness. Your letter from Washington lifted my spirit. How—oh, how I wish I might have been with you in the Mellon Gallery! There are times when I am hungry for pictures, yet I have never been strong enough, when I was in Washington, to go to a gallery. Always, I am in the hands of a doctor, and that leaves nothing over. I saw my last "real pictures" in Florence in the spring and early summer of 1937. Then I would steal away, with Mrs. Duke, from the villa at Fiesole, where we were visiting, and we would spend the morning in a church or a gallery. Sometimes I would see only one picture, but that picture would be a Botticelli, and usually my choice would be the Birth of Venus. But there were many that I loved. Do you recall what Heine said of Mary Magdalen? "She was a catholic soul, and loved not only much but many." That was a happy June. I stayed in a villa that had once belonged to Marsilio Ficino,[1] and it was still called by his name. The garden was a paradise of all the flowers that God ever made. We spent, too, a whole day, far up in the Apennines, at La Verna, among the singing birds of St. Francis.

I have read your letter over again, and I feel as if we had talked together as we talked for hours on those two days in Richmond. Yes, we started life in the same way, only my sadder childhood was different. But I feel very near to you, and I felt this at our first meeting. You are right in thinking we met first in my sitting-room in some New York hotel, long before I began to stay at the Weylin. It was the Chatham, I believe, and we met that first time with a strong sense of friendship. That is the kind of recognition one never forgets, and, strangely enough, because it is so sudden, it rarely betrays one. The feeling does not come often, but when it comes, it has a kind of inevitability, as if one discovered a

[1] Fifteenth-century Italian philosopher and writer.

kinship of personality. I suppose this gives an extraordinary value to your insight into my prefaces. Certainly, I treasure that, and your complete understanding of motives beneath my life and my work. You have so much to give, and of all blessings I have missed most, and needed most, the intellectual sympathy that overflows from your mind, and the warmth and tolerance of your perceptions. Your visit gave me happiness, and you must come again, when I am over this relapse and this dark mood that appears to wait upon influenza. The "peace at last" seems now to have receded . . . or, perhaps, it has only declined for the moment.

My friendship with you and Henry has been a great joy in my life. Will you give him my love and will you keep my heart's share for yourself. After all, you did not send me the book of first poems, and you did not write in the volume I have, *On My Way*. I feel in your verse the quality that I found in you, and that is a rare kind of nobility, detached and yet strangely human.

Devotedly, dear Marion,

ELLEN

I must stop or the pain may come back. Forgive me for my long silence. . . .

TO MARION GAUSE CANBY

Richmond, April 12th, 1944

Dearest Marion:

Your poems[1] were late in reaching me. The book came only two days ago, but I have had it beside my bed, and I have turned back to it in the dark hours.

These verses bring you closer to me, and I think they express your natural inner self, and your Heart in the flush of youth. Even if they were written later, they are poems of

---

[1] Mrs. Canby's first book of verse, *High Mowing*, Houghton Mifflin, 1932.

youth. The first two make a deep appeal to me, because I might have written them when I was young and defiant. I am still defiant, but I am no longer young, though I have not yielded an inch in my rebellion against the cruelties of the world. In "Delivered of My Life," you have uttered my secret, as well as your own, the "Lift of air upon the topmost sky." That is asking of life more than life can ever give.

What more can I say? I love the poems, and I love you.

Your visit is still a bright gleam in a dark winter. How I should love to see you again this spring, but it looks as if you would have to wait till autumn to come. Do you recall the alcove in my guest-room? Well, a few days ago the whole ceiling fell, and the place has been a mass of plaster and wood. We are trying to have the ceiling put up (a new one, of course), but it will not be possible to have it painted until later in the summer.

This is a very old house, but nothing like that had happened before, and, most fortunately, no one was staying in that room at the time. I am so thankful that Irita and you had come earlier, and my sister had put off her visit.

But I shall look for you in the autumn. This has been the most wretched spring, rain and wind, and only one or two days of fair weather.

I am hoping to go away for the summer, but this is only a hope. I shall not know for a week or two.

All my love, dearest Marion, and my love, too, to Henry.

Yours ever . . . and ever,

ELLEN

TO J. DONALD ADAMS

Richmond, May 22nd, 1944

Dear Don:

An afterthought: *The Crest of the Wave*[1] is—or so it sounds in my ears—somewhat magniloquent. Wherever we are, or are likely to be, we are certainly not on a crest, either spiritual or physical. Could you suggest an ascending wave or the curve of a wave? So far, we are nearer the trough than the crest, even if we are rising, not falling.

To me, the worst trait in the modern mood, or at least in the modern literary mood, which appears, in some ways, curiously detached from life, is the fascination of the repulsive. I do not mean the immoral—that concerns me less, because our ideas of morality have so little to do with either the true or the good, but the attraction of the loathsome or the simply disgusting. But this may be a personal idiosyncrasy. My moral sense has always been less delicate than my stomach.

As the work goes on, send me a line to Castine, Maine.

Affectionately,

ELLEN

[1] Title considered for Mr. Adams's book *The Shape of Books to Come.*

TO FRANK MORLEY

Richmond, May 24th, 1944

Dear Frank:

The other three volumes of Toynbee[1] have just come—by "just" I mean three days ago—and I could not be satisfied until Anne Virginia stopped packing long enough to paste my bookplate in every volume. I am overwhelmed by this

[1] Arnold J. Toynbee's *Study of History,* six volumes, Oxford University Press, 1934, 1939.

simply gorgeous gift, and I rejoice to think that at last this long-wanted history is my own and occupies the brightest spot on my book-shelves.

I am still deep in Volume IV, for I must read slowly; but, as I wrote you before, the breakdowns of civilization have always been more exciting to me than the building up of what must, inevitably it appears, come down again. What a marvellous phrase he, Toynbee, creates in "The Nemesis of Creativity."

But, when the earlier part reached me, I turned back, for a brief dip, into Volume I, and read the pages in which he interprets Faust and Euripides and Christ, and enters into that fascinating discussion of "Yin and Yang" in the universe, or of the knowledge of good [and] evil. I am trying to read as much as I can before I go away, because I shall take no books with me, and use my eyes as little as possible for the next few months. But ill as I have been, I have enjoyed the work amazingly. My only quarrel with Toynbee is his treatment of Gibbon, and I feel, now and then, that he begins to lean a trifle too far in his acceptance of the opinions of the early Fathers of the Church, and indeed of a rather hazy Christian tradition. But, then, I was closely confined in Christian tradition.

And this reminds me that my sister Rebe, who is Mrs. Cabell Carrington Tutwiler, of Lexington, Virginia, has found a lovely, but very small, photograph of Aunt Rebecca and of "the little girl in blue." Both pictures were taken in the very year and month when we were both eager followers of Mr. [Dwight Lyman] Moody, the evangelist.

Well . . . we are packing (at least Anne Virginia is packing) and planning to go to Castine on June 7th. It is a choice of risks, but any risk appears light in preference to the intolerable summer in the heat and terrific noise and vibrations of this ruined quarter in Richmond. I cling to the old house, because I am not able to move elsewhere, and I love

the more than hundred-year-old interior. In winter, it is possible to shut out the surrounding streets; but in summer,
with the windows open and the smoke and shrieks pouring
in, the air is almost unbearable to the nerves. Yet the house
outside appears more attractive in its green mantle of creep-
ers and clustering trees. My magnolias have flowered beautifully this year, and the blossoms came early. After all, in
spite of the scorn Northern reviewers heap upon the now
completely discredited "magnolia and moonlight tradition,"
there have always been many magnolias in the South, and
even in the fallen grandeur of the present, moonlight has
never wholly deserted the Southern scene. Someday, I suppose, all this will be discovered over again.

Well, dear Frank, you are wonderful to me, and, surely, I
have been blessed in my friends. In all the years, I cannot
recall that one has ever let me down or failed in loyalty and
consideration.

We are utterly ignorant of what we shall find at Castine.
Maine in wartime is not the Maine we have known all these
summers. Our house is up high above and beyond the village,
and we are told that it will be impossible to install a telephone. Mr. Conti of the New England Telephone Company
has made an appeal for us, but if this has to go to Washington, we shall probably hear nothing more of it. I imagine the
appeal is buried beneath a million others. However, as I told
you, any risk that takes me away appears a good risk.

I am playing with the idea that living would not be too
trying for Christina[2] and you to have a glimpse of us, but I
should hesitate to ask you to come while things are so much
upset. We do not even know that we shall have a cook. There
would be nothing for you, when we cannot drive, and I imagine you do not play bridge, which is the salvation, apparently, of summer visitors.

[2] Mrs. Morley.

But I shall let you hear later, *when and if* we really arrive and are settled in.

Always affectionately yours,

E.G.

TO VAN WYCK BROOKS

Castine, June 25th, 1944

Dear Van Wyck:

I rejoice that Eleanor and you are both over your illness. What would have been bad news has become good and happy, because all the serious danger is over and you are thinking of that life-giving trip out to California. Go, if it is possible, not only to see the grandson, but to breathe that sunlit air for six weeks. The only good thing that came to me from the First World War, I am fond of saying, was a summer in California, and I spent almost the whole time in San Francisco. The air made me over. Even the fog every morning was delightful and exhilarating.

I am so glad that you have satisfactory accounts of your boys. One is always anxious in war-time, and there is a constant tremor along the nerves of those of us who stay at home and wait to hear, day by day.

How wonderful to be at work so soon again, and how I envy you! My working days, with my life, which means so much less to me, appear to be finished and over. Doesn't your other book[1] come out in October? How eagerly I wait for it.

Yes, this was a glorious year for roses in Virginia. Lilac time is long past there, but when we reached here, on the 9th of June, all the lilacs were blooming profusely around this house. They are the real lilacs, too, not the Persian or any other new variety, and their fragrance was heavenly until a nor'easter bore down on us three days ago. The gale is still blowing outside, and my nerves are in a state of recoil.

[1] *The World of Washington Irving.*

[*350*]

I can understand what Voltaire meant when he said, the English temperament was formed by the east wind.

How I wish I might see Eleanor and you. The trying part for bystanders in this war, and all wars, is the way one is separated from one's friends, both abroad and at home.

My love to you both,

ELLEN

TO CARL VAN VECHTEN

Castine, June 25th, 1944

Dear Carlo, how good to have a word from Fania and you.

After one of the worst winters of my life, here I am, yet once again, on my hilltop at Castine. . . .

I expect to stay here until the first week in October. Send *The Voice* [*of the People*] whenever you find it convenient, and I shall be glad to inscribe it. The first edition is bound in tan buckram, with a pattern of green oak leaves set in a square. Merle Johnson and not a few others have listed this edition incorrectly. But the later revised edition is much better reading.

Carrie is with me. We both send affection to Fania and you.

ELLEN

TO VAN WYCK BROOKS

Castine, September 7th, 1944

Oh, my dear Van Wyck, what a magnificent book![1] I read it first straight through, with a kind of breathless interest, and then I turned back and read it again, chapter by chapter, very slowly, lingering over each page. All the time, I was asking myself, How does he do it? How is it possible to keep that high level of vitality, of excellence, of pure crea-

[1] *The World of Washington Irving.* Dutton, 1944.

tive impulse? Fine as *The Flowering of New England* is, I think this book has a broader reach and even a more vital grasp. The sheer breadth of the portrayal, the wide view of the varying subject, and the complete unity you make out of diversity—all this impresses me from beginning to end.

The book comes to life with the first paragraph, and every character starts out of the printed page and moves with its own energy. Even Parson Weems takes on flesh as you describe him. Greater or lesser, this is true of every figure in every landscape, and I feel that it is especially true of your superb chapters on the West and the South. No other writer has made Jefferson appear so human, so friendly, so true to himself, and so commanding in intellect. Audubon, the great romantic, I see clearly, for the first time, against his background of forest; and he will always remain, for me, the Audubon of your book. What a gorgeous scene you paint, and how often it will come to me in the dark hours when I lie sleepless! Then I shall see the flap of bright wings and I shall follow the "tall figure with the springing step and the glance of an eagle." There will be the frontier with Audubon out on the Indian trails. Or the Louisiana swamps. Of the South you write as if the beauty and the tragedy were in your nerves and in your blood, without that vein of cruelty which seems to me to run through the beauty of all things Southern, wherever that South may be. As for Poe, you might have looked on the shabby splendour of his genius. For the splendour was his own, the shabby cloak was the outward form of his destiny. I have always felt a curious (because an improbable) kinship with Poe, and your study of him moves me profoundly. I can think of no other critic who has penetrated so deeply, with such unerring insight, into his obscure nature. Your chapter on his life in Richmond rings true in every word. I have always resented his hard fate when we compare it with the easier treatment the world, and especially America, gave to the more complacent Northern poets.

And where else can one find a more thrilling resurrection of Paine—of Paine, the long-buried and the half-forgotten yet [un]forgettable? Limited as his space remains, the dry bones stir and take on, once again, the dignity of greatness and the pitiable corruption of human nature.

But your finest achievement—or so it appears to me, is in the work as a whole, as a complete entity. Striking as the individual figures appear, they are, each and all, subdued to the superb grouping of masses as a background for life. I see the landscape, the horizon, even the clouds in each section. For this is a book of true American stature, with the moving actuality represented against the august shadow of legend. Every section is sufficient in itself, and yet each chapter falls into the larger pattern of history. I had almost said that the dominant idea is one of unity in variety.

This is a scrappy letter, for I am not equal either to the pen or the typewriter. After writing all my life, I appear to have forgotten how words run together. I am obliged to do little by little in the way of an effort. But I hope you will feel my enthusiasm and my joy in this book, which has given me my only real pleasure in this dreary summer. Forgive the smudges for the sake of the good will.

My love to Eleanor and to you. How I wish I might see you, but there is small chance of my coming to New York this autumn—or, I think, any autumn.

Castine has not worked its old magic, and I am dreading the strain of the trip home. I am planning to leave by October 16th.

Did you go to California? How are your sons and the grandson you had not seen?

Affectionately always, and always with greater pride and admiration in your work,

ELLEN

TO SIGNE TOKSVIG

Castine, October 8th, 1944

Dear Signe:

. . . You have been in my thoughts, but this has been a most trying summer, and I have waited to write, in the hope that I might be equal to a long letter. I have suffered physical pain, and, for the first time, this summer, I have felt no wish ever to return to Castine. Not that I wish to go anywhere else. Castine is still lovely, and so peaceful, so bathed in the air of tranquillity. Yet there are moments when surrounding tranquillity stabs into the mind as if it were violence. Autumn, the most beautiful of our seasons is coming on in a flame of colour, and there are moments, too, when colour may hurt one. We are planning to leave on October 22nd, and we must spend four nights on the road, because my heart compels me to go slowly—I, who have always hated to go slowly and softly!

All you think and write of *The Sheltered Life* interests me deeply. It is, to me, the second favourite among my books. I mean, after *Barren Ground* I like it best of my novels, and I think the middle section called "The Deep Past" contains the writing I should wish to be remembered by in the future. This reflective vision pierces more deeply, I have always felt, than most visions. General Archbald was profoundly real to me, and I seemed to discover in him level after level of downward seeking and upward springing, which I thought of as the inner poetry (or rhythm) of life. While I was writing this, I used to wonder whether others would see what I meant and was trying to do. It was a surprise to me that so many readers appreciated so quiet and subtle an analysis of the mind and heart of age. Even when I was very young, I liked to write of old people, because the old had attained a kind of finality. You are right about John Welch. Of all the characters in that book, he interested me least. He had the stiffness he would have had in the actuality, and indeed he was suggested, more or less, by an actual person. Yet he had his place, and there are many of his sort still in the town I call Queenborough. Compared to the General, he is inanimate, for I feel, with you, that General Archbald lives and walks and is rounded out in his own special shape. Jenny Blair is true in every fluttering heartbeat, and so is Eva Birdsong, and George I have known, and known well in reality.

To turn to the Germans. Yes, as a Dane, you know them far better than I ever have, or ever can know them. At this moment, they fill me with horror, yet I cannot see any end either to them or to the horror they will continue to make in the world and in the pages of history. What can be done to make them safe, or at least harmless, neighbours? My own belief is that nothing will be done, just as nothing was done after the First World War. We had the opportunity then, and we did nothing, because we were mad for sensation, avid for the taste of pleasure and the delight of whirling back into the life we had remembered. Have you read Henry J. Taylor's *Time Runs Out?* [1] It is a good book, and I recall the shock he felt, when he came to England from a newly liberated Europe, and found that people in London were thinking only of how or where or when they might enjoy themselves. I hope everything will be different after this war, but . . . but. . . .

No, I have not read your husband's book on Denmark.[2] That nice Terence Holliday, of the Holliday Bookshop (do you know it?) has advertised for it, without success as yet, and he told me earlier in the summer that Doubleday had no copies in stock. I am resentful of the way publishers let good books drop out of print; and yet they never seem to lack pulp for the printing of trash. And it angers me, too, to

[1] Doubleday, 1942.
[2] Francis Hackett's *I Chose Denmark*. Doubleday, 1940.

think of all the beautiful trees that have been sacrificed to make our many horrible and hideously cheap magazines.

My love to you, dear Signe. How I hope we may meet this coming autumn or winter. But it is now autumn, and I shall expect to be in Richmond by the first of November.

Write to me there when you have a free moment. I was interested to see that Francis Hackett will take John Chamberlain's place on the *Times*. Though I subscribe to the *Times*, it stopped immediately after that announcement, and I do not know whether the change has occurred. Something must have happened to the circulation department, for I have received my paper at rare intervals, and the post here is uncertain, as Mr. Pickwick observed of the morals of coachmen.

As always,

ELLEN

Forgive this scrambled letter. It is the best I am able to do. I have written it in bits, and it sounds stilted.

TO SIGNE TOKSVIG

Castine, October 19th, 1944

Dear Signe,

I was grieved to hear that you had suffered this summer (I have a horror of hospitals), but I rejoice with you that the malady was "benign." Yes, it is a curious word, but what tremendous significance it contains!

Your article[1] is especially sympathetic to my mood, for I lived in a world of Nature spirits when I was a child, and sometimes I still feel or see their genial forms, or formless happiness, in my memories. As a small being, I used to think that all the trees around our country house were separate and distinct personalities. I had names for them, every one, human names, and how I loved them! But that was in the long

[1] "Nature Spirits of North America" appeared in the magazine *Tomorrow* in 1944.

ago, and as I grew out of my child's world, I lost my friendly unseen spirits, with other lovely, and never entirely forgotten, things.

I should like, by the way, to subscribe to that magazine. I have never seen a copy, but I liked particularly a very penetrating review of my latest book in *Tomorrow*. That seems to me an excellent reason.

I am so glad that you sent me Francis Hackett's reviews. How has he kept, after all you must have seen and felt of two world wars, that remarkable freshness of mind and of writing? Distinction is so rare a quality today that I prize it, I believe, above every other merit in both poetry and prose. I wish you would send me the other reviews from the *Times*. That paper has the most careless circulation department. By the same post, on the same day, with the same amount of money, I ordered, before I left Richmond, the *Times* and the *Herald-Tribune*. The *Times* came infrequently, and finally stopped entirely a month ago, while the *Herald* has reached me every day since I came to Castine.

But I was pleased when Francis Hackett met in print and remarked upon vulgarity, which has a curious kind of renown —I had almost said, an evil prestige in contemporary fiction. And I use "vulgarity" in the American sense, not in the English, which seems to imply merely commonness. We have no exact word for that trait—nor, I imagine, had the Greeks such a word. "Obscenity" will not do, for that suggests a mature lewdness of behaviour, and the modern taste for vulgarity (I am obliged to fall back upon the word) resembles rather the snigger of a nasty-minded small boy when he writes bad words on back fences. When we grow up, I suppose, these giggles will no longer amuse us.

And how I enjoyed the comment on *Boston Adventure*.[2] The publishers sent me that endless exercise, but I could only gasp, "How terrible," and "Why Boston?" Any other town,

[2] By Jean Stafford. Harcourt, Brace, 1944.

east or west, on the map might have done quite as well. To anyone who has known Boston and Back Bay, the setting of that adventure is more ludicrous than amusing.

Yes, I should be delighted to have you lend me the book on Denmark. Post it to Richmond, for we are leaving on Sunday, and we are now packing and house-cleaning, though I can do very little to help. The man is waiting for my typewriter, and even if I had the strength, which I have not, I should not be able to copy this untidy letter. It is so beautiful here, and I have just come in from one of my last walks in the birchwoods. Beyond golden leaves, I look out, when I lift my eyes, on the rippling bay in a high wind, and on the deep blue shadows blowing over the Camden Hills. How I wish you could have come to this charming village. Though I am Southern in every drop of my blood, I find a strong kinship with the people and the background of New England. I like the cold, pure outlines of these autumn and winter landscapes.

How dear of you to send me this new translation of the *Bhagavad-Gita*.[3] I have loved that song of songs, the noblest expression, I think, of man's spiritual groping after the highest Good. I placed a verse from the *Bhagavad-Gita* on the tomb of my dearly beloved sister, who died thirty-three years ago. "The unreal has no being. The real never ceases to be. . . ."

No I have seen no review of Dunsany's novel.[4] Could you send me that and any others of which you may have extra copies . . . though, for that matter, I shall return them. I did so heartily enjoy the two you sent me. Well, goodbye for a little while. My typewriter is going before me to Richmond. I am looking eagerly forward to seeing you . . . really see-

[3] The translation by Swami Prabhavananda and Christopher Isherwood. Marcel Rodd, 1944.

[4] Lord Dunsany's *Guerrilla*. Bobbs Merrill, 1944.

ing you, dear Signe, before the year is over. That will help me to keep well, or at least not to fall ill again.

Devotedly,

ELLEN

TO SIGNE TOKSVIG

Richmond, November 1st, 1944

Dear Signe,

The post here is entirely too slow. I had no sooner mailed the postcard to you than your copy of *I Chose Denmark* was brought to me. I am reading my copy now, and yours will go back to you today or tomorrow. The book has an enchantment. I, too, who once lived in Arcadia, would choose Denmark if it is all that F.H. observed or imagined. The bare cleanliness! The fresh purity of the earth and sky! So far, because I must go slowly, I have read only half of the book; but I have lingered over the charming impressions, alive and brilliant in color, of the Signe I know in my mind and heart.

That first glimpse of you at the *New Republic* was wholly delightful. I could wish, much as I enjoy the other part, that there were more of you in each page. There aren't many women one would like, if one were a man, to be married to; but even when you are absent from this book, you leave an impression of perfect companionship.

Yes, I like the reviews you sent me, most of all, I think, I like the distinction of mind, the feeling that manner is not a thing detached from life, but that it is a part of morality. By manner, I mean what we used to call, and still should call (for God knows we need it!) "good taste." For good taste expresses and involves the knowledge of right and wrong, of good and evil.

Oh, there is so much I wish to say, if only I were able to write!

[*359*]

Thank you, Signe dear, for the new version of my old friend, the *Bhagavad-Gita*. I am reading it over with much interest and satisfaction, and I am glad that this volume contains the magnificent legend of Yudhisthira, for Yudhisthira has always been, for me, the King among kings. I have a very beautiful translation, in poetry, of that legend. Though I am overjoyed to have this modern translation of the Gita, it does not (perhaps because of a certain scientific bareness) come so close to me as my older version, with its more poetic phrasing. For example, a single word may come in one's way, and I find myself unmoved by the word Atman, while the phrase "the self within the self" stirs some far-off memory or association of ideas. But poetry will defy translation; and, for me, poetry (I mean English poetry) has taken the place in life that other persons may give to music. This may be only because I am a lover of words. All modern versions of the Bible provoke me, while I love as literature, the King James version. Do you recall the Lytton [Strachey] remark: "And, in any case, who remembers prophets? Isaiah and Jeremiah, no doubt, have gained a certain reputation; but then Isaiah and Jeremiah have had the extraordinary good fortune to be translated into English by a committee of Elizabethan bishops." The pity is that the many scholars who have known Sanskrit have had so little feeling for English. Yes, I agree with you, Aldous Huxley "somehow alienates me whatever he writes."

And I have a very small opinion of the Theosophists, especially of their lunatic fringe. Yet I am grateful to that society for one thing, and for one thing alone: when no one else would publish the Vedanta works, they brought out some really beautiful translations from the Sanskrit. . . . What a curious mixture I am! A lover of the Vedanta, of Plotinus, and of the later Mystics, and yet, inherently, a sceptic regarding the evidence of things seen or unseen, or believer or an unbeliever whose only creed holds that it is better to fight on the side of the Eternal . . . for the Eternal, whether we recognize its likeness or not, must be the Good.

Now, the warning comes to me, and I must break off. How I wish I might go on. No, I have never written of my feeling for what we call nature. Castine was satisfying, but I am thankful that you chose Connecticut for your home. The war has done its best to ruin Virginia. Connecticut, as I drove through, appeared lovely, but I have never imagined such dust or such dirty streets as I found here in Richmond.

As always devotedly,

ELLEN

I liked the end of "Hypothesis and Belief" [1] better than the beginning, which had, I thought, the flavour or lack of flavour I feel in Huxley. I do not believe that Science and Faith can be reconciled. For who knows what is "true science" or what is "true faith"? The diving bomb, the tank, the poisonous gas? Or the praying hands and the incense of goodness?

[1] Christopher Isherwood's essay, which was published in *Vedanta for the Western World,* Marcel Rodd, 1946.

TO DOUGLAS SOUTHALL FREEMAN

Richmond, December 1st, 1944

My dear Douglas:

After your great work, I feel that no other historian will ever again dare to write of the Army of Northern Virginia. By contrast, any later book on that tragic theme must always appear as an anticlimax. Though I am far from sentimental regarding the war for the Confederacy, or indeed regarding any war ever fought, a rare mist gathered over my eyes when I was reading your last chapters. But it was the victory of Lee over fate, not the defeat of the Confederacy, that moved me so deeply. How amazingly vivid the long struggle becomes in your pages! I am especially grateful to you because

[361]

your fine sense of the living fact and of the timeless moment has saved Lee's heroic figure, with his gallant army, from the colorless plaster of most American history.

Illness delayed my return from Castine, and since reaching home, I have not been well enough to write even a brief letter. But I have spent many days with your book, and I thank you from my heart for your thought of me.

I used to say that I knew little of American history, because American history books are such dull reading. But any season that gives us, in one month, *Gettysburg to Appomattox* and *The World of Washington Irving*[1] must make a great year in American letters.

Affectionately yours,

ELLEN GLASGOW

[1] The third volume of Dr. Freeman's *Lee's Lieutenants* and Van Wyck Brooks's new book.

TO SIGNE TOKSVIG

Richmond, December 4th, 1944

Dear Signe,

I loved your letters and I should have written long before this; but I have had a sad time since I came home from Maine. The sudden drop has been almost too much for me.

How unerringly you interpret my books! Your insight penetrates and finds the hidden meaning that so few readers ever discover, or even suspect. What you write of *The Miller* and of *They Stooped to Folly* means more to me than you will ever know. Yes, I have always felt that the chapter bearing Mrs. Burden's stream of memory was a part of my best work. If only I had sprung up in New England or, better still, in the Middle West, or even the Far West, I suppose it might not have taken me forty years to achieve recognition. But the North has its own peculiar delusions regarding the

South, and the South has no delusions about books, because it never reads them. Occasionally, perhaps, after it has heard a Northern critic discourse before serried rows of complacent ladies in pursuit of culture in programmes.

And, now, what about your visit to Richmond? I am trying to find several addresses for you, but the town is flooded with an overflow from Washington, and the war, as I think I wrote you, has destroyed all the native charm of Virginia. How I wish it were possible for me to ask you both to come straight to me. In happier days this would have been my first thought; but my long illness and the many war problems have changed my whole way of living. I can no longer have guests, and I never know, from day to day, how well or how ill I shall be. What distresses me is that I shall be able to do so little to make your stay pleasant. I was talking this over with a close friend only yesterday, and we both regretted the excursion we used to make to the places on James River. In the spring, these old places are lovely, with a singular and very special poetry of the past. But all such visits are now over, at least for "the duration," detestable phrase! I hope in my heart that you will come. I shall love to see you both, and my only fear is that Richmond will bore you, and you will find life here uninteresting. As for me, I feel, too, that I am merely the shadow of myself, and that you will meet only a part of what I have been in the past. A few of my friends still think the hard trip is justified; but, for the most part, the war has cut me off from New York, and from my friends there who speak my own language. I am trying to write frankly, because I should not like to feel that you and Francis were disappointed. . . . I hope . . . I cannot keep from hoping that you will come and that I shall be much, much better.

And now for possible places, none good, I fear, but places are no longer good even in New York.

These persons might, or might not, be able to take paying guests for a few days. Most of them, I believe, take in guests for months or even for a year.

Miss Munford, 307 West Franklin Street, Richmond 20. This house has a romantic history, but you would find only old or elderly guests, all in the greater Virginian tradition. For years, the house was run by four sisters, who were girls in the Civil War, and have never lived far beyond the battles around Richmond, when their adored young brother was brought, dead, to them, up this same tree-shaded Franklin Street. Theirs was one of the great Virginian families, but after the Civil War, the four women, still young girls, were completely impoverished. Like other women in the South who had neither an aptitude nor an income, nor any special strain of intelligence, they turned, instinctively to teaching as a means of livelihood. I have described this in my *Virginia*. Some day you must read that book.

But, as a small child, I went to school in this house, and was taught by a Miss Munford, who was still a great lady.

Other addresses will come, I hope. One of the advantages of going to this house is that it stands in a secluded block only a little way from my corner. Then there is always the old Jefferson Hotel, with a distinguished past but a wholly inadequate present. Many persons I know live there, but I could not honestly recommend any hotel in Richmond. I know the food must be uninteresting, but the Van Wyck Brookses preferred it to the commercial John Marshall, and so does Frank Morley, who stays there when he comes down to see me. That, also, is very near my corner, only two blocks away. I think you know Frank, and you might ask him about the hotel.

Dear Signe, I am finding an almost forgotten thrill in this search for a place.

I must thank you, too, for the pleasant and very apologetic letter I received from the *Times*. They wished to send me the paper for two months, but I have a satisfactory arrangement with the Jefferson, and I send every morning for the day's paper. I am enjoying F.H.'s reviews, but I looked in vain for your article. It will come later, I suppose. . . .

I forgot to tell you that only one of the four Munford sisters is now living. She is or was the youngest, "Miss Etta," and was born, I imagine, some years after the War Between the States. I have not been to the house since, as a little child, I climbed up four steep winding stairs to the schoolroom at the top. The three elder sisters have all died, I think, of old age; for I thought of them as old when I was a child. I am sure the house must be very depressing; but it had its tragic history.

Much love to you,
ELLEN

TO SIGNE TOKSVIG

Richmond, February 5th, 1945

Dear Signe:

Your letter lifted my spirit. You have been much in my mind, but I suffered a sharp setback at the New Year, or just before, and I have not recovered my strength. I hope the spring will revive me. You cannot know how I look forward to seeing you and F.H. A few years ago what gorgeous times we might have had on James River!

Your note enclosing the clipping by F.H. has just come. I love those notes. They have a rare quality. I taste the salt in the mist. It is easy, I think, for a Virginian to understand the Irish mood of that coast. We were brought up on dreams, so many of us, because, after the Civil War and the Reconstruction Acts, we had so little else. Though I came in the next generation, I still heard and felt the loss of satisfying realities.

I must stop now, but I must tell you to look up Norma

[365]

and Herschel Brickell if you ever find yourself near them. When they came by Richmond a week ago, I had no hope of being able to see them. However, that was one of my better days, and I had a glimpse of them when they stopped to speak to Miss Bennett. I made her bring them upstairs, and I found that Norma was overflowing with her recent discovery of the Isherwood translation of *The Bhagavad-Gita*. She had found it, quite by accident, when she was in a hospital in South America. I should like her to tell you what it meant to her. So far, I can follow her, but I take wings and fly away at the faintest shadow of Theosophy or Christian Science. I have a painful suspicion that most of these modern direct intuitions are cheap emotional transports.

But none of this is true about Norma. We talked only of the Gita, and I shared her enthusiasm. She is interesting and very attractive. They are both dear friends of mine, and I should like you to know them.

Yes, F.H. must write his memoirs. The book would make a companion volume to *I Chose Denmark*.

Devotedly,

ELLEN

I loved your Chinese rose at Christmas.

TO ELEANOR STIMSON BROOKS

Castine, October 12th, 1945

Dearest Eleanor:

I am still saying to myself, "If only I had an Eleanor!" How you do it, I don't know, but a mountain of worries appears to dissolve in vapour before you. All the summer you have used your strength over the details of living, and now you are starting, or so it seems to me, with lighthearted courage on that long journey.

The letters from Van Wyck and from you have done me a world of good in this dreary time of my life. Do let me hear of your arrival in California. I shall be so interested, and I know that, in spite of this charm, or because of that endearing quality, it is useless to warn you against Peter, the Pincher. He must be a darling, or Van Wyck could never have stood the pinches so mildly.

How I wish I might have shared your summer. Not seeing you in so long a stretch of months has been a great disappointment to me. Even letters are still too much of an effort, but I send you both my love and a whole wide world of good wishes. I am glad you are going to a climate that will be healthful, and I hope you will find that happiness is awaiting you in the sunshine.

But I shall always think of you in a garden on a hill, with a view of rippling blue water.

We expect to leave on the 22nd, and I dread unspeakably the return to Richmond, and to a house, with the surroundings where I have suffered so deeply. In many ways I am better, but I am not yet entirely well and strong. If it were possible, I should go on to New York and see your physician, but, before trying anything else, I must go back to my roots. Taxes and this long illness together have almost drained my resources. But later, perhaps.

It was dear of you to take all that trouble about a doctor, and I appreciate your thoughtfulness, in the midst of so many worries, with all my heart.

I cannot see you now, but I send my unfailing devoted friendship to you both. Never forget that I am thinking of you every day.

With my love,

ELLEN

TO SIGNE TOKSVIG

Castine, October 14th, 1945

Dear Signe:

What a series of mischances! What an enormous (Yes, I meant just that) disappointment! Some way, somehow, I had an idea that you were going to stay with friends in Augusta, but even that is too far away. No one here knows just how far. Some tell you 63, some 73 miles.

I am sending this greeting and goodbye in the midst of a turmoil. The visiting members of my family set off this morning, and the house is torn up for packing. We are leaving in a few days, provided we secure the right rooms at places to stop for the night. It is a long trip and I dread unspeakably the return to a place where I suffered so deeply last spring.

You and F.H. must come from Washington. I shall feel as if I were a ghost haunting a house which was once kept so beautifully. Now the walls are really crumbling about me, because we could find no workmen in wartime. But come you must. Fate must not be so unkind as to prevent our meeting at last.

Thank you for sending me that quotation from your brother. How is he able to write English prose so perfectly? I liked more than I can tell you your Huxley review. Yes, I had missed the reviews by F.H., and I rejoice in his good fortune.

Now, I am called to take my morning walk in the woods. Autumn has brushed them lightly and tenderly. The leaves have not yet fallen, and the trees are mantled in flame and dark splendour. You, I suppose, are settled in your lovely Connecticut, the most attractive state, I think, for a home.

Devotedly always,

ELLEN

TO VAN WYCK BROOKS

Richmond, November 5th, 1945

Dear Van Wyck:

How good it was of Eleanor and you to take time from your packing to write to me! I can never tell how much your letters have meant, and I have followed you, day by day, on your journey to California. It must do you a world of good to spend the winter in that clear, bracing air.

I am thrilled by what you tell me of your book.[1] It is a joy to think of your working so well and so easily, and I find myself hoping that my heart will be beating, with a stronger pulse, when your latest volume is placed in my hands. To imagine you, in that concluding volume, writing of my work is the happiest prospect I see in the future.[2] I can hardly wait through the years for those volumes that treat of the Civil War years and then afterwards. Surely, America has had nothing like this in its literature, nothing so broad, so deep in feeling, and so penetrating in the varied forms of action and of insight.

Yes, I am in Richmond again. Maine did me much good, and my heart bore up well through the summer; but, unfortunately, we came back to endure a long spell of summer heat in October, and I have been less well in the past two weeks. The theme you suggest makes an appeal to me, and I play with the idea of another novel ahead. But I am not interested in little things, and I doubt whether my heart and my nerves will ever again become equal to the work of a big book. That you should do these things with such easy power fills me with admiration. Only very lightly have I dealt with the flight of the Southerners after the Civil War, and that

[1] *The Times of Melville and Whitman,* Dutton, 1947.
[2] Mr. Brooks wrote of Miss Glasgow's work in *The Confident Years: 1885-1915,* Dutton, 1952.

[*369*]

was in *Life and Gabriella*. But I play with the theme when you speak of it. And who knows what may happen? I may even be free of this nervous tension, and vibrating once more to the old lost sense of creation. Just now, the days go by, somehow, in some monotonous movement of detail. I may imagine myself at work, but in reality I find the smallest action an effort of the will.

My love to you both. Do not pause in your work to write to me, but your letters have given me a renewed feeling that the life of the mind still goes on. Eleanor and you make a world of your own, and I seem to have a part in it.

Affectionately yours,

ELLEN GLASGOW

Ellen Glasgow died on November 21, 1945. The sequel to
In This Our Life *about which she wrote in her later letters
was not finished to her satisfaction and was therefore never
published. Her autobiography,* The Woman Within, *was
published posthumously in 1954.*

*A letter to the editor from Marion Gause Canby dated
August 23, 1955, can perhaps serve as an epilogue to the self-
portrait of Miss Glasgow revealed in her own letters. The
visit mentioned in Mrs. Canby's letter is referred to in Miss
Glasgow's letters to her in February and April 1944. Mrs.
Canby has given her gracious permission to quote the following:*

There were always so many people about, almost always
when I saw Ellen—so I took a train to Richmond . . .
specifically to talk at length and at ease with Ellen. The talk
came in Ellen's big, charming, very personal bedroom while
she lay on her sofa; this room was so like my mother's room,
sofa and all—and I'm confident it was a reversion to Ellen's
mother's room, chiefly because of her own ill-health (the two
mothers' variety was Victorian ill-health!). That morning
Ellen spoke a number of times of how her inner life had been
lived in her study, and in this big room. Her visits to New
York, while pleasantly friendly in her hotel-room, were
mixed up quite justly with being a "great writer" among
other writers. *That* life was hers at such brief and rare intervals. And in Richmond, with a few exceptions, she was her
"Southern" self to friends—as of course you know. But in

her own room—an Ellen eagerly warm and every inch the creative artist!

Yet in reading *The Woman Within* (of which she spoke often that morning) I was amazed to see that the "vein of iron" which always sustains her books, had not been *her* personal support in times of sorrow. It seemed she had no *philosophic* acceptance of human tragedy to help her through, with its awareness of "scale," (Man against the stars, etc.). Each sorrow broke her heart all over again as though no one had ever died or met catastrophe before. Her lifelong research on the "vein of iron," or in clearer words, the tragedy of life on earth, didn't seem to apply to her. She was like a little girl in her grief over mother or sister, and I believe all this was the psychological explanation, anyhow, of her ill health. But perhaps this lack of what might be called a *good hardening* was after all one of the things that kept her so warm and free of personality, giving herself, always. And she never had to go against the grain. She was very actually emotionally and intellectually hungry, but her daily life was filled with devoted care and, being indulged, she indulged herself in sorrow—perhaps! I don't know—but somehow *The Woman Within* seemed to *me* in many ways a different person from the Ellen I knew.

INDEX

[*373*]

Index

Index

Index

Index

Index

Index

Index

Index

Index

Index